BALANCING
ACTS

SUNY series in Women in Education
Margaret Grogan, editor

BALANCING ACTS

Women Principals at Work

LISA SMULYAN

State University
of New York
Press

Published by
State University of New York Press, Albany

Production by Susan Geraghty
Marketing by Patrick Durocher

Printed in the United States of America

For information, address State University of New York
Press, State University Plaza, Albany, N.Y., 12246

Library of Congress Cataloging-in-Publication Data

Smulyan, Lisa.
    Balancing acts : women principals at work / Lisa Smulyan.
        p.   cm. — (SUNY series in women in education)
    Includes bibliographical references (p.   ) and index.
    ISBN 0-7914-4517-8 (alk. paper). — ISBN 0-7914-4518-6 (pbk. :
alk. paper)
    1. Women school principals—United States Case studies.
    2. Educational leadership—United States Case studies. I. Title.
II. Series.
LB2831.92.S58 2000
371.2′012′082—dc21
                                                                    99-15652
                                                                    CIP

10 9 8 7 6 5 4 3 2 1

CONTENTS

ACKNOWLEDGMENTS

My deepest thanks go to the three principals who allowed me to spend a year following them, asking them questions, and being a part of their lives and work. They are impressive people and educators, as demonstrated in their daily balancing acts and in their willingness to share their lives in an effort to help others understand their work. They provided me with professional assistance and became personal friends; I will always appreciate their support. I am also grateful to the teachers, administrators, parents and students who permitted me access to everything going on in their schools. I felt warmly welcomed by all who gave of their time and space.

A number of colleagues read and responded to various versions and drafts of this manuscript. Joy Charlton often provided me with the push, the encouragement, and the questions that moved me forward. Kathy Mooney was an amazing reader and editor, asking questions that led me to insights I did not know I had. Annette Lareau, Susan Liddicoat, Kathy Schultz, Wes Shumar, and Eva Travers provided valuable feedback, as did anonymous reviewers from SUNY Press; I thank them all. Amy Roberts, a student at Swarthmore College, helped with coding and asked good questions in the earliest phases of the research; Kelly Wilcox, another student, provided detailed assistance with the bibliography at the end. Grants from the Spencer Foundation and from Swarthmore College helped support this project, giving me the time needed to do in-depth, ethnographic data collection.

Many of us who work in the field of education hope that what we do makes a difference in the world of schools, and so in the world of children. Sometimes it is difficult to remember those goals in the face of theories, deadlines, and the arduous processes of research and writing. I dedicate this book to my children, Benjamin Smulyan and Amanda Markowicz, and to all the children they represent for me. It is coming back to my children that has helped me remember my most important reasons for engaging in this kind of work.

INTRODUCTION

A QUESTION OF BALANCE

As I began to write the cases that comprise the center of this book, the metaphors that emerged from the subjects' own words were those of balance: "Dancing on Water," "Handling it Graciously," "Playing the Referee." Unlike other studies of principals that focus on administrators' skills and leadership styles, these cases highlight a dynamic process of negotiation that occurs on a daily basis. What, I began to ask, creates the balancing acts these women elementary school principals carry out each day? How do these constantly shifting negotiations impact on their work as principals? How do the multiple contexts within which they work influence the tradeoffs they make?

The principals' balancing acts occur on several levels. All three women juggle personal and professional lives, deciding how much of one can or should be sacrificed to the other, or whether it is possible to have them in balance. In one case, for example, Ellen Fried is a forty-five-year-old white woman principal in a lower-working-class school community. During her eighth year as principal, the year of this study, she finds that her mother's illness and death force her to put more time into her personal life. To her surprise, she discovers she can still do her job well. Ann Becker, a sixty-seven-year-old white woman who has served as head of the elementary division of an elite private school for five years, describes holding friends at arms' length and limiting the number of friendships she develops at work. She knows from experience that she has difficulty balancing the relationships required as friend and authority. Jeanne Greer, a fifty-year-old African American woman in her fifth year as principal in a predominantly white suburban district, begins to make more room in her life for personal growth. She joins a church that meets some of her spiritual needs, and she finds that she can begin to act on personal values within the school and deal with the repercussions that follow.[1]

In addition, all three balance the demands of their middle management position. Principals serve teachers, parents, children, and central office administrators. Sometimes, these constituents require the same responses; other times, principals must choose whose needs or preferences they will emphasize. Jeanne juggles the district's mandate for school-based management with her teachers' conflicting needs to be involved and to be given clear direction. Ellen works to help her teachers implement a new, districtwide math program that few of them like. She conscientiously carries out the demands of the district while also supporting her teachers and empathizing with their misgivings about the program. Ann tries to respond to parental and administrative concerns about the first-grade reading curriculum while assuring teachers that they are doing a good job. Even when their actions conflict with the expectations of parents, teachers, or the central administration, all three principals consistently maintain and act on the belief that the children's well-being and growth is their first priority.

These three principals also balance attempts to implement school change with the inertia that characterizes institutions like schools (see, e.g., Sarason, 1971). Jeanne's efforts to develop more inclusive curriculum and instruction meet (usually silent) resistance from some teachers. Ellen's work to dismiss an incompetent teacher challenges the status quo maintained by her school district. Ann focuses on maintaining the organizational stability she has worked hard to create, despite calls from a new headmaster for curricular change. Their cases provide some insight into the personal and institutional characteristics that limit and support the occurrence of school change.

One of the most striking balancing acts all three principals undertake is managing the tension inherent in being a woman in a position generally held by men in an institutional structure predicated on male definitions of power, authority, and leadership.[2] This negotiation affects all of the others mentioned above. It influences how each principal interprets the personal/professional dichotomy in her life; how she understands and responds to the demands of students, teachers, parents, and the central office; and how she works for change within a relatively stable and sometimes resistant institutional environment.

Several other researchers have begun to examine the tensions experienced by women administrators. Susan Chase (1995), in her study of women superintendents, found a "discursive disjunction" in the narratives of superintendents about their professional work and their personal lives. Although these women could identify issues of gender inequality in their personal experiences and relationships, they spoke about their professional work in terms of individual success, power, and accomplishment. Rarely did they connect conversations about inequality with narratives about their work. They ultimately developed individual, personal responses to work concerns as a strategy for negotiating issues of power and success in the school environment, rather than using their understanding of inequality to construct collective responses or forms of resistance to the male-dominated structures and norms within which they operated.

Similarly, Schmuck and Schubert (1995), in a study of twenty-eight women principals, described the contradictions they heard in their subjects' descriptions of their work. Although the majority reported experiencing no sex discrimination in their careers, "many of these same women reported differential treatment because of their sex . . . but did not label this behavior as 'discrimination'" (p. 279). Like Chase's superintendents, these women wanted to succeed within the prevailing structures. They may have been somewhat unaware of the forces that constrained them, and they, too, tended to see their experiences as personal, individual, and unique rather than as a part of larger social structures and inequities in the institution.

> First, women want to become integrated into the prevailing administrative culture; they want to deny their unique status as minorities, and their identity as women in a predominantly male administrative culture. Second, women principals, like men principals, are uninformed about how school policy and practice intentionally or unintentionally serve to perpetuate sex inequity. (Schmuck and Schubert, 1995, p. 281)

As women learn to be administrators they may unconsciously silence a part of themselves. They may also find ways to redefine the authority and power inherent in the administrator role so that their own voices can emerge. These conflicts and negotiations are not necessarily negative or disabling; they do, however, complicate the process of an individual's growth and development as a person and an administrator.[3]

THE ROLE OF CONTEXT

My own children, ages seven and ten, attend two different elementary schools. My son goes to a small private progressive school; my daughter attends a public suburban elementary school near our home. I am an active parent in my children's classrooms. I also work with both schools (and many others) in my capacity as a professor of education at a local college. I often joke with teachers and colleagues about the different hats I wear, sometimes simultaneously. I bring to my parenting, my teaching, and my varied interactions with schools a strong commitment to issues of equity and an awareness of the power of schools to both reproduce and challenge existing social structures. I am also conscious of how my relationships with my own students and with parents, teachers, and administrators in each school within which I work differ, as do my actions and interactions at each site. While I maintain a core set of educational values and a cohesive sense of who I am as I move from school to school in multiple roles, I am aware that the school, the community, and the institutional contexts in which I engage influence my approaches and responses in the different school environments.

Principals, too, act within multiple contexts, even within a single school. Thus another way of understanding the balancing acts in which each principal engages is to envision a series of interactions between the individual and the contexts within which she works.[4] Prior studies of effective principals, which emphasize the tasks, skills, and roles of a good manager, ignore the range of frameworks within which a school leader acts. More recent studies, especially those that focus on gender or race and school management, have begun to examine the organization of schools and the ways in which this organization reflects larger social structures that perpetuate gender, racial, and class inequities (e.g., Chase, 1995; Dunlop, 1995; Adler et al., 1993; Ballou, 1989). As an institution with a culture that encourages a particular set of values and certain ways of knowing and interacting, the school constrains the relationships and behaviors of the principal who works within it. This structural approach problematizes the relatively static notion of effectiveness. It locates differences in management styles in larger institutional and social realities and examines the effects of those structures on behaviors and outcomes. But this same approach may overemphasize the social and cultural determinants of behavior within the institution, ignoring the individual's ability to act, adapt, and sometimes change the frameworks within which she works.

This book uses life history and ethnographic methods of research to examine the work of three female elementary school principals. The goal is to illustrate the complex interactions between women administrators' personal and professional lives and the social and cultural frameworks within which they work. By developing a detailed picture of the principals' daily experiences, we can examine the tensions that arise when a community, an institution, and a principal experience differences in class, race, religion, and expectations about gender and age. In order to understand how principals operate effectively in schools, we must examine their actions and responses in the contexts within which they work.

By contexts, I mean the multiple forums within which all individuals operate, each context unique and yet overlapping in influence. In particular I focus on four contexts that are especially salient in principals' lives and work. The first, the *personal context* of the individual, is comprised of her home and educational background and her training and path to the principalship. This personal context influences a principal's perceptions, values, and relationships to people and institutions; she carries it with her into all of the other contexts within which she works. The second, the *community context*, consists of two constituencies: the families served by the school and the teachers who work within it. Community members' class, race, social, religious, and educational experiences, and their expectations about what constitutes leadership, create a context to which principals respond in a variety of ways. Similarly, teachers' backgrounds and expectations provide a framework within which principals work. At times teachers' and parents' perspectives are parallel; often they differ. Taken together they create a shifting set of demands and relationships a principal must negotiate in order to be effective within the context of the school community. The third context, the *institutional context*, includes two components—the people in positions of power who control process and product, and the structural regularities of schools and districts that govern the actions of school principals. As a middle manager, the principal must find ways to operate successfully within this context, even when its demands and structures challenge her personal style and values or conflict with the requirements of teachers and families in the school community. On some occasions, she may adapt to the norms of the institutional context; on others she may find ways to resist and change it. Finally, the *historical and social context* encompasses and reflects all of the others. It includes the historically accepted patterns of behavior, hierarchies of power, and norms of interaction that shape us and that we, in turn, both perpetuate and resist. Social constructions of meaning, of roles, of power, and of relationships influence a principal's actions and experiences in all areas of her life and work. Consequently, the historical and social context is interwoven through the other three.

Analytically, each of these contexts might be considered unique and separate, and could, perhaps, be represented as a series of concentric circles within which the individual functions. Yet these contexts also interconnect in a complicated pattern. A response in one context inevitably draws on or affects another. For example, gender expectations, a historically and socially constructed set of responses, ideas, and values, influences how an individual principal is seen within a community or how she chooses to respond to an institutional demand. Redefining a principal's effectiveness in context, then, requires the interweaving of several layers of understanding, an analysis that reveals a dynamic process of negotiation too complicated to be characterized by a list of skills, traits, or roles. The principal both constructs her role in context and is constructed by those contexts.

The balancing acts described above can be seen, then, as the principals' responses to demands within and across contexts. In order to balance her personal and professional life, for example, a principal explores how her prior experience and approaches interact with the institutionally and historically constructed parameters of the role of principal. Being a middle manager often involves negotiating the demands of parents, teachers, and central office administrators. The principal may discover that the needs and expectations of the people comprising the community context differ from the more regularized and hierarchical requirements of the larger institutional context. Tensions inherent in being a woman in the principal's role can be examined as the result of social constructs that affect her interactions across the contexts within which she works.

This book uses case studies to illuminate the ongoing processes of negotiation, balance, and change experienced by three women elementary school principals. It recognizes the importance of gender as one factor contributing to the complex and dynamic personal and professional lives these women live and examines how their experiences as women principals both reflect and challenge the current literature on gender and school administration. Case studies make it possible to explore the role of gender in the contexts of the individual's life history, her community and school, and in the historical and social constructions of school and school administration. This approach also allows us to recognize other variables that affect a principal's life and work, including her race, religion, age, and class. By examining the details of these women's experiences we can challenge prior notions of what constitutes the work of the principal and allow the voices of the women themselves to be heard. What emerges is a view of the principalship as a work in progress. As the principals themselves suggest, they are dancing on water, handling conflicting demands graciously, and playing the referee. They are creators, negotiators, and interpreters of the rules, working within given frameworks and, simultaneously, developing new visions of what those frameworks might be.

OUTLINE OF THE BOOK

Studies of the principal, past and present, tend to prescribe the characteristics of an effective principal. Such prescriptions fail to examine the historical, social, institutional and community contexts within which school leaders work and neglect the personal and professional influences they bring to their decisions and actions. Only when these contexts and individual variables are considered can we begin to see how school leadership is a dynamic process of negotiation that takes into consideration the demands of the moment, the institutional structure, and historical definitions of power and relationship. Chapter 1 examines how past research on the principal tends to focus on relatively static descriptions of effective principals. It also considers how more recent research on gender and school leadership begins to provide a more dynamic perspective on the process of the principalship. Finally, chapter 1 presents four themes that emerged from my examination of the experiences of three women principals and that are used to frame the case studies in chapters 3, 4 and 5. The themes, *Becoming a principal, Serving others, Meeting institutional expectations*, and *Balancing continuity and change*, reflect how a principal negotiates demands within the personal, community, institutional, and historical and social contexts within which she works.

The substantive insights about school leadership I present in this book and the methods used for collecting and presenting the data are intertwined. Qualitative case study and life history approaches provide new perspectives on the complex interactions that characterize women's lives and work as principals. They lead to new categories of analysis, different ways of understanding school leaders and their work. The same methods created dilemmas for me as a researcher and writer. In chapter 2, I introduce the three principals and explain the processes of entry, data collection and analysis, and writing that characterized the development of the case studies. I also reflect on the dilemmas inherent in doing this kind of relationship-dependent research, tensions that required a constant reevaluation of my roles and relationships in the schools in which I worked.

Chapters 3, 4 and 5 each comprise a case study of one of the three principals. I begin each case with a vignette, taken from my field notes, which provides an initial insight into that principal's style and the contexts within which she works. The case study chapters are then organized around the four themes, introduced in chapter 1, that characterize several aspects of the dynamic process of principaling experienced by these women. All three of the cases use narratives, stories that reflect the ongoing dilemmas and responses of the actors involved, to help us understand the complexities of the principals' actions within the multiple contexts within which they work. Whenever possible, I use the words of the principals themselves, or others with whom they work, to illustrate their perspectives and experiences.

In the final chapter, I again use the four themes to examine what these cases tell us about the dynamic process of school leadership. How do gender and context influence that process? How does a more dynamic view of the principalship contribute to our understanding of the role of the individual principal in school change? How might we move from an analysis of the individual work of these three women to an understanding of the limits they experience and the possibilities inherent in these stories of their lives and work?

As they balance the constraints and opportunities present within their personal, community, institutional, and social contexts, these three women principals demonstrate that change is possible. Although their cases complicate traditional, more static definitions of effective leadership, they provide insight into the complex interactions between the individual principals and the social structures within which they operate. The work of these principals makes clear that a school leader can improve teaching and learning in schools. Their stories also illustrate the constraints that need to be addressed for schools to benefit fully from what these individuals have to offer.

CHAPTER 1

Studying the Principalship

At one point in my career, I planned to become a school principal. In that role, I believed I could continue to work closely with children *and* have a greater impact on the curricular and structural elements of schooling that frustrated me as a teacher. A principal could, I thought, be instrumental in developing a supportive, positive school environment in which both children and adults could learn and grow. I began to read more of the literature on principals, looking for insights into my potential role. Sometimes, I recognized my own relatively stereotypical views of the principal as an "effective leader," someone who managed people and buildings in order to increase student achievement. I also found, however, that prior work on principals did not always reflect my version of what a principal could be or how I envisioned myself in the role. The given lists of skills and attributes seemed removed from the messy realities of schools, and the list makers generally omitted any mention of the actual person doing the job. As I worked with the principals in this study and experienced with them the complexities of their daily lives, my initial reservations about traditional work on educational leadership increased. What did the research mean by its definitions of effective leadership? What was left out of those relatively limited definitions? How could we begin to capture more accurately the dynamic process of principaling that I witnessed each day in the three schools in which I conducted this research?

In this chapter, I explore these questions, examining traditional portrayals of school leadership and the historical and social contexts within which these descriptions have developed. These contexts help us begin to understand the current frameworks within which school leaders function. I then consider how investigations of gender and school culture begin to challenge the norms of effective leadership described in the mainstream literature. While these latter studies add complexity to our understanding of leadership, they too have some limitations. In the final part of this chapter I propose an approach to educational leadership that uses both individual and contextual frames of analysis to provide a more complete and complex view of the principalship.

THE EFFECTIVE PRINCIPAL

Over the last thirty years, the school principal has been identified as a key player in school improvement and change. Studies of the principalship burgeoned when effective schools research in the 1960s showed that schools needed an effective leader in order to create an environment that would lead to student achievement and teacher satisfaction (Richardson et al., 1993; Donaldson, 1991; Porter et al., 1989; Lomotey, 1989; Boyan, 1988; Burlingame, 1987). The early studies defined the effective leader as someone who helped the school achieve the qualities associated with effective schools: teachers with high expectations for student learning, a positive school climate, increased time on instructional tasks, regular and systematic student evaluations, community support, and adequate resources (Richardson et al., 1993; Spring, 1989). Some current studies of effective school leadership continue to describe the school leader in these terms; even when they examine the principalship from other perspectives, researchers frequently use the term "effective principal" in the title or the text of their work, suggesting the framework, or at least the historical precedent, within which they are working (e.g., Blase and Kirby, 1992; Wooster, 1991; Lomotey, 1989; Mortimore and Sammons, 1987; Deal, 1987; Blumberg and Greenfield, 1986).

Analyses of effective principals typically emphasize three aspects of the position: the *tasks* the principal performs, the *skills* she brings to the job, and the *roles* she plays in the school and system. The first two approaches tend to support the view of the principalship as involving management and problem solving toward preestablished (or principal-determined) goals. The third approach, which focuses on the principal's role within the system, may incorporate a more ecological view of the school. Within this perspective, the principal is one of many players affected by the interpersonal, political, and physical context within which she works. Each of the three perspectives is described in more detail below.

The *task approach* to school leadership, although less prevalent in recent literature, provides a picture of a principal whose responsibilities include curriculum leadership, teacher supervision and evaluation, district and parent communication, and, at times, student discipline. Often this approach emphasizes the crisis management aspects of being a principal; that is, the principal has defined tasks to perform but often must instead (or in addition) respond to immediate crises. The principal's day consists of a series of seemingly unconnected events and interactions that must be addressed before she can complete the tasks expected of one in her role (Acker, 1990; Wolcott, 1973).

The *skills approach* to the study of school leadership, while it may also describe the leader's tasks and roles, explores particular competencies that result in effective management. The National Association of Elementary School Principals' publication *Principals for 21st Century Schools* assumes that because school-based management and teacher control and decision making will increase, future principals need to learn how to manage and facilitate these processes. The publication notes that effective principals' skills and competencies include the knowledge of good instructional practices; the ability to motivate and guide teacher-leaders; expertise in communication, interpersonal relations, planning, and implementation; and skills in site-based management, in building partnerships with parents, in gathering data for decision making, and in developing a school climate and culture that are conducive to empowerment (National Association of Elementary School Principals, 1990).

Another skill-oriented view of the principal describes her as a craftsperson, a characterization that combines the ideas of playing a certain role and having a set of skills (Blumberg 1989, 1987). A craftsperson has an end product in mind and the ability to produce it. The craft of a school administrator involves "the idiosyncratic use of self to make prudent decisions concerning problematic situations in school life . . . the exercise of practical wisdom toward the end of making things in a school or school system 'look' like one wants them to look" (Blumberg, 1989, p. 46). Like many other approaches in this field (Blase and Kirby, 1992; Buell, 1992; Parkay et al., 1992; Smith, 1991), the craftsperson model describes a principal as someone with a vision for the school, what Greenfield (1987) calls a "moral imagination," and the skills to move herself and her colleagues toward that vision.

Surveys and first-person accounts of effective principals also focus on the competencies needed to allow faculty and staff to teach and nurture students (Donaldson, 1991). Blase and Kirby (1992) describe strategies identified by teachers as those used by effective principals. These include the use of praise; the ability to influence teachers by involving them in decision making and granting them professional autonomy; the ability to lead by standing behind teachers, offering material, instructional, and emotional support and encouragement, and providing feedback and rewards; and the appropriate and minimal use of formal authority derived from the principal's position in the system's hierarchy. Teachers in Blase and Kirby's study also note personality characteristics or traits they feel make a principal more effective, including honesty, optimism, consideration, and the ability to model the behavior expected of teachers.

Occasionally, when the skills are defined as interpersonal and the process advocated is one of participation, skill-oriented descriptions of the principalship include elements of emancipatory leadership, or leadership for empowerment. Beck and Murphy (1993), for example, describe the principal of the 1990s as more than a manager. They argue that not only must the principal as educator empower others to learn, she must also be a "social architect," one who takes responsibility for addressing critical moral and social issues through her role in the school. This approach to leadership emphasizes both individual growth and development and a moral imperative to help schools accomplish social change (Grundy, 1993; Sergiovanni, 1990). For the most part, however, the skills-focused literature describes the competencies a principal needs in order to succeed in specific tasks that will result in students and teachers reaching high levels of achievement in a comfortable learning environment.

All of these skills-oriented analyses focus on the principal as the visionary, the goal setter who uses her skills to help others in the school reach academic and personal goals. This perspective suggests that once a principal has gained these skills and accomplished these tasks, she can create a positive school environment in which teachers are decision makers and children achieve. These approaches tend to ignore the concept of the school and school system as institutions with processes, demands, rituals, and roles of their own that change over time. Skills-oriented analyses also pay little attention to the fact that the schools themselves exist within larger social and cultural frameworks that in turn circumscribe the behaviors, ideas, and interactions of the individuals within them.

Literature examining the principal's *role* more frequently looks at the school or school district as a system and the principal as a key player within an organizational structure (Griffin, 1990; Deal, 1987). Blumberg and Greenfield (1986) suggest that we need to throw away the "great man" approach to understanding effective school leaders and examine both the systems within which principals operate and the range of roles principals assume beyond that of the "leader." School systems, as loosely coupled organizations that value loyalty and maintenance of the status quo, provide few opportunities for communication and collaboration among principals. This kind of system reinforces its own structure, tends not to support creativity or change, and leads to a principal's isolation and sense of powerlessness vis-à-vis the larger system. Principals therefore turn their energies inward, toward their schools. Since schools themselves are loosely coupled, principals may find it difficult to orchestrate collaboration or to influence the entire school. They may therefore focus instead on individual, interpersonal relationships rather than the organization as a whole. Given the limitations implicit in the organizational structure of schools, an effective principal must hold a vision for what the school could be, take initiative in structuring her own role in ways that keep her from getting mired in administrivia, and act resourcefully to avoid expending all her energy on organizational maintenance. Blumberg and Greenfield (1986) suggest that instead of thinking of the principal only in the role of leader, we examine the role of school routines and regularities in the principal's life and consider the school as a political and decision-making arena in which the principal is one player.

Each of these approaches—seeing the principal as fulfilling particular tasks, having necessary skills or strategies, and playing key roles—provides a perspective on the work and life of a principal. She does indeed have tasks that need to be completed, required by the system and the school and expected by the district, parents, teachers, and students. She draws on a variety of skills and strategies, some learned prior to assuming the principalship and others learned on the job, to carry out those tasks. And she plays a range of roles, depending on the situation, the others involved, her own past experiences and work, and her own and her school culture's notions of effectiveness. Only by combining the three approaches do we begin to develop a more complete and complex view of what a principal might do in order to be effective, what the process of negotiating the demands of the principalship might look like in practice and over time. Even in combination, however, I found that these approaches to studying the principalship provided only limited insight into the experiences of the three principals with whom I worked. The descriptions in the literature failed to capture the individuality of the women who filled the position of principal in the schools where I spent an intense six hours a day. Nor did existing studies include any reference to the contexts within which principals work. My field research persuaded me that the person and the contexts are key variables in understanding how a principal functions in her role and interacts with others.

In addition to overlooking the importance of person and context, the general literature on the tasks, roles, and skills of an effective principal rarely addresses the influence of gender (or race or class) on an administrator's actions, interactions, tasks, roles, or skills. By failing to acknowledge the impact of gender, this literature implies that all principals experience common demands and need similar strategies to be successful. Occasionally, studies refer to variables resulting from different school and district cultures and requirements (see, e.g., Blase and Kirby, 1992; Barth, 1990) and, less frequently, from the social, psychological and intellectual history the individual brings to the job (Blumberg, 1989,

1987). Blumberg refers to the latter as the individual's "baggage" (Blumberg, 1989, p. 48) and comments that despite idiosyncrasies in how each person interprets events and acts in situations, there is a common character in the things principals do and how they think about them: "what is most personal is generalizable" (Blumberg, 1989, p. 205). Although there are certainly generalizable characteristics of principals and their jobs, calling the effects of gender, race, and class either baggage or idiosyncrasies minimizes the impact of these social constructions and power relationships and suggests that the influences of gender, race, and class are individual interpretations rather than powerful, socially constructed aspects of experience.

In the few places gender is mentioned in this more general literature on school administration, authors emphasize the difference between our stereotyped views of women's characteristics and the attributes of a principal. In describing the 1990s "principal as servant," Beck and Murphy (1993) explain that "enabling leadership has a softer, more feminine hue to it. It is more ethereal and less direct. There is as much heart as head in this style of leading" (p. 191). The connection of servitude, softness, ethereality, and heart with femininity contributes to a sense of women's styles as different from men's, and until now at least, inappropriate when applied to educational leadership. The stereotypical skills women have, the tasks they emphasize, and the roles they play in society conflict with the expectations described in much of the literature on effective principals. On the other hand, approaches authors have described variously as leadership of the 1990s (Beck and Murphy, 1993), emancipatory leadership (Grundy, 1993), and transformational leadership (Sergiovanni, 1990) parallel emerging descriptions of women's leadership styles in schools (see, e.g., Astin and Leland, 1995; Regan and Brooks, 1995).

Work in gender and administration challenges, informs, broadens, and replaces some of the existing frameworks used to examine the principalship and the concept of effectiveness. Even if principals are more influenced by the requirements of their organizational role in the school culture than by other variables, including gender (Eagly et al., 1992), gender, race and class remain key variables in the tasks principals choose to address, the roles they play, and the strategies they use to carry out both. And gender influences the processes of negotiation and balance principals carry out in every context within which they function. In the sections that follow I examine the literature on gender and school administration and begin to question how it complicates this field of study, providing a more process-oriented understanding of the position, the person in it, and the contexts within which she works.

GENDER AND SCHOOL ADMINISTRATION

In one interview I had for a principalship, an administrator asked me how I would "handle" veteran male teachers. When a different interview committee found out that I was recently married, they asked if there were any circumstances I could foresee in the next few years that might keep me from doing the job (i.e., did I plan to have children any time soon?). Gender, in a multitude of unspoken ways, influenced my experiences as I considered and was considered for the principalship.

The historical development of educational administration has, however, led to a field of study and practice that neither questions nor reflects on the place of women in the system. In the United States, teaching and administration have long been considered separate professions. By the mid-1800s, teaching had become "feminized" (Spring, 1986; Hoffman, 1981), acceptable and appropriate for women as an extension of their work with children in the home. With the development of public schooling and the organization of school districts in the late 1800s and early 1900s, teaching came to be defined as a female profession and administration as a male domain. The management structures and styles of the developing bureaucratic and capitalistic system of the early twentieth century carried the implicit message that just as men controlled industry and government, so should they manage schools and teachers: "Reform and adoption of the business model, in which administrators and professors of administration controlled the structure, the knowledge, and the values for education, took place without much interference from the community, minority groups, teachers, or even from school boards" (Ortiz and Marshall, 1988, p. 125).

Schools followed a pattern of early-twentieth-century municipal and corporate reform and development to become more hierarchical as well as more professional. John Philbrick, principal of Quincy High School in Massachusetts, described this structure in 1856: "Let the principal or Superintendent have the general supervision and control of the whole, and let him have one male assistant or sub-principal, and ten female assistants, one for each room" (quoted in Spring, 1986, p. 135). The emphasis on hierarchy, efficiency, and scientific management led to the creation of the myth of the neutral professional educator: "Business managers, school board members, and other social groups encouraged school administrators to become more professional, to apply scientific-management ideologies in their work, and to build power on neutral apolitical expertise separate from the politics of the community" (Ortiz and Marshall, 1988, p. 125). Hierarchy also contributed to the gendered division of labor in education; women, in their roles as teachers, assumed the "appropriate" subordinate role in the institutional structure.

Schools thus came to resemble other competitive bureaucratic institutions that emphasized management and control. Educational historians such as Katz (1987) and Tyack (1974) have pointed out that this "one best system" was not inevitable but the result of a series of choices made by those who gradually assumed power over educational organizations and practice in the early 1900s. These choices led to patterns of success and training for school administrators that continue to dominate: "The myths that become standards for success as a school administrator are male models of discipline and power, business (also male) models of administrative science, and anti-intellectual models of training that focus on mentoring by skilled and traditional veterans" (Gosetti and Rusch, 1995, p. 21).

Research in educational management has followed a similarly narrow course. There have been few studies of women and minorities, in part because women and minorities have been underrepresented in positions of educational leadership and in part because traditional patterns of research in the field have reflected the male-dominated nature of school administration. Yeakey et al. (1986) and Blackmore (1993) trace the neglect of gender in this literature to the acceptance of the "rational man" model of organizations that emerged from the early 1900s emphasis on school administrators as professional experts who should run their schools as effective businesses. Yeakey et al. also point out that the study of educational administration is grounded in the positivist tradition of the 1900s that emphasized "noncontroversial, detached 'truths' that remained impervious to larger equity issues, social realities and social problems" (p. 113). As a result, the field of educational administration has failed to examine the larger social and cultural constraints and norms within which educators function:

> The traditional management of knowledge in educational administration has had the combined effects of (a) separating educational administration from education; (b) blinding educators to inequities and incongruities that have become part of the accepted system of schooling; and (c) promoting a base of theory, research and knowledge disconnected from the voices, needs, and realities of individuals who do not comply with or benefit from the ethos of hierarchical control. Conventional management knowledge has also inhibited the exploration or explanation of social system characteristics that have maintained the separation of men from women in education and, particularly, the unequal access of women to significant administrative careers. (Ortiz and Marshall, 1988, p. 126)

The history of educational administration has, therefore, contributed to knowledge, policy, theory, and research in this field that emphasize hierarchical control and efficiency. Acceptable study of school administration has focused on issues such as organizational size and structure, teacher productivity, and budget and management rather than teaching-oriented issues such as pedagogy and the goals of schooling. Studying women in educational administration challenges some of the key assumptions underlying theory, knowledge, and practice in schools and in school leadership.

OVERVIEW OF THE STUDY OF WOMEN IN EDUCATIONAL LEADERSHIP

The explicit study of women in educational administration has experienced shifts in emphasis during the past twenty years. Early studies examined the numbers, documenting the underrepresentation of women in all levels of educational administration, and probing the reasons for this discrepancy (see, e.g., Edson, 1981; Wheatley, 1981; Biklen, 1980; Clement, 1980). These studies focus on discrimination and stereotyping that limit women's entry into and success in the field and document patterns of socialization that prevent women from developing the expected behaviors, aspirations, and values that would allow them to apply for administrative positions. This earlier research tends to ignore larger systemic issues of power and ideology and often fails to see the individual as able to act, either on her own or in coordination with others, to challenge the existing system.

A second group of studies examines differences in male and female management styles. To a large extent, male management styles provide the norm; studies of women look at what women do differently from men, without attempting to explore why the documented differences exist.[1] Current studies that emphasize management differences tend to redefine traditional terms such as leadership and power so that women's management styles can be examined on their own merits rather than in comparison to men's (see Regan and Brooks, 1995; Adler et al., 1993; Ozga, 1993; Astin and Leland, 1991). But these new definitions run the risk of essentializing women's characteristic approaches.

More recently, studies have begun to focus on the organizational structures of schools and their reflection of larger social structures that perpetuate gender, racial, and class inequities. "What is provided is a different view of organizational reality. By grounding organizational social theory in the larger social structures, in the organizational realities from which it emanates, the weight of the evidence reveals that the position of racial minorities and women in organizations is inseparable from the relative position of women and racial minorities in the larger social system" (Yeakey et al., 1986, p. 118). While this approach continues to emphasize a gender difference in style, it locates that difference in larger institutional and social realities, questions its source, and examines its effect on outcomes. The sections that follow examine the key issues of access, management style, and institutional structure and culture in more detail, exploring how each contributes to a more complex understanding of the principalship.

Access Issues

Much of the earliest research on women in educational administration examines issues of access, probing the reasons behind the decreasing numbers of women principals between 1930 and 1980. In the first three decades of the twentieth century, the number of women in elementary principalships increased, the result of the feminist movement, the organization of women teachers, the right to vote in local elections, and the economic advantage to a school district of hiring lower-paid women (Shakeshaft, 1989). Even during this "golden age" of women administrators (Hansot and Tyack, 1981, as quoted in Shakeshaft, 1989, p. 34), women were only about 55% of the elementary principals but constituted almost 90% of elementary teachers (Shakeshaft, 1989). Between 1930 and 1980, the number of women in principalships declined, despite the fact that the number of women elementary and secondary teachers remained between 80 and 90%. Traditional concerns about women administrators resurfaced: women were constitutionally incapable of maintaining needed discipline and order; they did not fit the picture most school boards held of a school administrator; they were expected to leave the profession early for marriage; and they lacked men's abilities to interact with other men in power and to deal with community issues and problems. In addition, the Depression, the consolidation of school districts, and the slowing of suffrage and union movements led to a decline in support for women in administration and an emphasis on providing jobs for family heads, that is, men (Shakeshaft, 1989; Stockard and Johnson, 1981). Even though the percentage of women principals has increased marginally in recent years, the disparity between the proportion of women teachers (83% at the elementary level and 53% at the secondary level) and the proportion of women principals (36% and 11%, respectively) continues to raise questions (National Center for Education Statistics, 1994).

Explanations for women's underrepresentation in administration have focused on external barriers, internal constraints, and the mixed experiences of women who do become principals. In her study of 142 women who hoped to enter educational administration, Edson (1988) explains that women *do* want to become administrators. They want the professional growth and challenge, they believe they will be good administrators, and they hope to do something positive for children. Yet even women who aspire to school administration face barriers of discrimination in hiring and promotion that often limit their movement. One of the key barriers is that those in positions to hire, school boards, superintendents, and other school administrators, are usually men. These "gatekeepers" tend to hire people with whom they are comfortable and who most resemble themselves in attitudes, behaviors, career path, and values (Bell and Chase 1993; Edson, 1988, 1981; Marshall, 1984; Stockard and Johnson, 1981; Wheatley, 1981; Clement 1980). Existing stereotypes of what constitutes leadership, in contrast with women's traditional strengths and roles, also work against the hiring of women for these positions. As discussed above, school leaders historically have been managers, organizers of people and schedules who are able to negotiate successfully with superintendents, school boards, and communities and evaluate, hire, and fire teachers. Women have been described as lacking in independence and task orientation and as being too emotional, dependent on feedback from others, and collaborative to fit into the bureaucratic hierarchy of school administration (Ortiz and Marshall, 1988; Biklen, 1980; Clement, 1980). Ortiz (1982) describes the experiences of women teachers who aspired to principalships and who consequently had trouble getting tenure; their principals told them that if they did not want to stay in teaching they should get out of it. One principal told Ortiz, "Teachers who start out thinking they're going to be administrators aren't as committed to children and their learning problems. Those persons just aren't as successful in the classroom" (Ortiz, 1982, p. 59). A double standard exists for women and men who pursue administrative careers; women educators are expected to be dedicated to their classrooms and their children while men may move on and still be seen as committed to the field.

Other external barriers limiting women's access to educational administration include a lack of available information about positions and few structural opportunities to gain the skills and visibility needed to advance in the system. Women, especially elementary teachers, tend to be bypassed for selection for attendance at conferences and meetings, access to special funds, and selection for training programs, since this form of recognition is distributed informally by male administrators who, again, may choose to reward and encourage those most like themselves or those who they feel will most benefit from or be likely to use the new skills in the future (Yeakey et al., 1986; Edson, 1981; Wheatley, 1981). Women may engage in less GASing (Getting the Attention of Superiors), a form of anticipatory socialization that men use to gain access to information and positions (Ortiz, 1982). Without information and experience, women may not know about possibilities for advancement or may, in the eyes of those who hire, lack the preparation required for the job. In addition, those in positions to hire may see women as lacking in the motivation to advance and to take the steps needed to prepare themselves for administrative tasks. Again, we hear a dependence on the historical notion that women make good teachers, but, because they lack ambition and commitment, they do not make good administrators.

Women sometimes lack the information and experience that would provide stepping stones into the bureaucracy because they do not have the networks and mentors frequently available to male teachers who aspire to (or are encouraged to consider) administrative careers (Edson, 1988; Miklos, 1988; Fauth, 1984; Biklen, 1980). Given the lack of role models and the social and structural barriers to advancement, women may need extra encouragement and support; many women who do become school principals point out that they were "pushed" into the role by others who told them that they had something to contribute (Ozga, 1993; Pavan, 1991; Yeakey et al., 1986). Yet fewer women than men connect to mentors and to networks that would provide this support. For the most part, the men's network is unconscious, informal, and private, and yet it operates to give young male teachers greater access to the people and experiences that prepare them for selection into a principalship. Lack of mentorship contributes to women's later (in comparison to men) entry into the principalship and to feelings of isolation for those women who aspire to and assume positions of leadership (Edson 1988; Fauth, 1984).

Studies that focus on internal or psychological barriers to access examine socialization patterns that lead both men and women to perceive that women lack skills and behaviors needed for administrative success. Women, the research argues, have been socialized to internalize traits perceived by themselves and others as incompatible with leadership roles, such as a sense of self as helper rather than leader, as warm rather than ambitious, as emotional rather than rational, and as passive and deferential rather than active and independent (Grogan, 1996; Pavan, 1991; Yeakey, 1986; Weber et al., 1981; Biklen, 1980). Acting in ways that challenge these traditional roles may lead to conflict or stress for women administrative aspirants. It may also limit the numbers of those who apply for administrative positions, even if they aspire to the role.

Some argue that women have chosen not to pursue educational administration both because they have a realistic sense of what is possible in a discriminatory system and because they do not want to take on the tasks of school management as these have traditionally been defined

(Ozga, 1993). If women cannot maintain and use their existing values and styles of interaction and leadership (some of which may be seen as traditionally feminine), they do not want to enter the field of educational administration. In addition, the perceived rewards of administration— power, influence, money, status, increased sense of competence—may be neither the kinds of rewards women want to work for nor the way in which they define success (Clement, 1980; Sassen, 1980). These patterns of behavior may also conflict with the choices a woman has made about her family responsibilities and roles and the quality of life she wants to lead (Pavan, 1991; Biklen, 1980). In looking at some of the reasons why many of the 142 female aspirants to administrative positions had not reached their goals, Edson (1995) explains, "While the world of teaching more easily accommodates the dual world for many women, the demands of administration still often presume one has a 'wife' at home" (p. 44). The prevailing definitions of leadership and power in schools thus contribute to many women's decision to opt out of leadership positions. While this approach allows us to see women as agents (rather than victims) who make autonomous choices about their lives and careers, it tends to sidestep the fact that these "choices" are influenced and limited by gender role patterns deeply embedded in our social structures.

Several studies have examined the similarities and differences in men's and women's career paths into educational administration (Grant, 1989; Shakeshaft, 1989; Edson, 1988; Fauth, 1984; Prolman 1983; Clement, 1980). This work suggests that the traditional notion of "career" needs reexamination when applied to many women in education (Smulyan, 1990; Grant, 1989; Sikes, 1985). Women choose teaching, remain in teaching, grow and change as teachers, and enter educational administration in ways that reflect both personal and social/historical pressures on their lives. These factors differ from those affecting men, whose life patterns have been used as the norm against which women are examined. For example, research suggests women generally enter teaching because they "love children," because it is a socially acceptable role to family and friends, because they can envision making a difference in the world through teaching, and because in some cases they perceive limited opportunities for women in other fields (Pavan, 1991; Prolman, 1983). When they become teachers, women generally have no plans to enter administration (Polczynski, 1990; Grant, 1989; Sikes, 1989). Women who do leave the classroom tend to do so after many years of teaching, and possibly after raising a family (Marshall and Mitchell, 1989). Those women who do leave teaching usually work in special curriculum areas (e.g., reading, curriculum development) rather than in school administration, maintaining their connection to teaching and instruction rather than shifting to management

(Mitchell and Winn, 1989; Shakeshaft, 1989; Prolman, 1983, Paddock, 1981). When we include women's experiences in descriptions of leadership, becoming a principal emerges as a less linear and more complicated process of balancing personal and professional needs and internal and external expectations of role and success.

Gender Differences in Management Style

Many studies of gender differences in management style define school leadership in terms of the principal's control over certain aspects of the schooling process. The assumption in these studies is that there is an organizational role (described above as modeled after an early twentieth-century male executive norm) that may conflict with assigned or socialized gender roles when the organizational role is filled by a woman. The organizational role itself is rarely questioned or examined; if anything, researchers seem to applaud when women appear to outshine men in these positions.[2]

This literature suggests that women principals tend to pay more attention to curriculum, interact more frequently and regularly with students and teachers, involve teachers in democratic decision making, and focus more on developing the school as a people-centered community than do male administrators (Eagly et al., 1992; Shakeshaft, 1989; Schmuck et al., 1981; Gross and Trask, 1976). There appear to be few gender differences in the level of concern principals have for academic achievement, in their desire to involve parents in school activities, or in their level of task orientation or desire to get the job done well (Eagly et al., 1992; Charters and Jovick, 1981; Gross and Trask, 1976). These studies present conflicting views of possible differences in male and female principals' levels of interaction with their faculty and colleagues; for example, while Gross and Trask (1976) found that male principals maintained a greater social distance with the staff outside of school than female principals, when other variables were controlled, this contrast seemed to occur primarily as a result of differences in marital status. Charters and Jovick (1981) suggest that both personal and situational factors (e.g., size of school) seem to influence leadership style as much as does gender. They do, however, substantiate Gross and Trask's claims that female principals communicate more with their faculties than do male principals and that both male and female teachers tend to be more satisfied with their working conditions under female principals, given these principals' closer personal relations with teachers and their concerns with the educational affairs of the school. Again, this research provides a sense of the quantity of interactions that occur, but not the quality of those interactions and the dynamics behind them.

The different career paths of male and female administrators contribute to differences in both the particular roles and tasks they emphasize and the style in which they carry out those tasks within the community (Shakeshaft, 1989; Marshall, 1985; Tibbetts, 1980). Spending more time as teachers and in positions emphasizing curriculum may lead women principals to focus more on instruction and on the work of the teachers in the schools; they tend to see their job as more that of a master teacher or educational leader than that of a manager. Teaching and learning are of primary concern; women principals emphasize achievement, coordinate instructional programs, know teachers and students as individuals, and work to help them develop (Shakeshaft, 1989). Given their own negotiations in their personal and professional lives, and the position of "outsider within" (Collins, 1991) in the historically male-dominated culture of school administration, women may bring different perspectives and skills to their work.

In both research and first-person accounts, women administrators describe themselves as different from their male administrative colleagues. They write, or tell researchers, that they listen more and that they are more patient, committed, open and honest, caring, vulnerable, communicative, and connected to their school community of teachers, students, and parents (Ozga, 1993; Young, 1990; O'Rourke and Papelewis, 1989). They also emphasize their interactions with others:

> One of the reasons why I have a bigger in-tray is because I spend a lot of time on my staff, the door is always open. Most of the male managers I have worked for get through their in-tray enormously quickly, I'm not saying they all do, but for many it forms a large part of what they do, whereas I spend more time with the punters and customers. I do the paperwork around people, whereas the contrary is that you see the people around the paperwork. (Adler et al., 1993, p. 121)

Other research has yielded similar conclusions: "Although the activities that men and women undertake to fulfill their job responsibilities are primarily the same, there are some differences in the ways they spend their time, in their day-to-day interactions, in the priorities that guide their actions, in the perceptions of them by others, and in the satisfaction they derive from their work" (Shakeshaft, 1989, p. 170). Some women administrators point out that the incorporation of the skills and processes they emphasize could enrich definitions of good management that have developed from more male, hierarchical structures in schools (Traquair, 1993; Regan, 1990).

Shakeshaft (1989) and Marshall and Mitchell (1989) connect their understanding of the management style of women school administrators to the work of Gilligan (1982), Lyons (1983), and Noddings (1988), which suggests that women tend to operate within an ethic of care while more men function within an ethic of justice.

> Relationships with others are central to all actions of women adminis-trators. Women spend more time with people, communicate more, care more about individual differences, are concerned more with teachers and marginal students, and motivate more. Not surprisingly, staffs of women administrators rate women higher, are more productive, and have higher morale. Students in schools with women principals also have higher morale and are more involved in student affairs. Further, parents are more favorable toward schools and districts run by women and thus are more involved in school life. (Shakeshaft, 1989, p. 197)

This notion of different cultures, gendered ways of knowing and responding to the world, is controversial because of its tendency to polarize and essentialize what we consider male and female (see, e.g., Hare-Mustin and Marecek, 1990). This framework does, however, pro-vide greater insight into how and why women and men may carry out and experience the principalship in different ways than do approaches that count the number of times women and men principals talk to teach-ers or to central office staff.

Efforts to examine gender differences in management style from a structural perspective have contributed to a gradual reshaping of the prevailing definitions of leadership and power. Regan and Brooks (1995), for example, describe feminist attributes of leadership that arise out of women's experiences "below the faultline" of power in our soci-ety.[3] They point out that "school leadership might be enriched by a syn-thesis of below-the fault attributes, generally known and practiced by women, and above-the-fault qualities, grounded in men's experience, but taught to and learned by all women who become successful school leaders" (p. 18). Hurty (1995), too, describes a different kind of power evident among the women elementary school principals she studied. The power "to get the job done" rather than power over people and resources draws on five strategies: a willingness to expend emotional energy, an ability to nurture learning and development, an ability to talk with rather than at others, the use of "pondered mutuality" (i.e., employing a give-and-take approach to making decisions), and a com-mitment to working collaboratively with others toward school change. "The 'different voice' that emerges conspicuously from the data as women speak about their experiences as school leaders is one of con-nectedness and coactivity, of shared and expandable power, and of empowerment" (Hurty, 1995, p. 395). Rita Irwin (1995), in a case study of a woman supervisor, describes this new kind of leadership:

> Leadership framed from a feminist (socialist) viewpoint would concep-
> tualize power as a sharing of responsibility, decision-making, and
> action among participants in an effort to share power with others or
> nurture empowerment. Through leadership, people are empowered to
> improve practice. (p. 153)

Astin and Leland's (1991) investigation of women in positions of
educational leadership from the mid-1960s to the mid-1980s raises
questions about the adequacy of traditional frameworks for explaining
women's leadership behavior. To encompass certain "feminist" aspects
of administration, these authors redefine leadership to include desired
practices and outcomes: "Leadership is a process by which members of
a group are empowered to work together synergistically toward a common goal or vision that will create change, transform institutions, and
thus improve the quality of life" (pp. 7–8).

These studies of leadership and power argue for the need to redefine our notions of leadership, to provide models that challenge the
assumptions and values of the dominant culture of leadership, that
legitimize women's experiences, and that provide alternative strategies
for both women and men. They neglect, however, to examine the
impact of context on the ways in which women carry out their roles.
How does a particular community context affect the definitions of
leadership available to a particular principal? How do issues of class,
race, and age affect the relationships between a principal and the
teachers and families with whom she works? We also need to examine
how others' expectations influence leadership style, and what the
resulting patterns of interaction look and sound like. Do teachers, central office administrators, students, and parents *expect* women to be
more nurturing and caring, more focused on curriculum and on the
social-emotional well-being of students and staff? How do these
expectations create patterns of interaction and establish particular
roles for women that may differ from those of their male colleagues?
Work on women in university teaching (also a male-dominated profession in both structure and persons) suggests that students expect
women university faculty to be more caring and more understanding
than male faculty. When women professors do not live up to these
expectations, students find them wanting as teachers and faculty members; when they do, students find them less rigorous academically than
their more impersonal colleagues (Aisenberg and Harrington, 1988;
Hall, 1982). The case studies presented in chapters 3, 4, and 5 illustrate how this double-bind of expectations creates conflicts for women
principals, both in their interactions with their varied constituencies
and in their evaluations of themselves as school leaders. As long as the
norm of the effective principal remains male-oriented, women may

continue to see themselves as different or to describe their work as balancing what others expect from a leader and what they expect from a woman (Bloom and Munro, 1995).

Impact of Organizational Structure and Culture

Many studies of gender and management style tend to dichotomize male and female approaches and skills, emphasizing women's traditional skills of collaboration and care and obscuring the larger social fabric within which people work. When examined within larger frameworks of institutional power and control, however, these gendered patterns of thinking and action reported by researchers and by the administrators themselves suggest that women in educational administration consciously or unconsciously function within a male-oriented system of discourse, relationship, and power. Focusing on the school as a culture helps reframe the notion of difference, emphasizing less the polarities between the experiences and behaviors of men and women school administrators and more the interaction of life experience and institutional structure in the development of styles of action and interaction.

While all principals have the experience of being in the middle, balancing demands of parents, teachers, and school or district administrators, women and men experience the social system and the bureaucratic structures of the institutional context differently. They operate within different constraints and may respond differently within similar situations as a result of actual and perceived differences in status, experience, and roles. A school or school system can be seen as a culture dominated by masculine language, values, patterns of interacting, definitions of knowledge, and standards of appropriate behavior (Marshall, 1993, 1988; Ballou, 1989; Shakeshaft, 1989; Weiler, 1988; Connell, 1985). These cultural beliefs, behaviors, and values contribute to the production and reproduction of gendered relations and actions at the institutional level (Blackmore, 1993). Given this frame of analysis, new questions emerge in the study of gender and schooling. For example, what are the preferred values and behaviors in the existing culture and what are the values and behaviors of those who tend to be marginalized within or excluded from school administration (e.g., women and minorities)? How do "deviants" (again, women and minorities) operate within that culture (Marshall, 1988)?

In psychology (Bem, 1993; Schaef, 1985) and political science (Ferguson, 1984), researchers have argued that male-dominated institutional structures influence all aspects of women's experience and behavior. It is not gender per se that causes difference but women's and men's

positions in a social structure "so androcentric that it not only trans-
forms male-female difference into female disadvantage; it also disguises
a male standard as gender neutrality" (Bem, 1993, p. 182). Women thus
bring to their work social, interpersonal, and institutional experiences
that differ significantly from men's experiences in society and that operate as subsystems within the larger patriarchal structure. Schaef argues
that a White Male System "surrounds us and permeates our lives. Its
myths, beliefs, rituals, procedures and outcomes affect everything we
think, feel, and do" (Schaef, 1985, p. 2). Women live within their own
Female System and yet learn to function within the White Male System
in a variety of ways, including acting like men or playing out the role of
the traditional woman.[4] Ferguson (1984) has argued that "women's
experience is institutionally and linguistically structured in a way that is
different from that of men" (p. 23). The male bureaucracy, which permeates all public and most private institutions, creates self-perpetuating
mechanisms that make it difficult for individuals, especially those (such
as women and minorities) who occupy token roles, to see, let alone
resist, the structures. Both Schaef and Ferguson suggest that women can
begin to create alternatives once they recognize the larger structures
within which they operate; but these authors also describe the limitations to resisting the existing bureaucracies and structures that characterize institutions such as schools.

When women enter the "administrative culture" of schools, they get
signals that tell them that they can expect occupational segregation and
isolation, the pressures of tokenism, and work in a culture whose norms
were developed with the expectation that males would fill most positions. Marshall and Mitchell (1989) suggest that women principals
experience stresses in their job that men in the same positions do not,
including comments about their gender and flirtatious teasing. Others,
including both peers and their superiors in the system, may expect them
to have problems with discipline and authority, see them as a sex
objects, ignore or isolate them, and give them more work to do and less
credit for their achievements than their male counterparts. Women
administrators are expected to accept and adapt to male values, language, and norms of interaction in order to find a place in the system.

As women adjust to this culture they may learn to adapt in a variety of ways.

> Thus, for women, political lessons are: you must compensate, you will
> be excluded, and you must not make a fuss. Even though they will not
> really be "one of the guys," women should not call attention to that
> fact. Even though they must spend time alleviating other's anxieties
> about their presence, women learn to do this extra work and stay quiet.
> (Marshall, 1993, pp. 172–173)

One result of the press of this male-dominated institutional context is that women tend to personalize any experience of discrimination or difference rather than see it as part of a collective experience (Chase, 1995; Schmuck and Schubert, 1995). Women often speak easily and confidently about their professional lives, accomplishments, and dilemmas. When asked about the role of gender in their experiences, however, they become more guarded and find it difficult to generalize from their own personal examples of discrimination or conflict. The desire to be judged by their competence and to be accepted as a professional overshadows the experience and language of inequity. Women administrators may, then, either ignore the issue of gender or develop individual solutions to inequities they and others experience rather than take an activist stance that makes addressing inequality a part of one's work. The institutional and social structures within which women leaders operate do not support a collective, ideological approach to gendered experience.

EMERGING THEMES IN THE STUDY OF WOMEN IN EDUCATIONAL LEADERSHIP

Prior studies of women and educational leadership have complicated traditional descriptions of effective administrators. They position differences in management style within an examination of the structural contingencies which contribute to and shape a principal's actions and interactions. But these same studies may overemphasize institutional and social frameworks of behavior and belief. They rarely describe the individual's adaptations to those structures, and they provide little insight into immediate or systemic changes an individual can accomplish. When I began to compare and contrast my experiences in the field with the theories and data presented in the literature discussed above, I found that existing frameworks of analysis did not always capture the emerging pictures of women's lives and work in my case studies. By listening to the principals themselves, observing their actions and interactions, and attending to the voices of others with whom they worked, I began to identify a set of four themes that characterized their experience. These themes arose primarily from an analysis of the data collected for the cases, although they also reflect some of the issues raised in the literature on gender and leadership. The first theme, *Becoming a principal: Negotiating the personal context*, uses the experience of the three principals in this study to consider the questions: How do women become principals, and how do their career paths differ from the normative paths established by the many men who have preceded them? How does each woman's personal context affect her entry into the principalship and her assumption of the role? The second theme, *Serving others: Defining leadership in the community context*, examines the questions: How do women principals serve their communities, balancing the varying definitions and expectations of leadership held by the teachers and families with whom they work? How does the community context constrain her work, and how does she shape these relationships given her own background and sense of self? The third theme, *Meeting institutional expectations: Negotiating the culture of schooling*, allows us to ask: How do these principals meet institutional expectations, serving the central office and playing out the role of middle manager? How does a principal both adapt to, and, when she sees the need, challenge the institutional context?

A fourth theme, *Balancing continuity and change: Negotiating within the system*, examines the relationship between the principal and institutional continuity and change. Within this theme, I investigate the questions: How do these principals balance continuity and change in a system that relies on both for success? How do a principal's actions contribute to historical and social expectations about schools and school leaders? How do they challenge these perspectives and structures? The literature on school change (discussed briefly below) provides an additional framework for understanding some of the ways in which women principals may be uniquely positioned to break through the status quo, as well as the ways in which the system constrains their efforts to bring about change.

Each theme reflects the principal's engagement in a different context, moving from a focus on the personal context of the individual, to relationships with others within the community context, to the larger institutional context of schools, to issues of school and social change within a given historical and social context. As I have suggested, these contexts overlap and intermingle; more than one may be involved in any given action, interaction, or experience. The historical and social context, especially, informs and influences each of the others. But in each theme, the balancing act undertaken by the principal focuses on a particular area of experience, providing an opportunity to examine the interaction between the principal and one salient context. The four themes, introduced in more detail below, provide a common frame for each of the case studies presented in chapters 3, 4, and 5 while still allowing us to examine the uniqueness of each principal's experience.

Becoming a Principal: Negotiating the Personal Context

> I can't go back [to teach in the inner city] because the abuse is too difficult for me—the abuse that children receive in black schools. . . . I

know it how it is for these kids, you know. It's available and those kids can't have it. And I can't make it happen, you know. I'm too old in a way, too. Now even more. So I have to do it from here. I have to figure out a way to do it from here. (Jeanne Greer, Interview, 11/91)

Although the personal context and experience each woman brings to the principalship is influenced by larger social and historical patterns in education, individual responses and perspectives differ. Each case study presented here provides insight into that principal's entry into the principalship and describes her initial assumption of the role. For each, certain personal issues and experiences are salient. Jeanne's race, educational and family background, and intense experience as a teacher provide her with a unique foundation for becoming a principal, as reflected in the quote above. Ann's late entry into education, her discovery of a new self in the role of administrator, and her determination to be an independent actor in the world influence her assumption of the principalship. For Ellen, concerns about the status of teachers, mentors who encouraged her work, and a fairly traditional path into the principalship provide a personal context for her future actions. This context helps us to understand how a principal balances personal and professional demands in order to develop a sense of herself as a confident and competent administrator. Negotiating the personal context in becoming a principal includes gaining access to skills and positions that prepare one for the role, developing a sense of confidence in one's own perspective, and beginning to define for oneself what a principal can and should be. This context consists of more than patterns of access or career development, more than the baggage or idiosyncrasies of the individual. It is an ongoing set of experiences that both shape and are shaped by individual history and institutional and social structures and expectations.

Serving Others: Defining Leadership in the Community Context

My families never make me feel anything other than just respected in all. Because most of them just have so much money, they just think everybody does. And it's old money; most of them didn't earn it, somebody else did. But I find in general—and I can kind of take it for granted now—that here on the East Coast there's so much history and so many schools and universities and things that I used to just hear about but not have any connection with. And so I have gotten used to it. And I guess it's partly that I can find my way around, but it is definitely not my world. (Ann Becker, Interview, 2/94)

In the cases that follow, each principal draws on a range of approaches in her work with the parents and teachers who constitute her school community.[5] Ann demonstrates a somewhat impersonal, management-oriented style that allows her to negotiate as a professional with the upper-class, well-educated, and demanding parents described in the quote above. The same approach, however, sometimes feels unduly cold to her teachers. Jeanne looks most like the women leaders described in the literature; she is child centered, oriented toward teaching and curriculum, and more of a facilitator than an authority in a community that both accepts and questions her less directive stance as an educational leader. Ellen balances empathy and authority, presenting a firm, controlling hand within her school's working-class community. Parents and teachers generally accept her use of power; all concur that she has the children's best interests in mind in all that she does, even when they disagree with her decisions. All three principals face the conflicting expectations parents and teachers have of principals and of women; each negotiates this set of contradictions in ways that fit her own personal style and the community context within which she works.

The experiences of the three women described in this book suggest that school leadership is as much about the relationships with others in the community that allow the work to get done as it is about the specific tasks, skills, or roles of the principalship.[6] In the community context, gender influences a principal's approach, her definition of leadership, her emphasis on negotiating interaction with others, and the expectations others have of her in the role. The resulting leadership styles demonstrate the dynamic processes of accommodation and risk taking, adapting to the system and developing a unique voice that characterize these women's principalships.

Meeting Institutional Expectations: Negotiating the Culture of Schooling

> Administratively, I don't know how they [other district administrators] look at her. I think because she's so driven sometimes and [I] think some people feel sort of intimidated by that and tend to sort of make fun of it. Rather than appreciating it and saying wow, isn't that nice. I've heard someone say once that she's kind of a joke up there [in the central office]. . . . Unfortunately when you have a female, a woman who is very successful in their job and very driven—if it was a man it would be like again, "Oh, wow, isn't that wonderful." But instead it's, "Oh, she's so pushy. Oh, she's so aggressive." (Teacher interview about Ellen Fried, 2/93)

All three principals in this study operate within institutional contexts characterized by hierarchical and male-dominated norms. Their immediate contexts differ; for example, two of the principals work in public school districts and one in a private school.[7] But their institutional contexts share many attributes, the result of a common social history within which schools and administrative behaviors have been defined. All three women must find ways to balance their own personal styles and patterns of interaction with the demands of an institution which, to some extent, questions their very presence. Ellen, as the quote above suggests, must negotiate within a male-normed system of status and interaction. She is a team player; she knows how to work the system *and* hold onto her own voice, although she acknowledges the discomfort involved in the negotiations she undertakes. Jeanne describes giving the central administration "what they want" while struggling to maintain her own vision and goals. Ann falters, finding it difficult to sustain her own confidence and style within the framework provided by a new headmaster.

The school as an institution, a culture that constrains and encourages certain ways of knowing, of interacting, and of valuing, frames the relationships and behaviors of the principals who work within it. Because it is a culture that developed around historically and socially constructed, male-normed definitions of leadership, power, hierarchy, and interaction, women adapt to it in ways that influence how they play out their roles as middle managers. Their interactions with central administrators, the ways in which they carry out central office mandates, and the processes they use to balance district, teacher, and parent demands all occur within this culture and are influenced by it.

Balancing Continuity and Change: Negotiating within the System

In the children's story, *Ming Lo Moves the Mountain* (1982), by Arnold Lobel, the main characters, Ming Lo and his wife (whose name we never learn), are unhappy about their home. They live at the base of a mountain, and rocks fall from the mountain onto their house, making holes that allow the rain and sun to enter. Ming Lo's wife decides she has had enough, so she sends Ming Lo to the village wise man to ask him how to get rid of the mountain. The wise man suggests to Ming Lo that he and his wife bang on their pots and pans to scare the mountain away. This plan does not work, so Ming Lo, at his wife's urging, returns to the wise man. The wise man ponders the problem, and then tells Ming Lo to make many loaves of bread and cakes and take them to the top of the mountain as an offering to the spirit of the mountain. Ming Lo and his wife do so, but the mountain remains where it is. Ming Lo goes again to the wise man, who tells him to take down his house, gather up his possessions, and do the "dance of the mountain." To do this dance, Ming Lo and his wife must face the mountain, close their eyes, and put one foot behind the other. If they dance for a long time, the wise man tells him, the mountain will move. Ming Lo and his wife pack up their house and do the dance of the mountain. When they open their eyes, the mountain has moved, and they live happily ever after.

Many who have studied schools suggest that they are, if not impervious to change, at least as difficult to move as the mountain was for Ming Lo. Seymour Sarason (1971) and Daniel Lortie (1975), for example, talk about the behavioral regularities that characterize school life—the cultural patterns, norms, relationships, and expectations that serve as barriers to change. Many of the attempts to change schools, especially in the past ten years, seem to resemble the banging on pots and pans and the offering of bread and cake to the spirits tried by Ming Lo and his wife. In the United States, reform reports like *A Nation at Risk* (1983), the *Carnegie Report on High Schools* (Boyer, 1983), *The Study of High Schools* sponsored by the National Association of Secondary Schools and the National Association of Independent Schools (Powell, Farrar, and Cohen, 1985; Sizer, 1984), and John Goodlad's *Study of Schools* (1984), among others, have documented the problems and called for a range of changes in American high schools. For the most part, the result has been negligible. When the noise died down, schools had actually changed very little.

Where do individuals like Ming Lo and his wife and the three principals in this study fit into this picture? Are they merely the pawns of those who, like the wise man, order the changes? Are they completely helpless in the face of an overwhelming and intractable institution? Is it necessary to fool them into thinking change has occurred in order to make them feel good about their lives and their jobs? We might argue more positively that they are key players in any true change that will occur. The mountain will move only if the individuals most closely affected by it move. And the movement will be most valuable if those individuals move forward with their eyes open, rather than backwards with their eyes closed. In any case, their perceptions of the institution, of the process of change, and of the ultimate goals will all influence any real change that occurs.

The cases presented in chapters 3, 4, and 5 show how principals choose, consciously and unconsciously, to balance continuity and change. The changes they pursue arise out of deeply held values and often conflict with the institutional and social norms that govern the schools. Jeanne, for example, pushes parents and teachers to explore issues of race and diversity; Ellen works to have a veteran teacher dismissed. Ann resists changes in her school, preferring to maintain a stability she has worked hard to achieve. In each case, the individual balances her own and her school's desire for continuity with the efforts required to resist and change the historically and socially constructed status quo that circumscribes her work in schools.

Calls for school reform in the United States in the 1970s and 1980s emphasized specific changes that would lead to school improvement as measured by student achievement on standardized tests. In response to this past work, many recent studies have included an examination of the process of change (Lieberman and Miller, 1990). These studies, such as work by Goodlad (1975), Lieberman (1984), and others document the critical importance of collaboration, teacher participation, and a focus on practical issues in effective school improvement. Many calls for school reform and school restructuring that began in the late 1980s and that have continued into the 1990s focus on site-based management, developmental and child-centered approaches to teaching, alternative forms of assessment, and teacher empowerment and involvement in decision making. These studies emphasize the need to develop a professionally supportive work environment for teachers that parallels a positive climate of learning for students. To create such an environment, those who aim to change schools may need to draw on the resources of other institutions, parents, and communities (see, e.g., Lieberman and Miller, 1990; Bastian et al., 1985). Principals are targeted as key players in this process, people who can help or hinder changes in attitudes, structures, and roles.[8]

Few of these calls for and studies of change in schools examine the influence of gender on the cultural norms and interactions of schools, and yet, as the case studies in this book demonstrate, change is clearly affected by who is trying to carry it out, the process being used to make changes, and the kinds of changes proposed, all of which may be influenced by historically and social constructed expectations, norms, and relationships. In addition to displaying general institutional inertia, schools resist changes that challenge or threaten the male-dominated bureaucracy and the patterns of behavior that reinforce it (Ferguson, 1984). These changes include hiring women administrators, recognizing alternative forms of management, and developing programs or policies that incorporate previously untried forms of learning and interaction.

Adler et al. (1993), Ballou (1989), Marshall (1985), and Shakeshaft (1989, 1987) all argue that the male-dominated structures, processes, and value systems in society and in schools limit the number of women hired into administrative positions and then constrain their actions once hired. If women approach leadership as feminists and want to develop different approaches, goals, and processes, they may be frustrated and limited in what they are able to do. If their more "female" management styles are less conscious, they may be unaware of the constraints, less able to draw on the support of others, and more likely to blame themselves for their lack of success in certain areas. In either case, they are forced to balance the need to be successful and professional in a male-normed system with their awareness of their difference (Chase, 1995; Dunlop, 1995).

Women may choose to use gender as an issue as they act and respond as leaders or they may unconsciously make choices that draw on their experience as women in the larger society and in the school context. Leadership approaches described as "female" may be more constructively interpreted as conscious or unconscious acts of resistance within the larger school and social structures. Such actions have the potential to challenge the dominant culture of the school institution and of the larger patriarchal society (Dunlop, 1995). Although Ferguson (1984) avers that resistance leading to institutional change is close to impossible within existing bureaucratic structures, Ferguson, Schaef (1985), Chase (1995), and Grogan (1996) suggest that developing a feminist discourse which reflects women's experience may lead to the development of a female system that can challenge and redefine the dominant discourse and institutional structures. But the existing culture of schools, and indeed, the larger social structures within which schools operate, make this task difficult. Even if the changes women administrators want to make have little explicit reference to gender, women leaders may face institutional barriers that reflect both general inertia and a more specific resistance to a woman making changes. Women principals may learn to function successfully within such a system at the expense of their own values and perspectives:

> Schools are structured to run like rational bureaucracies with apolitical decision making, order, and communication chain of command, logical division of labor into specializations and promotion by competence for well articulated functions. But no one who looks closely (e.g., by ethnography) at the day-to-day operations or who listens to the stories told by educators about how to function in schools will really believe this myth. Instead administrators learn to use the rhetoric and the legitimized controls of bureaucracy to lend credibility for their actions. Administrators know that they must speak and act as if all actions are rule-based when actually they know how to function as street level bureaucrats to survive. They know to maintain the myth of contest mobility and affirmative action although they recognize how easily that is undermined in site-level discretionary allocations of responsibility and opportunity. They know to value the maintenance of order above all else, but many use their discretion to incorporate counseling and nurturance in their dispensation of discipline and in conflict management. Thus the bureaucratic myth is maintained. Women educators learn to maintain it as they become increasingly "competent" administrators. But in doing so, they are learning to support a system and a cul-

ture which may, in fact, be alien to values related to caring, support, and nurturance. . . . [F]or women to even appear at all in the administrative culture is to challenge it, but to appear different (e.g., by demanding reform, by articulating new goals, by redefining methods) is especially risky. (Marshall and Mitchell, 1989, p. 31)

School change is not impossible, but given institutional and cultural expectations and regularities, it is very difficult, perhaps especially for those who do not fit the norms of the institution.

Conversely, women principals may have an advantage in trying to implement school change; the leadership styles described in the literature on effective school restructuring often parallel those attributed to women administrators. As outsiders, with a different set of experiences and different ways of operating in the bureaucracy, women may be more able to see the system at work, more willing to take risks, and more aware of possible changes that would improve the teaching and learning environment than those who have never had to challenge or question their place in the institution of school.

GENDER AND SCHOOL ADMINISTRATION: SOME CONCLUSIONS AND CAVEATS

Gender is only one variable in determining an individual's leadership style and effectiveness. While gender shapes the female administrator's worldview, school and life experience, and modes of interacting with others, it is one of several interacting factors that influence her behavior and effectiveness (Charters and Jovick, 1981; Schmuck, 1981). In both the individual's life and in the community in which she works, issues of race, ethnicity, and class come into play, as do particular organizational structures in the school district and community, and other issues, events, and experiences in the life of the individual. Frequently, the literature on gender and school administration neglects this diversity in its examination of the experience of the women administrators studied. Just as women are rarely included in the general study of educational administration, so are issues of race, class, and context missing from the studies of women in administration.

Race is never mentioned in the general studies of educational administration as a factor which might interact with other issues in determining how a principal carries out her tasks, develops skills, or takes on certain roles. The limited existing literature on minorities in administration (work that focuses primarily on African American administrators) suggests that race does indeed influence career path, approaches to management, and the experience of the principalship. For example, the majority of African American principals in the United States tend to be assigned to large urban schools with all African American student bodies (Valverde and Brown, 1988; Ortiz, 1982; Doughty, 1980). Such assignments often represent and perpetuate assumptions that African Americans can (and should) work only with other African Americans (Coursen et al., 1989) and may limit administrators' opportunities to move up in a system whose gatekeepers are white men. The language used to describe the barriers and constraints encountered by African American administrators parallels that used to describe the experience of women: "Most theories of leadership behavior in educational organizations assume that schools consist of academically and racially homogeneous pupil groups managed by white males" (Valverde and Brown, 1988, p. 143). African American principals may face role conflicts resulting from opposing demands as they work to overcome stereotyping, explain why school districts are not working for minority students, respond to minority constituents, demonstrate loyalty to central office superiors, fellow administrators, and teachers, and serve as agents of change (Valverde and Brown, 1988). Conversely, Lomotey (1989) argues that having race in common allows African American principals to have greater communication with students and parents and greater ability to involve the community in the school, both of which contribute to their success in helping students in predominantly African American elementary schools achieve.

Edson (1988), in her study of 142 female administrative aspirants, found that both affirmative action and community pressure contribute to the hiring of minorities. Some of the minority administrators Edson surveyed believed that even if hired in part because of gender or racial "quotas," they would prove their competence once in the job; others felt that they were channeled into assistant or lower-level administrative positions as a result of race and gender discrimination. Most agreed, however, that they had achieved their positions through competence, not because of their ethnicity or race (Edson, 1988; Doughty, 1980). This interpretation echoes the more general desire to see difference as individual rather than collective and to give one's professional work priority over any collective response to discrimination (Chase, 1995; Schmuck and Schubert, 1995).

Just as the addition of the lens of gender complicates our view of the school principal, so does the consideration of other important social and personal constructions of self and other modify our understanding of school leadership. Issues of power, control, bureaucracy, relationship, curriculum, supervision, learning, role expectations—all key elements of the school principal's experience—arise within the multiple contexts of the social, economic, and political structures of the society, the school district, the school community, the school itself, and the personal history of each individual. Weaving together a complete story, a description of the life and work of a school principal, is a complicated task, one that cannot be simplified into a list of traits, tasks, responses, or management styles. In examining the balance between individual and institution, professional success and the experience of inequality, the case study approach (described in detail in the next chapter) provides an opportunity to illustrate, challenge, and expand our views of the styles and experiences of women administrators, even as it provides insight into the complex factors that shape individual principals' lives and work.

CHAPTER 2

Methodological Dilemmas

When asked about how it had felt to have me "shadow" her all year, Ann Becker said:

> Having you with me has been a very interesting thing. I would say to anybody that ever has the chance to do this, it certainly makes you think about yourself, maybe more than you might because you're talking about yourself more, and it makes you think about what you value in a school. And so, you know, it's just, it's been fun for me. (Interview, 7/94)

In response to a similar question, her school head, who had been working most of the year to ease Ann out of her job, responded:

> I think you've been wonderfully helpful for her. . . . I think that you've allowed her some perspective, you've been a good sounding board, you have kept her on her best behavior in some ways. She is not the person that you see every day. She's been a lot better more consistently, but your presence there and . . . having her know that you were going to interview the whole country has made a positive impact in a lot of ways. It has, at times, I think, also made it harder because she's tried to cover both sides of the fence, and you can't do that. . . . She really respects you, which helps, and you listen, you know? You're not there to judge anything that happens, and that makes a huge difference. And so I see that as a positive. We've gotten a free consultant; do you want to do it again next year? (Interview, 5/94)

These two comments reflect many of the issues and tensions inherent in the research methods used in this project. In developing rich case studies of the lives and work of three women principals, I found myself negotiating my roles and relationships with the principals themselves; with the teachers, parents, and administrators in the three schools; and, subsequently, with readers as I debated with myself about the stories, themes, and issues to present to others. These dilemmas appear to be inherent in critical, or reflexive, qualitative research (see, e.g., Kincheloe and McLaren, 1994); they are certainly characteristic of case study research (Hatch and Wisniewski, 1995; Stake, 1994; Goodson, 1992; Burawoy, 1991); and they have been of particular interest to feminist qualitative researchers as they seek to carry out ethical, rigorous, and socially transforming research (Chase, 1996; Josselson, 1996; Fine, 1994; Kelly et al., 1994; Maynard, 1994; Oleson, 1994; Stewart, 1994; Lather, 1991; Acker, Barry and Esseveld, 1991; Fonow and Cook, 1991; Stacey, 1988). In this chapter I examine the dilemmas which arose in this study, demonstrating that the methods chosen to discover and represent principals' lives and work are necessarily complex.

The research process and its outcomes are inextricably interwoven; understanding the principalship as a dynamic process of negotiation requires methods that provide insight into always changing actions, interactions, and meanings in the contexts within which they occur. Such methods are grounded in experiences and relationships that highlight the shifting multiple meanings present in the reality of the research settings. These approaches also allow for—in fact, almost require—an openness on the part of the researcher to changes in focus, in framework, and in analytic perspective. I began this study believing that gender was a key, and perhaps determining, factor in the experiences of these principals. Midway through the process of data collection, I was much less sure of that stance; the data and the principals' perspectives seemed to minimize the role of gender. At that point, personal background and style and institutional and structural constraints emerged as more dominant variables. I also questioned the validity of imposing a gendered framework on the experiences of those who did not share that perspective (an issue discussed in more detail below). In the final analysis, I have returned to gender as a salient category for understanding the process of the principalship. But this most recent understanding has been complicated and enriched by a dynamic, interactive research process that allowed individual and institutional patterns to emerge from the data and that maintained the voices and perspectives of those involved.

My overall goal in this study was to use qualitative methods of research, in particular participant observation, semistructured and unstructured interviews, and document collection and analysis, to generate case studies of three women principals. By using life history, case study, and feminist approaches, I can illustrate, challenge, and expand our views of the styles and experiences of school administrators. These approaches situate the behaviors of the individuals within the community, institutional, and larger social and cultural contexts within which they work and allow us to see how individual styles, issues of gender, and institutional contexts converge, interact, and change over time. This kind of research, and my own personal style, required that I develop relationships with each of the three principals that were founded on trust, mutual respect, and care for one another's personal and professional well-being. We did, indeed, form such relationships, which have continued beyond the life of the research study. But these same relationships created tensions as I carried out the research and as I made decisions about what to report and how to report it.

DILEMMAS IN THE RESEARCH PROCESS

Researchers across the social sciences have, in the last twenty years, begun to reflect on the dilemmas inherent in conducting research that involves more than a distant researcher-subject relationship. While we have always examined the ethical issues of engaging in work with others, there is a growing introspection around our own roles and responsibilities in the field and a more explicit acknowledgment that new definitions of research relationships raise previously unexamined personal and professional issues. For example, life history and case study researchers often call for a collaborative relationship between researcher and researched since each participant brings a particular viewpoint and set of meanings to the situation at hand (Goodson, 1992, 1991; Smulyan, 1992). At the same time, they recognize the tensions involved in the notion of collaboration, given the differences in power and purposes the researcher and research participants bring to the experience (Hatch and Wisniewski, 1995; Fine, 1994; Stake, 1994; Goodson, 1992).

In carrying out this study of three women elementary school principals, I faced many of the dilemmas described in the literature on case study, life history, and qualitative feminist research. These challenges may be grouped into the following four categories of questions.

- Why do case studies? And why study only women? How can only three case studies provide us with insight into the larger issues of the role of gender and context in school leadership? These questions were especially salient as I first designed the study and again as I returned to data analysis and writing.

- What were my roles in each school? Was I an observer and interviewer? The principal's friend and confidant? A vehicle through which teachers could meet their needs? A buffer? What use would we all make of the information I gathered in each school?

- What was my relationship with the principals involved in the study? Could I be a friend and a researcher? What should they tell me? What should I use? What kind of interpretations could and would I make about their actions and interactions that would preserve the trust we had developed and also serve my research goals?

- What effect might my being a feminist researcher have on these principals, women who typically did not use gender as a lens to frame their own experience? To what extent did my focus, my questions, and my presence change their ways of seeing and acting in their institutions? Should I, and did I, contribute to empowering them or changing the social world within which we operate? To what extent does my interpretation of their work and life situations reflect the framework I bring rather than the meanings they make in the situation?

I will consider each of these dilemmas in more detail below, and, in doing so, introduce the design of the project and the three principals.

The Case for Case Studies

The rationale.   Several years ago I found myself in a room of academic colleagues, being interviewed about this project in order to qualify for institutional funding. "Why are you only studying women?" one asked. And, "What can you learn from looking at only three cases?" queried another. For many of us engaged in qualitative, case study, and feminist research, the answers to these questions sometimes seem self evident. But to much of the academic world, they continue to require explanation.

My decision to do case studies of women principals grew out of a felt need, one described by Charol Shakeshaft:

> Histories, case studies, and ethnographies almost always center on the male principal or superintendent. Consequently, we know little of the individual lives of the women who occupy these positions. (Shakeshaft, 1989, p. 56)

In looking for books for a course entitled "School and Society," I found examples of teachers' lives and work (e.g., Cohen, 1991; Weiler, 1988; Connell, 1985), but only empirical studies of women principals (Shakeshaft, 1989; Edson, 1988) with no accompanying stories that would help students understand the complexity of the experience of women in educational administration. Wolcott's 1973 study of *The Man in the Principal's Office* is one of the few qualitative studies of principals, although new studies on women in leadership have begun to emerge, including Chase's 1995 qualitative study of women superintendents, Irwin's 1995 examination of two women leaders in a Canadian school district, and Grogan's 1996 analysis of the experiences of women aspirants to the superintendency.[1] Case studies, then, fill a gap in a body of literature that until recently has provided a limited understanding of the lived experience of women educational leaders.

Life history and case study research provide methodological frameworks for this study. Both approaches emphasize the importance of exploring the relationships between the individual and the contexts (community, institutional, and historical and social) within which she operates; it is through examination of an individual life that culture "speaks itself" (Reissman, 1993, p. 5). Sharon Kaufman (1993), who uses life history to explore the history of medicine in twentieth-century United States, explains how focusing on the individual contributes to our understanding of social structures and institutions:

> By viewing social change through the lens of individual experience, we are able to move away from infinite generalizations and abstractions and into the realm of individual constructions of meaning. For it is only at the level of the individual life that larger social and cultural phenomena acquire significance and the individual-cultural relationship is distinctly represented. Through the examination of several individual's lives, we gain access both to multifaceted meanings of the self-within-the-culture and to a richer, more detailed portrait of the culture which contributes to and is constituted by those meanings. (Kaufman, 1993, p. 326)

Given their particularistic bent, both methodologies also invite reflection on the generalizations possible from the findings presented in the life histories or cases. When challenged about the possibility of generalizing from single cases, researchers argue that case studies contribute to the development of grounded theory, and, in doing so, influence the ongoing conversation about our understanding of the world (Stake, 1994; Burawoy, 1991; Orum et al., 1991; Donmoyer, 1990; Schofield, 1990; Merriam, 1988; Yin, 1984). This kind of theory construction relies in part on the researcher's presentation of the case, but it also depends on readers' construction of meaning as they connect the new information to their own experiences and understandings (Stake, 1994; Donmoyer, 1990; Merriam, 1988). Traditional generalization implies movement from the particular case to all members of the population represented by that case. In contrast, case study researchers "identify general patterns, themes, metaphors and images across the cases through the process of comparison and contrast" (Rossman, 1993, p. 110). Even as they emphasize the importance of focusing on the particular situation and meanings developed within that situation, case study researchers also look for larger social patterns: "The importance of the single case lies in what it tells us about society as whole rather than about the population of similar cases" (Burawoy, 1991, p. 281). What we can learn from each case may be more important than what we learn from trying to generalize across a small number of cases (Stake, 1994). "Only three" cases can therefore be seen as three valuable opportunities to examine patterns and processes experienced and created by individual women principals in different settings. Using these three particular examples, we can begin to explore the relationships between a principal's experience and the institutional and social cultures within which she lives and works.

Like life history and case study work, feminist qualitative research in the social sciences often accomplishes its goals by focusing on women's immediate, context-based experience. These methods appreciate the value of allowing an individual voice, one that is often underrepresented, to be heard, respected, and legitimized (see, e.g., Reissman, 1993; Burawoy, 1991; Ball and Goodson, 1985; Beynon, 1985; Plummer, 1983 on life history research; and Stake, 1994; Merriam, 1988; Walker, 1986; Yin, 1984 on case history methods). Such a focus offers an opportunity to examine previously silenced stories within the larger social patterns framing women's lives (Franz et al., 1994; Reinharz, 1992).[2]

> What focusing on the everyday life of women should do instead is reveal that connection between public and private, between production and reproduction. In socialist-feminist research, the everyday world is not a self-contained world; quite the contrary, it is an integral part of the social whole. What's more, the relationships and values of that private, everyday world are shaped by larger social and economic forces. (Weiler, 1988, p. 61)

Detailed cases allow us to hear individual voices, relate them to our own experiences, and see how they reflect larger social patterns and issues. Especially in a male-dominated field, such as educational leadership, cases can provide insights that support, inform, and challenge theories of administration. Sandra Acker (1990), in one of the few ethnographies of a primary head teacher in England, explains that current studies of school management focus on lists of tasks, skills that can be taught, and the fragmentation and unpredictability of the head's day. These studies fail to describe the simultaneous, dramatic quality of events; they provide no detailed account of the daily activities and the emotions that accompany them; and they offer no sense of the continuation of issues and events over time. Narratives, on the other hand, provide insight into the complexities of the principal's actions within the multiple contexts of community, school, and society. Others who focus on the contributions of women to new definitions of school leadership, agree:

> Case studies are especially important because they provide us with examples of what transformational leadership actually looks like, insight into the qualities of the individuals who are transformational leaders, an understanding of the struggles to achieve empowerment, and finally, vicarious experiences of transformational leadership through stories or narratives. Elevating these examples allows for opportunities to find one's voice in the midst of many competing voices. (Irwin, 1995, p. 11)

It is therefore acceptable, and even beneficial, to do cases of women without doing similar studies of men; case studies of women allow us to give full attention to previously untold stories. They also provide an opportunity to reframe the story of the principalship, removing it from the normative discourses that have been created and sustained by men who have traditionally filled the role and carried out research on school administration (Grogan, 1996).

The combined approaches of life history, case study, and feminist qualitative research provide more than a set of values and methods that guide this study. These same approaches have also supported my other, more action-oriented research goals. In doing any research in schools, I have always aimed to have the work in some way contribute back to the immediate context within which I work (Smulyan, 1992; Oja and Smulyan, 1989). Feminist researchers call for an action orientation, although they recognize the difficulties involved in carrying out such research (Schultz, 1998; Kelly et al., 1994). Educational researchers, too, have frequently struggled with the combined goals of contributing to knowledge in the field and affecting practice (Lieberman, 1992; Oja and Smulyan, 1989). As a researcher, I want to do work that meets both goals: I want to recognize the "deeply political nature of everyday life" (Weiler, 1988, p. 63) and contribute to our understanding of the gendered nature of our experiences while working toward actual change in practice. Life history, case study, and feminist research, all of which emphasize a collaborative process between researcher and researched, allow for the possibility of addressing these goals, even as they lead to some of the dilemmas described in later sections of this chapter.

The three principals. The three principals chosen to participate in this study embody some of the variables I wanted to consider as I asked questions about the interactions among the individual, gender, and context. The three principals differ in age, race, and class; although they all head schools for children in grades 1–5, the institutions within which they work are quite different from one another. Two of the principals work in public schools; one is the head of the lower school in an elite private school. One of the public schools is in a middle-/upper-middle-class suburban area and the other serves a working-/lower-class community; the private school attracts upper-class families. All three are located in the metropolitan area of a large Eastern city. Each case stands alone as a unique story about how that principal negotiates her life and work in her community and school contexts. And yet, some themes resonate across the individual stories as well.

All three women are elementary school principals who had been in their current positions for at least five years at the time of the study. In all three situations, I first negotiated an agreement with the principal to participate in the study and then asked for and received permission from the appropriate school or district administrator. In all three cases, both the principal and the administrators agreed with little hesitation.[3]

Jeanne Greer is an African American woman who, after having taught for twenty years, became principal of the Greenfield-Weston Elementary School. Greenfield-Weston serves a middle-/upper-middle-class, predominantly white suburban community, and is the same school in which Jeanne had taught for twenty years. She had been principal for five years at the time of the study and had just turned fifty. I knew Jeanne prior to the study through my college's use of her school for field placements and our work together in a summer program for middle school students several years earlier. I consider her both a friend (we talk about our children, about schools, and about our work over lunch or dinner) and a colleague (I frequently use her school for my own students' placements and research). At her request, I wrote a letter of recommendation for her when she applied for the principalship; she, in turn, wrote for me when my husband and I needed references for an adoption. When I contacted Jeanne about being a part of the study, she asked for a day to think about it and then, the following day, said yes. We slipped easily into a new working relationship that was built on prior trust and experience with one another. Our personal and professional relationship has remained strong since the time of the study.

Ellen Fried is a forty-five-year-old white, middle-class, Jewish woman who had been principal of Fieldcrest School for eight years at the time of the study. Fieldcrest serves a predominantly white lower-/working-class community on the outskirts of a large city. My prior contact with the school was relatively limited; I had placed a group of students at Fieldcrest several years earlier to do a research project for a course, and a former student of mine had taught there for three years and had just left. I had heard that Ellen was a dynamic, effective principal, but I had never met her when I first called to ask if she would be interested in participating in the study. She told me several months later that, after our first meeting, during which she agreed to be a part of the study, she panicked, wondering what she had gotten herself into. She was somewhat formal and reserved with me during our initial interview and the first several weeks of the study. This behavior contrasted with the fairly direct, outgoing approach I observed as I watched her in action in the school. Over the course of the year, however, she gradually opened up to me about personal and professional matters, even as I shared my own work and life with her in our many informal conversations. Ellen and I have remained in contact since the study, meeting for lunch or dinner on occasion and drawing on each other's professional skills when appropriate. I have, for example, written job-related references for her; she has helped me place student teachers and has been a guest speaker in one of my classes.

Ann Becker, a sixty-seven-year-old white woman from a rural, working-class community in the Midwest, had been head of Pepperdine's lower school for five years at the time of the study. Pepperdine, an elite private preparatory school, serves a predominantly white, wealthy clientele. My only prior contact with the school was, again, placement of a group of students to do a course-based research project. When I contacted Ann about participating in the study, she was pleased to be considered. She later told me that she became involved because "she liked my research and she was just used to helping out, like with graduate students who needed a place to work; she was flattered to be asked; and it could only be good for the school to get people to reflect on what they were doing" (Field notes, 9/8/93). Ann immediately made it clear to me that I could attend any meetings I wished or ask any questions; once she decided to participate in the project she committed entirely. She told me both implicitly and explicitly that she shared things with me that she would not tell anyone else (Field notes, 4/6/94). Ann and I have remained in touch since I left the school, although she no longer lives and works in the area.

Data collection and analysis.   To collect data for these case studies, I spent at least one day a week for a year in each of the three schools as a participant observer "shadowing" the school principal. The data for Jeanne's case was collected during the 1991–1992 school year and for the other two cases between June 1993 and June 1994. I took notes in the field (and was teased about my yellow pad in all three schools) and wrote extensive field notes each night following the observations. In these notes I recorded the principal's formal and informal meetings, actions, and interactions during the school day and her conversations with me as I followed her through her day. I also attended and documented Home and School organization meetings, Back to School nights, district administrative council meetings, faculty meetings, and some committee meetings. In addition, I conducted four or five two-to-three-hour semistructured interviews with each principal over the course of the year, asking about prior life experiences and current issues in her work. Midway through the year, I began to contact and interview teachers and parents from each school and other school administrators about their perceptions of the school in general and of the principal. I usually began with teachers and parents with whom I had had previous contact through my observations and then interviewed others to get a range of perspectives in the school. I interviewed between fifteen and twenty teachers and administrators in each school and district, although that represented a different proportion of the staff in the school (e.g., at Fieldcrest I interviewed about one fourth of the teachers; at Greenfield-Weston I interviewed about half of the teaching staff; and at Pepperdine I interviewed almost all of them). I also interviewed between eight and ten parents in each school, following up on leads about parents who had different relationships with the principals and schools and recognizing that this sample was limited. Principal, teacher, and some parent interviews occurred in the school; a few parent interviews were held in private homes. Most interviews were taped and transcribed; with those who preferred not to be taped I took notes and rewrote the notes within the same day.

In order to construct a detailed description of each principal's life history and school experience and effectiveness, I analyzed the data both during and after data collection using processes described by Becker (1951); Glaser and Strauss (1967), and Schatzman and Strauss (1973). I had few, if any, preexisting expectations of analytic categories; my goal was not to impose existing frameworks on the principals' experiences but to see what patterns emerged in the process of data collection and analysis. As I collected the data, I kept reflective notes on emerging themes and patterns and my own thoughts and feelings about the research process. These continuous reflections served as initial data analysis, often providing questions and ideas that led to future data collection via observations and interviews. Following the year of data collection and preliminary analysis, I developed codes based on key issues and themes observed in the data, and coded all field notes and interviews. The computer program Hyper-Research helped me to organize all of the data coded in a particular way, which contributed to the clarification and modification of patterns I had seen. In addition to themes in the data, I also identified one or two key "stories" (Acker, 1990) that developed during the course of the year for each principal. These stories form the core of the case study chapters in this book, illustrating the specific trends within each principal's life and work and the general themes that emerge across the three principals' experiences.

Finally, I showed a draft of each case to the principal involved. While I debated whether or not to do this, as have other researchers (Chase, 1996; Lieblich, 1996; Datnow and Karen, 1994; Acker et al., 1991), I felt that each participant deserved to hear and respond to my presentation of the meanings they constructed in their social world.[4] I have, when appropriate, included their reactions, without changing my interpretation of what occurred. I will discuss further, below, some of the complications involved in this aspect of researcher-participant relationship as I consider the multiple roles I assumed in each school, my developing relationship with each principal, and the impact of the study on the principals' sense of themselves and their work.

Multiple Roles

I sat, as unobtrusively as possible, jotting down notes at a meeting between the principal and several teachers at Fieldcrest School one morning in March. At one point, the teachers in the meeting, trying to reconstruct a list of ideas they had just brainstormed, turned to me and asked me to read back my notes to them. Startled, and a little embarrassed that I did, in fact, have their ideas down almost verbatim, I found the list and read it aloud. We all laughed at this use of my "unobtrusive" note taking and the meeting went on (Field notes, 3/12/94).

This incident illustrates the impossibility of being an uninvolved researcher, perhaps especially in schools, where people always seem to be looking for more time, more support, more people, and more resources. Datnow and Karen (1994), for example, describe how they planned to enter the schools in their study as nonparticipant observers to document detracking programs. Instead, they found themselves being asked for advice and support and making decisions about when and how to use their insiders' information to help people and programs succeed. Principals and other administrators also used their presence as an intervention to maneuver a change in their schools. Mehan (1996) describes how his research team consisted of people from the teacher education program of the local university who were also an active part of the K–12 educational community they studied. They describe how the "various entanglements" of researchers and participants "both facilitated and constrained their project" (Mehan, 1996, p. 22). Other educational researchers have made it their goal to foster relationships and collaborative ventures in schools that lead to school change although they continue to recognize the difficulties for both researchers and school practitioners in bridging the gaps caused by different training, institutional requirements, and perspectives (Lieberman, 1992; Oja and Smulyan, 1989).

In each of the three schools in which I was an observer, I was also a participant, and the roles I played influenced both what I saw and what others chose to tell me. On the one hand, principals and teachers in the schools saw me as detached, removed, and quietly separate from their lives. Ellen told me that, in describing my presence in the school to a group of graduate students taught by one of her colleagues, she said,

"This woman is so amazing because she is the most like—neutral, innocuous, and yet she's got all of us telling her everything. It's like we don't even know she's there." And Carol [the professor and colleague] said, "It's true. You know this is the quietest writer of notes we've ever seen!" (Interview, 1/94)

Principals, and the teachers, parents, and administrators with whom they worked, had difficult conversations in front of me about children, about classrooms, about hiring and firing, about what they needed and when they needed it. The life of the school certainly continued undeterred by my presence. If I was not ignored, I was often integrated into the ongoing processes and interactions at each school.

On the other hand, principals and teachers alike told me, both implicitly and explicitly, that they used me and my presence for their own purposes. Each, for example, used me as a way of controlling one another's behaviors. A teacher at Fieldcrest explained during an interview that she and her colleagues asked Ellen for things when they knew I was there because "it is more likely Ellen will listen and we'll get a response" (Interview, 2/94). Ellen pointed out that when either I or the new assistant principal came with her to meetings "people have this desire to put their best foot forward" (Interview, 1/94) and so seemed to be more cooperative and polite. At Pepperdine, a teacher stopped me and asked me what I thought of the new science teacher candidate. When I responded that other people I talked to did not seem too impressed, she pointed out that a person we both knew, who was the head of a school in the Boston area, would have been on the phone to elite graduate schools of education asking them to send him their best people. The teacher maintained that it was not her place to tell Ann what to do, but she wondered if perhaps I could suggest to Ann that she make such a call (Field notes, 6/1/94).

At all three schools, being in and around the front office and being an observer meant I knew people's whereabouts and schedules and the issues or concerns of the day. As a result, in all of the schools I sometimes helped people find the principal, answered questions about what meetings were happening when and where, and occasionally volunteered to cover the phones or walk a class down to lunch when I perceived that such help was needed. At Fieldcrest I worked a few times with a third-grade boy who had serious emotional and behavioral problems and whose teacher frequently asked him to leave the classroom. At Greenfield-Weston I talked several times with a teacher interested in the possibility of getting a degree or certificate that would allow her to supervise student teachers. I also occasionally helped Jeanne set up the room used for meetings or assemblies.

Questions about when to intervene and what role to play went beyond these usually unplanned and voluntary uses of my presence as an aide, buffer, and conduit of information. All three principals would ask me for my perspective on the issues at hand; each, at some point during the year, said, "You have to come in and see this meeting," or "I'm glad you're here. I want to ask you about. . . ." Usually they just wanted me to be there, without necessarily expecting explicit feedback or help. For example, Jeanne called me one evening and told me I did not want to miss the next day's faculty meeting; she had been preparing it for several days as her first real attempt at school-based management. She was not asking for help, only saying it might be interesting for me to be there. On another occasion, at Fieldcrest, I met with Ellen before her meeting with the fourth-grade teachers to discuss class lists for the following year. Ellen explained that she was concerned about some of their decisions, including the placement of only one African American child in one class, four in another, and none in a third. She wanted to raise this issue at the meeting and said that she was glad I would be there because I could provide some perspective. I was not sure exactly what she expected from me; it seemed inappropriate for me to enter into this conversation. At the meeting, she raised her concerns about the African American students and several other issues. She and the teachers did some major reshuffling of students, while I observed and said nothing (Field notes, 6/17/94). In this case, the conversation preceding the meeting seemed to have been more a means for Ellen to practice what she wanted to say to the teachers than a request for intervention.

At other times, principals asked me for direct feedback or help. On a couple of occasions, Ellen asked me to read the observation reports she had done of teachers' classrooms to see if I felt she was being clear and fair, given what she wanted to communicate about what she (and sometimes we) had seen. Jeanne once asked me to look at the workbook of a child who wrote and spoke nonstandard English. She and the child's teacher had been debating about whether and how to correct his writing, and Jeanne asked for my opinion. When Ann talked to me about her plans for the future, she sometimes sought specific advice. For example, in October she showed me her letter of evaluation from the head of the school. She said she did not want to sign it because it included a statement with which she disagreed; she asked for my perspective on that decision. In most of these cases, I tried to mirror back to the principals what I heard them saying, so they could hear it again and reflect upon it. I did, on occasion, offer my opinion as well, especially when it confirmed theirs and provided support for their intentions or decisions. If and when I did disagree with something, I tried to present my view as another possible option, or I kept it to myself. For example, in the situations above, I told Ellen that I thought her written evaluations meshed with what she had told me and would be something the teachers could read and respond to comfortably. I gave Jeanne some background information on the debates about teaching nonstandard and standard English. And I suggested to Ann that if she chose not to sign the letter, she might want to include a statement of her own saying why. But in each situation, I found myself wrestling, on the spot, with the difficulties of balancing my roles as researcher (not wanting to influence my "subjects'" decisions), educator (with opinions of my own), and friend (wanting to support each principal at that moment).

In another situation at Fieldcrest, described in more detail in chapter 5, Ellen was gathering evidence to be used to dismiss a teacher. I was well aware of the many issues involved; I had heard many of the conversations between Ellen and other administrators, Ellen and this teacher, and Ellen, the teacher, and some parents. I interviewed this teacher late in the spring, using my standard questions about his work and experience in the school and his perspectives on Ellen as an administrator. During the interview he described his work and his relationship with students, parents, and Ellen in ways that belied much of what I myself had observed and heard from other sources. I doubt he knew how well informed I was about his case, although he certainly knew that I talked frequently with Ellen and sat in on many meetings. That night, as I wrote up my notes of the interview (he had asked not to be taped), I wondered whether or not to share the information in it with Ellen.

> I thought about reporting this to Ellen and decided not to. I really feel an obligation to preserve confidentiality, even though I think this teacher should go and my not talking to her may withhold information that would help her strategize. (Field notes, 5/94)

In this case, my roles as researcher, as educator, and as supporter of the principal conflicted and I chose to err on the side of researcher. Here, the confidentiality of the teacher seemed more important than helping Ellen strategize and contributing to a process of dismissal that I believed was the right educational decision. Not keeping this teacher's confidentiality would, I felt, jeopardize all of the other promises I had made as a person and a researcher in this school. But it was not an easy decision.

At Greenfield-Weston, perhaps more than at the other schools, I sometimes felt the stretch of playing several roles simultaneously, since I continued to have other professional connections to the school besides my research project. At one point I found myself observing while Jeanne and the assistant superintendent interviewed one of my former students for a teaching position. On several occasions I had conversations with teachers in the school about joint business, such as a program bringing fourth-graders and college students together to work on a computer project. Also, because I was at the school so frequently, I heard from teachers about college student observers and aides who did not show up or about their interest in working with a student teacher. In addition, some of my academic colleagues who knew I had a working relationship with this school (although few knew about the research project) felt comfortable sharing their views of the school and the principal with me or asking my advice. In one case, for example, a colleague looking for information about an appropriate teacher for her rising first-grade daughter asked my opinion of Greenfield-Weston's various first-grade teachers. I described to her what I knew about the teachers and the classrooms. A few days later Jeanne told me that this colleague had called to request a particular teacher for her daughter based on information she said she had heard from some of her college students. I described to Jeanne the conversation this colleague and I had had, and I apologized for sharing information that was unavailable to some parents. Here, my role as researcher was complicated by my roles as college professor and member of the community.

Like other educational researchers, I faced the dilemma of balancing the roles of researcher and practitioner. As I collected information to contribute to a body of knowledge that seemed somewhat remote to the participants involved, I tried to maintain my other more personal or practice-based roles and connections in the schools. The value of maintaining our awareness of our multiple positions as we carry out research, encouraged by feminist researchers (e.g., Wolf, 1996; Fine, 1994), is ever present in this form of educational research. Our multiple positions and roles shape decisions that affect our relationships in the field, the data we can collect, and the ways in which we will interpret that data for others.

Researcher-Researched Relationships

Feminist researchers, in particular, have examined the dilemmas involved in establishing trusting, mutual relationships as a part of the research process (Chase, 1996; Josselson, 1996; Fine, 1994; Kelly et al., 1994; Acker et al., 1991; Fonow and Cook, 1991; Stacey, 1988). They argue that these tensions may be more salient for feminist researchers because the conflicts involved challenge some of the underlying goals and values held by those who define themselves as feminists (Wolf, 1996). Stacey's (1988) classic essay, "Can There Be a Feminist Ethnography?" raises questions about whether it is truly possible to avoid an exploitative relationship between researcher and researched and whether, in fact, a feminist approach creates a "delusion of alliance" between women researchers and their subjects. She asks if these approaches actually mask a kind of exploitation, and she argues that researchers' reflexivity about their own frameworks and constructions does not resolve the conflict between a collaborative process and a unilateral product within which the researcher imposes her own meaning on the situation and events. Others, too, examine the contradictions involved in trying to recognize and acknowledge the subjectivity of the participants (researchers and researched) *and* provide an analytic framework for interpreting that experience (Acker et al., 1991; Smith, 1977). Feminist researchers have come to recognize that the multiple positions they and the participants involved hold will always affect their relationships. Issues of power and control before, during and after the research project must be continually reexamined and negotiated (Wolf, 1996).

My relationship with each of the three principals differed, depending on prior interactions, our personalities, and the school situation. In all three cases, though, we became both friends and professional colleagues. Although I think that my "research" remained an abstract concept for all three principals, they seemed happy to help out. They recognized that the work was important to me, even though academic research was not necessarily familiar to them or immediately relevant to their daily work. They would say, on occasion, "Here's an interesting situation for your book" (Field notes 4/7/92), or would ask when the manuscript would be done. For my part, I made somewhat amorphous contributions to their daily work. Principals do not have a peer, a companion, or a sounding board on a regular basis; I was in the unusual position of knowing about their work and personal lives and could be present for them in a way that no one else was. I liked and respected them, and I was willing and able to listen and sympathize and, when necessary, respond to their concerns. At the end of the year, Ellen said,

> See, next year I'll probably lose my sanity 'cause you won't be here. I'll feel lonely. No really. You were a highlight, to have you here. Like I said Monday, I think every principal should have one [a shadow]. . . . I've loved it. I'm like sad that you're going. Can you stay? (Interview, 6/94)

I was struck, on occasion, by the eagerness with which each principal often welcomed me when I arrived at the school. "You picked a good day!" Jeanne said to me. Or, "I'm glad you're here; I wanted your opinion on something," Ann would say. I frequently reflected in my field notes on the fact that each of the principals seemed to appreciate my presence as a support, someone who knew enough to be able to empathize with and appreciate their experiences. Sometimes, I would comment on the generous amount of time each woman shared with me at the school. Each insisted that she looked forward to those times, that without me there she would never take the time out to reflect or talk through some of the events and issues of the day. I was pleased that my presence did provide something for the principals; I wanted my research to give something back to the people and the schools within which I worked, even if the "something" was rarely concrete or immediate. I also wondered, though, if I occasionally allowed myself to become complacent with the little I seemed to contribute, accepting our comfortable, apparently reciprocal relationship as enough (Wolf, 1996). In addition, the positive and personal relationship I shared with the principals made it more difficult to create and sustain analytic distance. The sense of responsibility I experienced within these relationships may have influenced both the data I collected and the way I have chosen to interpret my observations in this book.

At Greenfield-Weston, my prior relationship with Jeanne made our research-based relationship a relatively comfortable one from the start of the process. When the assistant superintendent asked her how she liked being shadowed, Jeanne responded (with me there) that she "loved it. It's nice to have someone to bounce things off of." When I remarked, teasingly, that I made myself useful by getting markers and things when she needed them, she added, "She even knows I need things before I ask" (Field notes, 12/12/91). We did not have many explicit conversations about the fact that we were friends and supported each other; we just did it. A couple of times during the year, after a difficult experience, I would ask Jeanne how she was. She would share her feelings of discouragement, or frustration, or determination to make things better, sometimes crying a bit in the process and apologizing for "letting down." One evening she called me, saying she needed to talk about a variety of personnel issues that had arisen over the course of the year and had recently come to a head, in part because of parent concerns. We talked for a while about the specific issues; I asked questions and made occasional comments or suggestions about things to try. In each of these situations I was glad that Jeanne felt comfortable enough with our friendship to "let down," that she trusted me to provide a sympathetic ear. I do not think much of what I said was immediately useful; I rarely, if ever, saw Jeanne follow up on an idea I had provided. My willingness to be a knowledgeable and sympathetic listener seemed to be more important than any specific advice I could give. And the process worked both ways. I would often share my own stories with Jeanne; the year during which I shadowed her I went through the process of adopting a second child, and Jeanne was frequently there for me as I lived through the ups and downs of that experience. I found, though, that while the research process asked Jeanne and the other principals to open up all aspects of their lives to me, I could choose what parts of my life and work to share: another example of the power and control the researcher wields in the process (Wolf, 1996).

As I wrote Jeanne's case, I wondered if I was presenting enough of the critical perspective that wove through some of the teacher and parent interviews, criticisms that I could document from my own observations as well. Could I be a "critical friend," simultaneously an outsider and an insider? I may have erred on the side of a sympathetic portrayal, because I myself see the overall picture as positive. When I showed a draft of her case to Jeanne, she told me that she found it difficult to read about herself. Eventually she forced herself to read the draft as a "learning process." She commented on how hard it was to see reflected in the case aspects of herself that she usually tried to avoid acknowledging.

> She said she was able in reading this to recognize pieces of herself she could not recognize in other circumstances. She's heard some of those characterizations of herself but wasn't able to see them. She's heard that she's defensive—and she could see what that meant from this piece—it made her stop, pause. It was a "golden opportunity to get another vision of myself from someone with whom I feel totally safe." (Field notes, 3/11/94)

Jeanne also commented that she had, at some point in the process, worried about whether or not I would still be her friend after doing this project. She no longer had those worries, having convinced herself that our friendship was not an issue. Although we have not discussed the project again in great detail, for a couple of years after the data collection year Jeanne would point out to me that she now did things differently, or that she had learned a great deal since the year I shadowed her. We have remained good friends and colleagues; the project is one in a series of interactions we have in our joint history. But I still do not know how objective or critical I have been in gathering and presenting the data for this case.

As mentioned above, Ellen was the most reserved of the three principals at the beginning of the project. More than the other two, it seemed as though she felt my presence as a responsibility, at least at the beginning of the school year. In her first interview, Ellen was relatively restrained, although once the tape recorder went off she loosened up a bit and told me I was "easy to talk to." At the end of the first several weeks of observing, I asked her how she was doing with my presence. She commented, "We'll get used to each other." Earlier that day she had also commented, in a half-teasing way, that she must have been "brain dead" when she agreed to do the project (Field notes, 9/13/93). I know that she thought about the project and my visits when I was not there because she would often save something to show me or write down ideas to tell me based on a prior week's conversation. She would some-times call me during the week to tell me her schedule or let me know what was coming up. Like the other principals, she would comment that I had chosen a good day that week. In Ellen's case this usually meant that she could engage me in a range of different kinds of activities with her—observing a teacher, interacting with students and parents, attend-ing a meeting—what she called an "educational" day, as opposed to a day filled with discipline or crisis management or paperwork. Although I do not think that Ellen felt she had to entertain me, I do believe that, of the three principals, she was most conscious of wanting me to have a good, well-rounded experience.

It also took longer for Ellen and me to share personal as well as pro-fessional conversations and insights. During the course of the year, Ellen's mother became quite ill and, in December, she died. In October, when her mother entered the hospital, Ellen asked me to leave the room when she had phone conversations with her father, sister, and brother. For some time she did not speak with me directly about her mother's illness; I had only surmised it from other things I had heard. Eventually, she did begin to tell me about it and we talked about how her mother's illness and death and her father's adjustment to the loss influenced her and her work. In the same way, Ellen kept to herself a new romantic relationship that started in late September. At an administrative meeting in October, Ellen intro-duced me to a principal who was a close friend of hers and then moved away for a private conversation. As they returned to where I stood, this friend asked Ellen if she had told me. When Ellen said no, the colleague teased, "You have to tell her everything!" Ellen promised that if anything good happened in the next eight weeks she would tell me, commenting that she had enough things happen in her life in the past eight weeks to be three different people (Field notes, 10/19/93). Again, we eventually began to have conversations that included these more personal aspects of our lives, but they came a bit more slowly with Ellen than they had with the other two principals. By midyear, our conversations about our work and home lives seemed very comfortable and open, the reserve replaced by a mutual respect and care for one another. Ellen's case seemed relatively easy to write; I respected her work and felt that she knew the pros and cons of her own actions and interactions. It seems possible that a rela-tionship grounded first and perhaps foremost in professional agreements and respect might have created an easier path for me as a researcher. In addition, I, like Ellen, am white, middle-class, Jewish, and an educator. These common characteristics may contribute to shared perspectives and attitudes that influence how I interpret and present her case.

Ann, more than either of the other two principals, used me as a sounding board for ideas and looked for advice and support. Her year-long struggle with the head of the school about her job and her tendency to distance herself somewhat from teachers and other administrators (both of which are described in more detail in chapter 4), probably contributed to Ann's interest in my views. Like Jeanne, though, she sometimes solicited my perspective but then used our conversations more as an outlet than as a resource for ideas to put into action. She mentioned on several occasions that I was a valuable support to her, or that she told me things that she never shared with anyone else about both her work and other aspects of her life. Again, this openness felt like a gift, a valued part of friendship, but also a responsibility.

In Ann's case, I had the most mixed feelings about my roles and our relationships. I liked Ann and admired her work; she honestly cared a great deal about the people she served and she set high expectations for performance—her own and others. On the other hand, I listened to administrators and teachers and knew their reasons for asserting that she should leave within the next year or two. As an educator, I agreed with several aspects of their arguments. I also knew how badly treated Ann felt, how much she needed someone to talk to, and how difficult the whole process was for her as a person and a principal. In this situation, I sometimes felt that I was being less than honest, not saying all I knew to anyone. When asked or told something controversial about Ann, I accepted it as that person's perspective and tried to mirror back to them what I heard being said rather than adding in my own complicated view. In most situations, people just wanted to hear that I could understand and empathize with their assessment of the situation. I did, at times, try to help Ann think about ways of handling situations that would make her more comfortable (e.g., if she chose not to sign the evaluation letter, she could write an explanation to accompany it), allowing her to deal with what seemed like her inevitable departure and maintain her own sense of self-respect. She had one other confidant in the school who gave her more direct advice; I, however, was with her on such a regular basis that I probably heard more specific incidents and concerns, and I wanted to support her.

I brought to these relationships an honest respect for the work the three women carried out. Because at one point in my career I had thought I might become a principal, this project allowed me to look at what I might have done. I talked with Jeanne, Ann, and Ellen about their work, my own teaching and past experiences, education in general, and the education of my own children. I left the field in all three cases extremely impressed with the work of the three principals and connected to each of them by bonds of friendship, professional respect, and mutual care. During the course of the data collection and analysis, and as I wrote the cases, I reflected on these relationships. I thought about how they affected me and the people with whom I worked, and how they had shaped what I could see and report. I believe that the kinds of relationships the principals and I developed allowed me to have much richer insights into these women's personal and professional lives, the meanings they construct, the actions they take, and the choices they make. In my experience, the collaborative, trusting relationships called for by life history, case study, and feminist researchers contribute a great deal to the meaning and depth of a research project. Because these relationships raise questions about roles, ethics, and interpretation, I tried to collect enough data through a variety of means—interviews, observations, documents—to validate the perspective provided in the cases. Still, that perspective remains inevitably colored by the values and relationships I brought to the project.

Feminist Research on Nonfeminist Subjects

The lens I brought to this study, and the findings that emerged from it, suggest that gender is one powerful dynamic in the experiences of the three women principals with whom I worked. Each of the women, however, tended to examine her own life and job from an individual perspective that rarely included gender as a theoretical or political lens. This conflict in our perspectives raised a number of dilemmas for me. First, a tension existed between my framework of analysis and the stories that these principals each told me, or the stories they believed they were telling me. Where I heard a gendered construction of experience that could fit into a general theoretical framework, they each heard their own individual story, unique to them. Should I present the story these principals believed they were telling about themselves, or should I describe the story that I heard and saw?

A related tension arose as I realized that, even when the three principals did see and describe issues of gender in their lives and work, they preferred not to credit gender with much influence and not to generalize from it as a way of explaining their own and others' experience. For Jeanne, Ann, and Ellen, to acknowledge the role of gender in their lives seemed to suggest an inability to function as a legitimate leader in the given structure of schools, an inability to control one's life and work. As I listened to their stories I heard a tension between these principals' descriptions of their experiences in the world as women and their ability and willingness to explore the implications of those experiences. This disjuncture had implications for my relationships with the principals and affected my decisions about how to tell their stories and mine.

Finally, I experienced a tension between the goals of feminist research and the actual outcomes of the project. Feminist researchers often aim to carry out research that contributes to social change, in particular the improvement of women's experience and position in society (Fine, 1994; Kelly et al., 1994; Maynard, 1994; Acker et al., 1991; Fonow and Cook, 1991; Lather, 1991; Weiler, 1988). Some feminist researchers have aimed to raise the consciousness of those with whom they work, assuming that this leads to empowerment grounded in the individual's new understanding of and ways of acting in her social world (Wolf, 1996; Maynard, 1994; Lather, 1991). As I developed strong personal and professional relationships with the three women in this study, I began to question the ethics of imposing my framework of meaning on their experience, even though that framework emerged from an examination of their lives and work. These women's perspectives allow them to function effectively in an individualistic, male-dominated system; challenging their perspective might mean undermining their strategies for effectiveness. I ended this study feeling that genuine changes in consciousness and empowerment were elusive and had to be documented as carefully as the different stories themselves.

When I presented this project to each of the three principals, I explained that I was interested in looking at the lives and work of women principals. I said that I wanted to investigate how the past lives and experiences of teachers and administrators affected their current work and response to school change. In addition I noted that some literature suggested that women administrators had management styles that differed from men; I wanted to see what different patterns of leadership looked like in real school situations. The principals who participated in this study were not chosen because they had strong feminist leanings or because they were especially aware of gender issues in their lives and work. Consequently, part of the research process became an examination of the effect of my research questions on their experience and understanding. In the sections that follow, I explore, first, how each of these women viewed herself when she looked through the lens of gender and, second, the impact of this study on the women's perceptions of themselves and their work.

Self-definition: The principals' views of gender. When presented with my plans for the study, all three principals commented that they did not think gender had made much difference in their lives and work. Often, after explaining that they were not feminists or that gender made little difference in their experience, each principal would go on to explain how, in fact, gender did influence her life. At our first meeting, for example, when asked about the role of gender in her life and career, Ellen said she always thought of herself as a principal, not as a female principal. She then went on to make fun of a statewide meeting of women administrators that focused on how to dress for success (Field notes, 5/6/93). At our next meeting, however, she held an index card on which she had written down a number of incidents or events in which gender had played a part, brought to consciousness by my questions. For example, Ellen related that as a reading teacher, she had told her reading supervisor that she thought she should get some experience teaching in a lower elementary grade classroom before considering administration in order to gain more legitimacy. Her supervisor responded, "How many men do you know that have taught a lot or taught all these levels? Do it if you want. It's not necessary" (Interview, 8/93). Ellen recognized the truth of this comment, using it to illustrate how she had not always seen how her own path was influenced by the gendered expectations of herself and others.

At other times Ellen said she was not sure if gender mattered. Again, she tended to follow a statement of uncertainty with an example of how being female had made some difference. When asked if gender affected the way in which she ran the school, Ellen replied,

> Not really. That may just be a bad sign of an inflated ego. I think there are times when, now, I'll give you an example, but I do think there are times when being a woman makes a difference. For example: I think the work with the architects and the construction people [during an earlier renovation] was beneficial because I can talk the lingo a little bit now and I'm not intimidated by it. At the beginning I was. But if I walk into room full of men and there are construction people there, I think it does matter that I'm a woman there because I have to establish myself a little bit. Like, I had some contractors in here—they were just taking the graffiti off the walls—the maintenance people sent them down. They never came in [to my office]. And I said, "I want to know [what's going on]. It's not a big deal, but I want to know." And they were like, "Oh, we're sorry." (Interview, 8/93)

Despite being unsure about the role of gender in her own life and work, Ellen worked hard to raise her colleagues' awareness about gender issues with students in the classroom. Since 1983, when the district formed an Equity Committee, Ellen has been its most active member (and usually its co-chair), going to training sessions outside of the district, finding and developing materials (worksheets, videos), and doing workshops for teachers throughout the district. None of these activities are common practices for most of the district's principals. Connell (1985) points out that many women teachers are stated or unstated feminists in their insistence on equality of opportunity for students, but fewer see feminism in terms of power issues for themselves. Like Connell's teachers and other women in administration, Ellen shied away from describing her experiences as the result of gendered discrimination.

She focused instead on ideas of individual success, power, and accomplishment that reflect the norms of the systems of education within which she was raised and worked. While she and her female colleagues in the district (one other principal and two central office administrators) interacted frequently and exchanged gendered stories, they tended to focus on particular events or issues rather than on more generalized theories or gendered explanations for what went on. This unconscious strategy may have allowed them to negotiate the institutional hierarchy more successfully given their relative isolation and lack of power.

Ann, like Ellen, tended to first deny the role of gender in her life and then expand on how it may have influenced her perception of herself in the role of principal. When asked explicitly if she was a feminist, Ann said:

> I don't believe so. I don't really know, Lisa. Number one, because I have three daughters, because my oldest one at [a large corporation] has faced a lot of things that I think could come under the discrimination kind of thing. I do feel that as a woman in whatever time in your life that you have to work awfully hard to prove that you can do something. And, you know, it's accepted that there are more women principals—whatever you want to call us—in lower school than there are in middle and there are more in middle than in high school. And oh my God, heaven forbid that you should be a high school principal. . . . But you know, I guess I don't really know what all would be involved in the women's' movement. I think that women have to be very careful as to what kind of image they portray. I think that you've got to have that balance between yes, you're feminine and how sexy you want to be seen, if you're going to play that game with men, you're going to take the consequences. And so I do feel sorry, especially for women that are very good looking and are trying to climb up any kind of ladder. It's better if you're homely, frankly, because then you cannot associate the two. (Interview, 8/93)

Ann seems to associate being female with needing to overcome gender stereotypes, or at least learning how to use them to one's advantage. She explains that she works to keep her emotions under control, and that she is very conscious of how she dresses (often in suits) in order to manage the impressions she gives as a woman head of school (Marshall and Mitchell, 1989). Ann implies here that to be principal you have to control external manifestations of femininity, although, again, she describes this in personal and individual rather than structural or political terms.

Jeanne's references to the role of gender in her life tended to be more implicit. One day, early in the year, I walked into Greenfield-Weston Elementary School and Jeanne said: "I'm in good spirits—I have a *Sweet Honey* song going in my head—'Tote that barge, lift that bale, Everybody knows I can work like Hell. Lord, I'm a woman!'" (Field notes,

10/7/91). In addition, for Jeanne, race, gender, and class intertwine in a dynamic that influence her experience, her actions, and the responses of others to her. For example, Jeanne was aware of the symbolic and political role of all three variables in her selection as principal; she knew that one central administrator wanted her to have the job, "Because he admired me. Because he's smart, you know, he's no dummy. That's a lot of tickets I bring in. I'm a black female principal. And I live in this town. And the people love me. But underneath it he's a poor, blue-collar person too. And it makes him feel good that I've made it because of him" (Interview 10/91).

Like the women in Chase's (1995) study of women superintendents and Schmuck and Schubert's (1995) study of women principals, the principals I studied tended to focus on their own individual actions and responses rather than the more generalizable experience of women as a framework for understanding their lives and work. Their stance may have resulted from a lack of opportunity and support for this kind of reflection. It also resonates with the norms of the educational meritocracy, which emphasize individual effort and success. But the possibility that these women's approach may also be an unconscious strategy for managing their interactions and experiences in a male-dominated profession and institutional structure presented a dilemma. Could and should I challenge their strategies for defining themselves and succeeding within their given work contexts?

Impact of the study on the principals.   To what extent did my openly stated interest in gender at the beginning of the project frame what the three principals told me? To what extent, if at all, did it change the way in which they came to see and interpret their experiences? To what extent is Patti Lather's expectation of feminist research, that it "encourage self-reflection and deeper understanding on the part of the researched as least as much as it is to generate empirically grounded theoretical knowledge" (Lather, 1991, p. 60) an imposition of a way of understanding the world as much as it is the first step toward social change? What should researchers do "when our understandings and interpretations of women's accounts would either not be shared by some of them, and/or represent a form of challenge or threat to their perceptions, choices and coping strategies" (Kelly et al., 1994, p. 37)?

As the above discussion suggests, my own framework did seem to contribute to the three principals' ideas about gender, providing them with a new perspective on their experience. I doubt that Jeanne, Ann, and Ellen would have generated examples of the effects of gender on their experience if I had not asked each of them directly about gender. Middleton (1989) and Weiler (1988) explain how women educators become politicized, gradually learning to use feminist ideas to articulate their own concerns as social and political issues rather than personal problems. Both note that feminist women teachers have all personally experienced discrimination or marginality. These experiences prepare them for later openness to feminist educational theories. Middleton and Weiler also suggest that women teachers who take a gendered stance have had access to feminist social and educational theories in a form that helps them to explain and articulate their own experiences.

Each of these three principals had experienced what I would identify as discrimination or marginality as a result of gender. Race, class, and age also influence their perspectives, however, perhaps making them less likely to focus on gender as a single explanatory framework. In addition, although Ellen had some familiarity with issues of gender equity as it applied to students, neither she nor either of the other two principals were familiar with feminist theory that might have provided a framework for explaining their experience as part of a larger system. All three principals usually preferred to attribute actions and behaviors to specific individuals and contexts rather than to larger social patterns such as gender.

Over the course of the year, my presence and occasional questions may have prompted them to think about gender as at least one way of conceptualizing their experience. Perhaps this serves as an example of what Kelly et al. (1994) describe as "challenging methods" (p. 38), ways of doing research that both create knowledge and question oppressive attitudes and behaviors, sometimes by raising with participants different ways of understanding their experiences. Without any prompting from me, one of them would occasionally ask me a question about issues of gender or comment on the gendered nature of an experience. Ann, for example, asked me about the pros and cons of coed versus single-sex schools for students in grades K–12 and college, and we talked about some of the issues raised by research in the field. At an administrative council meeting, Jeanne explained to the assembled principals, assistant superintendent, and the superintendent (all men) that she needed to talk about the use of extra classrooms and the library in her school. When the superintendent said she should not expect to move the library out to the other building at her school site during his tenure, she said she wanted to start working on it under his tenure so that when the new man—or woman—came along she'd be ready. There was general laughter around the room at her addition of woman. I wondered at the time if Jeanne would have added—"or woman"—if I had not been present or doing the study with her (Field notes, 10/7/91). Ellen began to use gender to analyze more of her interactions with the other administrators in her district, most of whom were male. Although she did not theorize about what was going on, she would describe the "old boys' network," or comment that she felt a little strange about being the only woman *and* having a different viewpoint or way of operating. On a day when she shared her office and adjacent conference room with the new head teacher, a social worker visiting the school to run workshops for students, and me (all of us female), Ellen stopped mid-sentence, looked at us, and asked if we thought a man could have shared his phone and space with so many people. She then went on to describe how she and two other women administrators had recently shared a hotel room at a professional conference. She commented that they had a great time staying up late talking—but they had wondered if the male administrators would have shared a room to save the district money (Field notes, 1/25/94). Although she did not necessarily draw consciously on a gendered understanding of her experiences in the course of a day's work, Ellen indicated here that, perhaps as a result of my questions or presence, she recognized that gender affected her administrative experience.

Still, it was not simply the lack of a theoretical framework that kept the three principals from using gender to analyze their experience. For example, while Ellen sometimes recognized that gender seemed to make a difference, she shied away from that explanation; it seemed to place interactions beyond her control. Gendering a situation was something others did to you, or worse yet, you did to yourself. In either case you no longer had agency, the autonomy to act.

> When you did that first interview with me and I was—not exactly defensive, but I would say I was strident with you, and [I said] "Oh, well, no, you know, my father vacuumed, and I grew up in a household where"—you know, I even said to the class the other day, I said, "I always pull back a little from the word 'feminist,' but yet I think there are gender issues." And then I had that sort of myriad of little experiences where it was only the men, and I thought the men were sort of getting overbearing, and I thought to myself how could I ever—'cause the truth is even when they don't do it to you, you do it to yourself. (Interview, 6/94)

When the three principals read and commented on drafts of the case studies I had written about them, they tended to focus almost entirely on the particular comments and issues raised by others about them in quotes I had used. They often wanted to refute what they heard as a misunderstanding on the part of another person, and so would reexplain their perspective to me. They rarely, if ever, commented on the general argument that gender had contributed to the shaping of their experience. Their primary common concern was that no one would want to become a principal if they read these cases. This reaction suggests, again, that a more socially constructed perspective felt more negative and perhaps more paralyzing than the particularistic and individualistic lens they used to explain and cope with their daily lives and work contexts. Using gender as a frame for analyzing their own experience might undermine their own sense of legitimacy in the power structure. It may also give them a political agenda in the eyes of others, making it more difficult to carry out their plans and goals.

If the three principals asked me, and they did on a few occasions, whether or not I saw gender operating in their experiences, I would say that I did, in addition to many other variables and issues. I might give them an example of how I saw their actions or responses influenced by the gendered expectations of others, or repeat back to them their own stories of how gender seemed to influence a choice they had made. I made decisions in the research process, based on our relationships and my goals, about whether or not, and how, to impose this frame on their thinking. My general stance was to keep gender as a frame for analysis, to offer it when asked, to ask questions that might encourage the principals with whom I worked to consider it as one lens through which they could see their experience, but not to insist on that lens as the only possible explanation. I do not believe that the "disjuncture" (Chase, 1996) between my analysis and interpretation and the stories the principals told me reflected any break in our relationship, nor did it keep me from maintaining their voices in the stories.

To some extent, the respect and trust we developed over the course of the year of the research allowed us to share with one another these sometimes different perspectives, to keep them in dialogue, feeling that we could learn from one another about different ways of seeing and knowing without feeling that we needed to convince one another of a particular truth. In this way, this research project maintained the goals of critical, feminist research and of educational research that contributes to the people and schools within which it occurs. The principals themselves experienced no great epiphanies about their lives and work, nor did they completely accept the gendered framework I provided of their stories. They did, though, come to understand and respect my perspective as a way of seeing their world and, perhaps, began to see it is a way of understanding some of their own experience. And I respected their relatively atheoretical, context-based process of making decisions that allowed them to be responsive, effective, and self-confident administrators.

CONCLUSIONS: THE CONVERGENCE
OF METHOD AND OUTCOME

The dilemmas I faced in carrying out this research included balancing multiple roles, negotiating relationships with the three principals, and maintaining the integrity of the principals' voices while telling my own version of their stories. It is not coincidental that similar terms—balance, negotiation, roles, and relationship—emerge both when I describe the project's methods and when I frame its outcomes. The methods I chose simultaneously reflect and influence the story I tell about the dynamic process of the principalship. Methods and outcomes in this project depend on an understanding of social life as constraining of and created by individuals who construct meaning and relationships in multiple contexts. This understanding leads us, as researchers, to use methods that allow us to find and consider those various levels of reality and to present findings that reflect a consciousness of our own voice as one of many.

Life history and case study approaches, used within a feminist framework, allow for this individual, context-based approach in which the complexities of people's daily lives can be represented and examined as a part of larger institutional and social systems of power and interaction. Each relationship, each setting, each set of interactions changed over time, influencing decisions made by the principals and by me as researcher. Although such methods create the dilemmas described in this chapter, they also allow a researcher to reflect on those inherent tensions in the research process that ultimately contribute to our understanding of the complicated fabric that constitutes individual and social life. For this reason, we must continue to recognize and document the tensions that exist between the various stories, frameworks and goals in the research process, allowing the voices of researcher and researched to emerge, overlap, and when necessary, conflict. By describing both the research process and product we have a richer understanding of the relationship between individual and social context and between theory and practice. We emerge with a better understanding of the diverse strategies and perspectives that help each of us function in different contexts within the social structure.

CHAPTER 3

Dancing on Water

Jeanne Greer, principal, calls Amy Grant [a young woman in her second week of teaching who has decided to quit] into her office. Jeanne says, "Here's what will happen. I will come up and talk with the class with you there—we'll sit on the rug. I want the kids to ask questions, so I can't tell you exactly what I'll say or what will happen. Then I'll introduce Evelyn [the new teacher] to them. Listen to the kids during the day, the questions they ask. They can drag things on inappropriately, too, so you'll have to listen to them." Jeanne says she will tell the children she wants them to go back and be students today, but Amy will have to sense if they're just being clingy or if they need to talk. Jeanne says the kids may feel a loss, anxiety. "So—go up and do it." Jeanne continues, "This may be the beginning of your maturity, leaving home. You are taking charge of your life, making a decision." As Amy leaves, she asks, "Do other teachers know?" Jeanne replies that some do— Elizabeth and the other first-grade teachers Evelyn would be observing that day.

Half an hour later, in Amy Grant's classroom, Jeanne sits on the floor in the reading area and goes around the circle trying to say each student's name. If she doesn't know, she asks what it starts with. She asks all the kids to sit on their bottoms. She explains that she will be called out in a while to go to an assembly, but right now she wants them to sit and listen and then ask questions. "Last night I had a meeting with your parents to announce that Ms. Grant was not going to teach at the school any more. When something big happens, sometimes kids think, 'What did I do?' but Ms. Grant's reasons for going are not you. I want you to know for sure, it's nothing you did. Ms. Grant wants to leave to be with younger children, but there are no younger groups in this school so she has to go somewhere else. So we don't have a job for Ms. Grant. I have interviewed people and found someone to be here with you." Then she asks the kids to ask questions or say how they feel. A couple kids say they feel happy. One little girl says there are tears coming out of her eyes but she doesn't know why—

she's not sad. Other kids said they are worried the new teacher will be mean. Jeanne asks what a mean teacher does. When kids tell her, she says, "But doesn't your mother say things like that sometimes—is she mean?" One kid says, "My father does that." Another comments, "My mother said you wouldn't hire a mean teacher." Jeanne says, "That's right—have you had a mean teacher here?" Jeanne promises the new teacher is not mean, and says they will see for themselves. A couple other kids say they feel weird. A couple say they really like Ms. Grant a lot and wish she could stay. Amy says she likes them too but wants them to have the best teacher they can have. Jeanne corrects her: "The most experienced teacher." (Field notes, 9/12/91)

When this study began in 1991, Jeanne Greer had been principal of the Greenfield-Weston Elementary School for five years. The school serves a middle-/upper-middle-class, predominantly white community (Greenfield) and a smaller white working-class community (Weston). A fifty-year-old "American black" (her term), Jeanne taught in this same school for twenty years before becoming its principal. Jeanne's child-centered approach and her unique way of capturing the best in people shine through in the vignette above. In addition, we see Jeanne's ability to take control, telling a teacher that she is "taking charge of her life" just as Jeanne has begun to take charge of the principalship. Management and decision-making skills do not come as naturally to Jeanne as do the "people parts" of her job, leading some of her constituents and colleagues to praise her for her warmth but question her ability to lead. Jeanne has worked hard to clarify her "vision" and find ways to begin to translate it into reality. Increasingly, that vision has included ideas about how to diversify and improve the experience of all children in the school. To implement her ideas, Jeanne struggles with balancing the traditional demands of administration in a relatively traditional school district with her own sense of who she is and how she wants to do the job. A parent, reflecting on Jeanne's attempts to meet the diverse demands of a vocal community, describes her as "dancing on water" (Interview, 6/92). The image is apt: Jeanne is a powerful presence in the school and community. As she negotiates personal, community, district, and historical contexts, she does not just stay afloat. She works to create a dynamic work of art on a constantly shifting surface.

Overview of the Themes

Jeanne's story of *becoming a principal* illustrates a process influenced by gender, race and class. Like many other women administrators, she taught for many years with no intention of becoming a principal (see, e.g., Polczynski, 1990; Grant, 1989; Shakeshaft, 1989). First as a child, then later as a teacher, Jeanne experienced school as a place in which people cared about her and she could succeed. When others convinced Jeanne to apply for the principalship, despite her lack of training and experience, she and they knew that her gender and race made her a good candidate for a variety of complicated and sometimes conflicting reasons. Her prior personal and professional experiences lead Jeanne to focus on meeting children's needs and developing a caring school community. At the same time she works hard to develop the more traditional management skills expected of a building principal.

As she *serves others* in the Greenfield-Weston School community, Jeanne has to balance her own style with contradictory expectations others have of her as a woman and a principal. Effective principals, by tradition, lead with authority and directness, drawing on historically male models of hierarchical control (see, e.g., Blackmore, 1993; Ortiz and Marshall, 1988; Yeakey et al., 1986). In contrast, the literature often characterizes women leaders as caring, collaborative, and empowering of others (see, e.g., Hurty, 1995; Regan and Brooks, 1995). When Jeanne exhibits a leadership style that emphasizes more characteristically female patterns of behavior, parents and teachers praise her attention to others and criticize her lack of firm leadership. When she takes a more authoritative stance, as she does around issues of diversity, they sometimes question her right to do so. Race again enters into the process, affecting others' expectations of Jeanne and her own conscious positioning as an "outsider within" the community (Collins, 1991).

In order to *meet institutional expectations*, Jeanne has to negotiate her role within school and district cultures whose norms reflect hierarchical patterns of interaction and decision making (see, e.g., Marshall, 1993; Ballou, 1989; Shakeshaft, 1989). When the district mandates a shift to school-based management, Jeanne explores ways of learning the process of democratic decision making and teaching it to others. Teachers sometimes resist the process, expecting a "real" leader to make unilateral decisions. Democratic practices also conflict with the district's authoritative power structure. Jeanne must develop strategies for meeting the demands of the male-dominated central administration while not losing her own voice in the process (see, e.g., Marshall, 1988; Schaef, 1985; Ferguson, 1984). She adapts to the prevailing culture but also finds ways to resist and challenge it.

Jeanne's attempts to meet institutional expectations while resisting some aspects of its culture contribute to her ability to *balance continuity and change* (see, Grogan, 1996; Dunlop, 1995; Marshall and Mitchell, 1989). Her personal background and teaching experience lead her to develop a vision of a school that better meets the needs of African American children and that helps all children, teachers, and parents become more knowledgeable about issues of racial and cultural diversity. Jeanne takes a more directive stance than she usually assumes in order to carry out this goal, challenging unspoken and often unrecognized biases that limit community members' perspectives and actions. In doing so, she begins to provide a model for leadership that challenges historically and socially constructed norms for school administrators.

Those who study women in administration run the risk of essentializing the characteristics and experiences of women leaders. By examining Jeanne's work within the contexts of her own life history and the community and school district within which she works, we can begin to explore how historically and socially gendered expectations of leadership frame and often constrain her actions. Her principalship challenges the discourse, the expectations, and the norms of both leadership and "female" leadership. Jeanne's story demonstrates that race, as well as gender, contributes to the dynamic process in which she engages, both constraining her in her role and giving her a powerful voice with which to pursue change.

BECOMING A PRINCIPAL: NEGOTIATING THE PERSONAL CONTEXT

So I'm learning how to be an administrator. I didn't want to be an administrator, either, you know. I sort of got pushed, and it seemed the wrong thing not to do. You know what I mean? It seemed cowardly—and I didn't think they'd pick me. I was as surprised as anybody. And then I kind of thought, "Well heavens! If they think I can, then I guess I can." (Interview, 10/91)

Jeanne's movement into the principalship reflects a typical female path of advancement. Like the women in Adler et al.'s (1993) study who explain that they entered both teaching and administration by "drifting" into it or through "luck," Jeanne had no plans to become a principal. Her assumption of the principalship, like her entry into teaching, results from the previously unforeseen convergence of personal and professional opportunities and decisions. Her experience, like the experience of other women, forces us to redefine notions of "career" to include both traditional female role expectations and responsibilities (Grant, 1989) and broader structural factors. An individual's career is "socially constructed and individually experienced over time" within the context of larger political and economic circumstances (Ball and Goodson, 1985, p. 11). Jeanne's experience also demonstrates the negotiations that comprise a dynamic process of principaling. During the first five years in the role as principal, Jeanne learns to balance personal needs and professional demands, both of which are affected by her race and gender.

Access and Entry

Jeanne was raised in and around Cleveland. Although she did not leave her family home until after she had entered college, Jeanne describes years of growing alienation and emotional abuse from her family, especially her mother. Her father enrolled in bible school when she was nine and preached on Sundays but always had other jobs during the week. Her mother cleaned houses and raised foster children along with her own. Her parents believed in education; Jeanne attended a rural Catholic school until eighth grade, when her family moved into the city. Jeanne often returned to this school, seeking out advice and counsel from the nuns who had been her teachers. Following one year in the regular Cleveland public schools, Jeanne tested into a public college preparatory high school. She describes herself as having had to work very hard simply to maintain her place there: "I hung on at Forrest Academy by the skin of my teeth. Just barely" (Interview, 10/91). From high school, she went to the University of Cleveland Teachers College on a scholarship from the high school's parent-teacher organization. She fell into teaching much as she later tripped into the principalship: "Ever since I was little I wanted to be a nurse. But someone gave me a scholarship, so I just walked off. . . . Everybody I knew and loved were teachers. People I cared about. I fell in love with teachers. They saved my life. . . . I didn't plan to be a teacher, but never did I look for any other thing to do" (Interview, 10/91).

Jeanne's first teaching job was in inner-city Cleveland, where she describes herself as a "person of privilege" in her own eyes and in the eyes of her students. She knew how to reach the students and their parents and how to use the resources available to help kids succeed.

> I was good. But I taught in a school, first of all, I taught in a school that I knew. I was a student-teacher there. There were American black kids in the ghetto. And I knew how to teach American black kids in the ghetto. . . . My father is a preacher, you know. I visited all my families before Halloween and let them know who I was. And kids produced. And I took them, I dragged them off to Unitarian church on Sunday. You know, just, it was like I knew what to do. I was, by that time a woman, a person of privilege. I knew where the sources were so I could get kids involved in things. (Interview, 11/91)

Within two years she was given the Cleveland Teacher of the Year award. Although she acknowledges that she was a good teacher, Jeanne minimizes the importance of this award, arguing that it had more political than educational meaning:

> I knew how to make kids mind, you know. And I knew how to organize and I could see what people wanted. I mean, I was a manipulator to survive in my own family. And it didn't take me long (as a teacher) to figure out, "What, you want some of that? I can do that." That's just how you survive. . . . I was a good teacher, but I don't know how they found me. There were other black teachers, people told me this. But it was still politically right, you know what I'm saying. But when I came here [to Greenfield] it was on my resume, because it happened. God, Greenfield took it up and carried it around like it was a gift from the king on a purple platter. Everywhere I went, people were saying I was Teacher of the Year. (Interview, 10/91)

While teaching, she met her husband, a Unitarian minister who was her father's age. In 1968 she moved from Cleveland to Greenfield with her husband, whom she credits with introducing her to a greater understanding of the social and political system within which she lived. They had a son and Jeanne stayed home with him for a few years; she returned to teaching (in Greenfield) when she and her husband divorced. The divorce, initiated by Jeanne, was painful for all of them.

> It fell apart because I was a child. Because I didn't know who I was. Because my husband really psychologically was not solid. And I certainly wasn't psychologically solid. Um, or balanced, I guess is the right word. And, I got tired of feeling badly, you know. (Interview, 11/91)

Jeanne kept her son during the week and his father had him on weekends. She describes a long period of self-reflection and emotional work, starting with the divorce, during which she tried to learn to "love herself" and to find a stable place in the world that would feel like home to her.

During the years she spent single-parenting and teaching, Jeanne often worked a second job (tutoring, clerking in a fast food restaurant, drawing blood in a hospital lab) to cover the cost of her son Darren's schooling. She sent Darren to private schools, both day schools in the area and boarding schools, in order to meet his emotional and academic needs. When her husband died, he left their son some money that eased Jeanne's financial burden enough so she could leave the extra jobs behind.

Perhaps not surprisingly, given her unplanned entry into teaching and the demands of her personal life, Jeanne gave little thought to entering administration. During her twenty years of teaching in Greenfield-

Weston, she earned the reputation of being a very creative, child-centered teacher, someone who truly focused on students and learning. Earlier in her career, when others approached her to consider a move into administration, she declined, explaining that she "had too much impact in the classroom" and "wanted to be that kind of a model." This response echoes the interests and concerns of other women principals. In general, women move into administration after having taught for much longer than their male counterparts; women teach for an average of 14.3 years before moving on, men for an average of 8.5 years (Marshall and Mitchell, 1989). Compared to men in administration, women with families more frequently balance the decisions they make about changing jobs against their family responsibilities. These deliberations and considerations sometimes lead to questions about women's level of commitment to the administrative positions for which they do apply (Grogan, 1996; Biklen, 1995; Bell and Chase, 1993; Edson, 1988; Fauth 1984).

More men than women have administrative experience before taking their first principalships. Men also tend to get their advanced degrees in administration before taking those positions, suggesting they have planned this career path. Women tend to begin graduate work, or push to complete it, once they accept an administrative position, and their graduate work is more often in curriculum development, supervision, special education, or counseling than in administration (Fauth, 1984; Weber et al., 1981). Jeanne did return to graduate school in administration prior to considering the principalship, but she did so in order to get a salary increase. She chose graduate work in administration through a process of elimination; she did not want to be a counselor and she did not know she could take library courses and still get the salary increase. She purposely took the minimum number of graduate credits required, "'Cause it wasn't my intention to be a principal" (Interview 11/91). Once hired, she had to return to school to complete the hours necessary for principal certification.[1]

Five years before the study began, when the former principal of Greenfield-Weston resigned, the assistant superintendent in the district encouraged Jeanne to apply for the position, although she had indicated little interest in administration prior to this time. Both the assistant superintendent and the superintendent considered her a "master teacher" who had been open to learning new things as a teacher and could perhaps encourage other teachers to be similarly creative. Both also recognized her lack of training in administration and management, but, given her gender and race, they thought she would be a good candidate to promote in this politically liberal but sometimes difficult-to-please community.

I don't really know how many candidates there may have been, but Jeanne was definitely the person I was interested in seeing in that role, with her elementary experience. And I thought the signals that it sent were all good: taking a master teacher who happens to be a black woman and making her principal. Obviously I was looking for some-one who was talented and had spark and could do the kinds of pro-gram things that I thought would be valuable for the district. (Admin-istrator interview, 4/92)

In retrospect, Jeanne suggests that she had not so much chosen to apply for the principalship but was propelled into it by others. Being "pushed" seems to help women overcome both the external and inter-nal barriers that may keep them from considering the position. Once the wheels started to turn, Jeanne found it difficult to stop them:

I really didn't think they were going to choose me. I did it to get a lot of people off my back. And at one point, you know, it occurred to me when the numbers started getting fewer that, you know, I might get chosen. And I really was scared. I mean, I was so frightened. I became disoriented, I cried at night. . . . The people that I had been in love with, who supported me, said I could do it. But what they hell do they know? . . . So that's how it was with the principal[ship]. I couldn't turn back after I got that close. Who was—what credibility was I going to have? I'd already told the superintendent I wasn't going to do it, and here I was. What credibility was I going to have by turning back? So I had to go through with it. It was like labor. You can't turn back once you're pregnant. You can't turn back once it hurts. You just have to go through it. And once you get through it, it's like bad pains, stomach, digestional (sic) problems, once you get through it you think, "Whew! Shit, I can do that!" (Interview 11/91)

Race seems to have been a spoken and unspoken aspect of Jeanne's entry into and experience of the principalship, as it is for most minority administrators (see, e.g., Edson, 1988; Doughty, 1980). Jeanne is aware of the role of race, gender, and class in her selection as principal; she herself comments that one central administrator advocated her selection because she was black, female, and a member of the community. Another central administrator clearly considered race an element of the choice, as suggested in his reference, above, to promoting "a master teacher who happens to be a black woman." A parent on the search committee confirmed that race was an unspoken issue in the search pro-cess.

He [the superintendent] didn't push Jeanne in any way, but that was fine. That might also have been the year that he started the minority liaison committee . . . but it was certainly a factor in my mind. He wanted a name as the superintendent of a district that was sensitive to minorities. I mean it was before PC was even as trendy as it is now. And this would have fit right in. He had this community committee, which I served on and it was a joke. And now he has a black female principal. This is going to put him on the map. (Parent interview, 8/92)

Others in the community raised similar questions about the selection process.

I always worry a little bit, was she hired as a token? Either female or black or both—or neighborhood person. I truly—I keep hearing rumors all over the place—since the day I came. Before I came. Is this temporary just to show they would hire? Is this true? (Teacher interview, 3/92)

In addition, community members who questioned the sincerity of the superintendent's concern for the communities of Greenfield and Weston asked whether perhaps he wanted a principal whom he could control or, possibly one who might not be able to be a strong advocate for these vocal communities' interests. They noted Jeanne's lack of experience and training, and they wondered if the superintendent expected to be able to manage her and the school, or perhaps even blame her for problems the community brought to him. Implicit was the suggestion that, given her gender and race, it might be easier to control and, if necessary, blame Jeanne for problems as they arose.[2]

Jeanne has always been conscious of her race in this predominantly white community (a theme that reappears in sections to follow), and she considered both gender and race as she struggled with her decision about entering the principalship. Compared to ten years earlier, when she could not have made the shift into administration, it was a good time to change gears. Her son Darren was settled in college and much more independent, and she was comfortable and confident in her work as a teacher. She was also, as later sections illustrate, personally ready to take on more responsibility, in particular thinking about how to meet the needs of all children in the school. In her choice to apply and to accept the position, Jeanne balanced her uncertainty about taking on a new role for which she had little preparation with her changing personal needs, abilities, and visions.

Taking on the Role

Jeanne saw the principalship as "a chance to give back to a community that had given me my womanhood . . . a chance to give back to a lot of people who were going to be really pleased" (Interview, 11/91). She did not appear to have had a clear vision of what she wanted to do or be as a principal, nor did she have the experience or skills that would make the transition to this position an easy one. She had not thought about what aspects of her teaching or prior work in the district would transfer to the principalship, what challenges she would face, what style of leadership she might try or where she might turn for support. She became the principal because others told her she could do it and do it well. Thus, when she entered her new position she felt well supported but had few plans or ideas of how to proceed.

Jeanne asserts (and others confirm) that during the first five years of her principalship she learned a great deal. She also began to establish a style of leadership and a school atmosphere that clearly reflected her own values and goals for the school. Parkay et al. (1992) identify stages of socialization experienced by first-time principals. New principals focus first on issues of survival and control, move through a period of stability and maintenance, and then develop an interest in leadership and professional confirmation in which they work to create a vision for the school and a school atmosphere that allows teachers to work with them toward that vision. To some extent, Jeanne experienced these stages, although the process was much more complex than Parkay et al.'s description would suggest. As a woman who had no administrative aspirations or experience, Jeanne may have developed approaches that allowed her to maintain traditionally expected roles, adopting enough of the male ways of functioning to be acceptable (Marshall, 1985). At the least, we need to recognize the extent to which Jeanne was an active shaper of her own environment and the interactions that occurred within it. She was not only socialized; she actively engaged in the school, the community, and the district in ways that have determined her experience and others' experience of her.

The administrator who preceded Jeanne, Elizabeth Allen, had been principal of Greenfield-Weston for seven years. She left the school and the state two weeks before Jeanne was hired, providing no overlap and no communication. As one parent explained, "[Jeanne] was just given the files and the desk, and that was it. And she was dealing with just trying to set up the office and the people she would work with, some of whom never ever had an administrative job. It would have been different if she'd been a principal somewhere else, but it still would have been unfortunate" (Parent interview, 8/92). Jeanne's warm, open style immediately differed from Elizabeth Allen's more rigid approach, one that made both teachers and parents feel disempowered and unwelcome. Elizabeth Allen had required teachers to sign in the hour and minute at which they arrived and left the school. She was fairly unavailable to parents and rarely consulted the community in making decisions. Jeanne, by contrast, has always made a concerted effort to make her teachers and parents feel like members of the school community.

And people will tell you a very different story about those years [prior to Jeanne's arrival] and I didn't experience them. But apparently [Elizabeth Allen] was a very difficult person and I don't think people felt they could go in and they could complain to her or talk to her, or involve her in the way that people do Jeanne. . . . I think people, I think Jeanne has very much to do with that feeling of welcome and availability and accessibility. (Parent interview, 8/92)

Some of Jeanne's efforts in these early years reflected her personal style; some resulted from her need for help and support in running the school.

Her first year, in addition to administering the K–8 school, Jeanne also had to coordinate a Middle States Review of the school, organize a steering committee from the school to participate in the discussions about district reorganization, and set up the district's new kindergarten center. She also took evening courses to complete her graduate work for principal certification. She knew to ask questions and request help; she depended heavily on her parent organization president that year. She sought help, as well, from the assistant superintendent, who spoke with her at least once a week during the first two or three years. Finally, Jeanne hired a secretary, Sarah Winston, on whom she relied as a colleague and assistant during the first several years. Sarah's skills in organizational detail and budgeting allowed Jeanne to delegate (sometimes intentionally and sometimes de facto) many managerial tasks. Jeanne and Sarah often brainstormed how to solve problems and address issues in the school. During these first three years, as Jeanne learned some of the "survival skills" necessary to run her school, she also began to make decisions, hire teachers, establish processes, and set a tone in the school that influenced the kind of principal she would become and the kind of school within which she would work.

The next several years, including the year of the study, appear to have been a time of increasing stability for Jeanne. External factors (especially the stabilization of the school configuration and the decrease in the number of faculty and students served by the school) contributed to this process of growth and mastery. Jeanne has become more confident in her abilities; more willing to take a stand with teachers, parents, and the administration; and more politically astute in working with the community, the staff, and the central office. She describes certain kinds of personal growth as especially significant during this period: learning to write more easily and effectively, learning to plan ahead rather than just reacting to crises and issues as they arise, and learning to be more efficient in handling district and school-based details. She sees the overall process as one of compromise, of learning to work the system by giving what it demands, but still finding ways to accomplish her own goals.

I gave very little thought as to what it meant to be a principal. I had an idea about schools and how they should work, but that idea can't be carried out in the structure I work for. So I've had to back off of my ideas and that sometimes makes me very unhappy. On the other hand, when I'm faced with wanting escape it or to say, "I'm not compromising my stuff," I look at the positive that's happened or the positive input that I've been able to get. And pride. And I won't let go. So then I figure, "All right. I'll be this kind of principal and then I'll just run around and do the other stuff [too]." (Interview, 10/91)

During these first five years, Jeanne concentrated on being a better listener, forcing herself to wait and consider all the information before responding. This approach has helped her collect the information she needs to make decisions. It also provides others with a safe environment within which to share their ideas and participate in the process of decision making. A parent describes Jeanne's listening abilities this way:

The other thing I was very impressed with her with was her handling of those community meetings to prepare for the site-based management discussions. I was only at one of those meetings. . . . She was very receptive to anything that anybody had to say and she was very undefensive. For example, one of the things that she heard was that people wanted small classes. That was a real thrust of concern. And people wanted small classes even if at came at the expense of the specials— physical education, music. And Jeanne is very much of a humanities person. She thinks the arts are really an important part of the curriculum, and she didn't jump in there and argue with people or challenge. She just—she was able to listen and gather the information in a way that I thought was very helpful to the process of the meeting. Because nobody ended up feeling "Oops, I better not say that because I'm treading on her toes." (Parent interview, 8/92)

Jeanne has also developed her ability to observe, question, and sit back and analyze a situation before speaking or trying to resolve a problem. One parent, noting this change, explains that Jeanne was, "Very very open. And it got her into trouble. She's learned. I think that sometimes she kind of wears her heart on her sleeve and sometimes says things that she doesn't want, in the enthusiasm if that's the word or in the moment, and then people maybe take it the wrong way and it can catch her up short" (Parent interview, 8/92). By the time of this study, Jeanne seems more inclined to step back first before speaking and acting. For example, during a hastily called forum for parents concerned about vertical grouping in the first- and second-grade classes, she tells the audience that she will not respond to their concerns that evening. Instead, she will listen to their comments, develop a coherent response, and get back to them. Her natural tendency to react first and think later still occasionally leads to difficult interchanges, especially with parents, but she has become more aware of the need to wait and plan her own actions to achieve the results she desires.

During the year of the study, evidence suggests that Jeanne is trying to become a better "manager," even as she holds onto the interpersonal approaches and emphases that are her hallmark (as illustrated in the story that begins this chapter). Being more in control of the managerial aspects of the principalship helps Jeanne see and work toward achieving her vision of what the school could and should be. "The pieces are all falling together—that this is an excellent staff, excellent school. And the vision is coming. And the mechanics are in place to start moving to the vision. Five years is a short time, but probably the only amount of time you could do it in" (Interview, 6/92). Seeing the bigger picture carries its own responsibilities: "You've got the vision, so you're scared. And you also have the pride. Like I said, I can't walk away from here until I've done a good job" (Interview, 9/91). When asked directly, Jeanne is unable to articulate exactly what constitutes her vision for the school. In her speech at the town's Fourth of July celebration, however, and in her reflections on what she wants to do in the next few years at the school, she focuses on two key ideas: serving all children and helping children learn to work with many different kinds of people. She is committed to providing an environment in which children feel in control, possessed of many choices, and excited about what they are doing.

In many ways Jeanne uses her first five years to take control over the principalship as opposed to having it entirely controlling her. As the stories below suggest, this is an ongoing struggle, a dynamic process of action and reaction among the many players in the school, district, and community. Jeanne not only learns particular skills, she also becomes aware of her responsibilities, her own responses, and her strengths and weaknesses. She begins to weigh these in relation to her vision for the school, assessing how best to achieve her goals. During the year of the study, Jeanne also takes control over other aspects of her personal life. She stops seeing a weight control specialist and takes on the work herself; she undertakes some long-planned home renovations; she plans and carries out a trip to Africa that she has talked about for years; and she provides her son with the money he needs to complete his final year of college. She also runs for and is elected to the vestry of a church that she had recently joined. At this stage, she seems to have regained the energy and determination to reach out and become involved in aspects of her life that had been missing during the first five years of her principalship, thus recognizing and learning to serve her own needs as well as those of others.

Becoming a Principal: Summary

Jeanne's entry into the principalship and her early experience of the role reflect many of the patterns described in the literature on women in educational administration. She becomes a teacher because it fit other's expectations of her, and she remains a teacher for twenty years before moving into administration. She becomes a principal at the urging of others, and with little formal or practical training or guidance, she finds herself figuring out how to reconcile her own goals as an educator with the demands of the position. She also gradually learns to balance personal needs and professional demands, doing her best to serve both parts of her life. Finally, Jeanne often recognizes and accepts the role expectations and constraints related to gender and race played in her work experience. Sometimes, as noted in the discussion below, she is able to use these limits and values to her advantage as she decides what actions to take as a school principal.

SERVING OTHERS: DEFINING LEADERSHIP IN THE COMMUNITY CONTEXT

Lacking role models, paths, patterns, and sometimes support for her own way of operating, Jeanne works to develop a style of leadership that integrates effectiveness in responding to school and district demands and her unique combination of creativity, energy, and care. Many parents, teachers, and students see the school as a place that cares about people, encourages growth and risk taking, and pays attention to individual needs and differences. They attribute many of these positive elements of the school climate to Jeanne's leadership and modeling. Even those who criticize her as a principal acknowledge Jeanne's wonderful work with children, are impressed by the fact that she knows every child's name, and appreciate the warmth and openness that characterize the school. Some with whom she works find Jeanne difficult, often because her actions and choices do not match their expectations of a "real administrator": someone who takes control, imposes decisions, and moves in a straight line toward a proscribed goal. Regan (1990) describes women principals balancing their "male" and "female" approaches to leadership; Jeanne weaves other strands of her life and work into this dichotomy. In her relationships and interactions with children, parents, and teachers she both supports and challenges gendered definitions of leadership.

Leadership in the Community

Greenfield-Weston Elementary School is one of three elementary schools in a school district that serves two larger communities, Greenfield and

Boyerton. Greenfield and Boyerton merged their districts approximately fifteen years ago. When the unified district was first created, it consisted of a single high school, a K–8 school serving Greenfield and Weston, and two elementary schools and a middle school serving Boyerton. Several years later, in 1990, the middle school students from both districts were sent to the single Boyerton middle school and the elementary schools became 1–5 schools. Although the initial merger of the two districts was fairly successful, tensions between Greenfield and Boyerton parents, teachers, and administrators reemerge periodically. A Greenfield parent group, for example, continues to contest the merge, calling for a return to a separate K–12 system of education for Greenfield alone.

In 1991–1992, Greenfield-Weston Elementary School served 407 children in grades one through five. Approximately 92% of the children were white, 3.5% Asian and 4.5% African American. The school had seventeen full-time classroom teachers, one resource room teacher, the equivalent of four and a half "special" teachers in reading, art, music, and physical education, and one full-time librarian. Parents often describe the school as a place where teachers and principal work hard to meet their children's needs, and where parents provide financial and in-kind support for the academic program. While the more affluent Greenfield community dominates within the formal school and district structures (e.g., school board representatives are almost always from Greenfield, as are Home and School presidents and other leaders of parent support groups), the more working-class Weston parents maintain a vocal minority presence as individuals and on committees.[3]

Parent support in a middle-/upper-class community is often accompanied by parental involvement in and questioning of school and district practice (Metz, 1990; Lareau, 1989). When Boyerton and Greenfield merged, the Boyerton superintendent became the superintendent of the new unified district. As suggested earlier in this chapter, some Greenfield residents continue to feel that he may not have the best interests of their community at heart. In turn, the superintendent and some of the other administrators find the Greenfield community demanding and difficult to work with. The superintendent, for example, describes the district as "Ford Country—because everyone has a better idea." The community of Greenfield, he says, "would find fault with anyone" (Administrator interview, 6/92). Jeanne, too, finds Greenfield a demanding community to serve; the parents are well educated and feel comfortable questioning and asking for what they believe their children should have in school. Weston parents sometimes raise concerns about the comparable resources and support available to Weston versus Greenfield children. These varied parental concerns complicate Jeanne's job as she tries to find ways to respond positively to them and to the range of expectations parents have of a school leader.

Many parents cite Jeanne's warmth, her desire to work with them and their children as individuals with special gifts and needs, and her openness to the ideas of others as the sources of the school's warmth and vitality. One parent describes how, at a tea for parent volunteers, Jeanne approached every parent present and commented on a particular interest or accomplishment of their child (Parent interview, 8/92). Another describes Jeanne's presence and style:

> I think that Jeanne is very alive and visible in the school. I think especially for the kids, they know that she's the principal. They like her; she knows them individually. You know, you can't buy that. And that's probably the most important thing a principal can do, is to be there and to be visible in a very positive way for kids. So I think she's good at that. I think she herself is flexible enough to allow innovation and change and individuals in our school to really grow. The down side of that is that sometimes that looks like chaos. And that bothers some people and it doesn't bother me at all—I think it makes her really outstanding. She comes up with an idea, you know, and she'll fly by the seat of her pants with it. And she won't necessarily get the kinks worked out. Sometimes these things work out and sometimes they don't. Her batting average is probably good, though. And I see that as really special. (Parent interview, 7/92)

Jeanne focuses on her relationships with people, spends time on the interpersonal dimensions of the job, and has created a school atmosphere that makes people feel comfortable and welcome. She is available to talk to others; she reads aloud with individual students and runs "community meetings" with groups of parents in their homes. These actions and traits reflect those found in the literature on women principals. Jeanne, however, explains that some of her approaches to parents and children reflect her own life history as a child growing up in Cleveland and as an African American living in Greenfield.

Jeanne's experiences as an African American woman in the Greenfield community have not always been positive. Early in her teaching career, a high school student spoke to her in a way that set off a violent reaction: "And what she said, she said in a way that my sense which can smell prejudice without—usually in a sniffle, now with more control—it just felt, you know. And I cursed her out, just cursed her out" (Interview, 10/91). Later, in a meeting between the student, the high school principal, and Jeanne, Jeanne began to apologize, "And the girl jumped up in rage and anger and said, 'My mother told me about people like you' and gestured. And I could tell right away, you know, I was vindicated" (Interview, 10/91). Jeanne's decision to stay and work in Greenfield was not always easy to reconcile with her sense of who she was. Still, she convinced herself that she had an important job to do and a contribution to make to that community.

> Now staying here, it felt right. . . . I know enough about being black that I can be black, you know. I can talk the jive I need, if I need to. I can survive. Nobody's going to hurt me walking into town or anywhere else. And I've figured out what I can do here. I had to figure out why—there was a crisis at some point about staying here and I chose to stay teaching here. Because there are enough black kids here . . . and there were enough white kids who needed to know about me. . . . And I know how I can be helpful here. . . . These kids are going to make decisions about a lot of people. For a lot of people. You know, that's input. It's powerful for every new kid that comes here [to see a black woman principal]. (Interview, 11/91)

Jeanne also notes that, as an African American woman who had experienced abuse at home and discrimination in her life and work, she has insight into other people that they do not have about her.

> We always thought as American black people, we knew white people better than they ever knew us. And I don't know if that's how relationships operate anyway or if that was really true, because most people who think they know me don't really know me. So I can't decide if it's the race element that's given me that shield, or that capacity, or whether it's just a part of my personality as it might be a part of someone else's. (Interview, 3/92)

Other African American writers have described this experience of being both within and outside of the system and explored how that multiple positioning provides a unique understanding of individuals, situations, and interactions (Collins, 1991; hooks, 1989). Jeanne seems to draw on that insight in her interactions with others. Her caring approach extends beyond the scope described by studies of women leaders; she seems also to see children, parents, teachers, and other administrators as individuals who are, themselves, in certain positions within the institutional and social structure. Her responses to and interactions with them thus reflect her own experiences and her understandings of theirs, experiences that have been shaped at least in part by both gender and race.

Some parents do not appreciate Jeanne's style of leadership. They raise the concern that her lack of attention to organization and detail fosters chaos, not freedom or creative energy. Many of those who criticize the school often focus on district-level policies, but they recognize that Jeanne's leadership may affect how Greenfield-Weston teachers and students experience district mandates. Criticisms include the lack of academic rigor in the school; the inability of classroom teachers to meet the needs of special students (e.g., gifted or special education), in part because of class size; and the lack of deeper understanding of issues in educational practice and learning theory that would allow for more effectively coordinated curriculum and teaching.

> I think that often the creative juices flow and the concept is wonderful, but I don't think that she always has the personnel to carry it out, or the wherewithal to carry it out herself. And I often think that she doesn't care as much about the details. . . . I guess if you study management you would say that the top person always sets the tone. So therefore, yes, she does have to take some responsibility for it not being a challenging elementary school for my children, and for a lot of others. But on the practical level, I'm not sure that there's anything she can really do. I think there are a lot of somewhat mediocre teachers; I think the classes are too large, and the classes are all heterogeneously grouped. And with so little aide time it's very hard for the teachers to do anything except to be the teacher to the middle. (Parent interview, 8/92)

Others—teachers and parents—note that the hierarchical structure of the district and the authoritarian style of the superintendent silence teachers and principals, undermining rather than capitalizing on their skills and strengths. After talking about the hierarchical nature of the school system, the inadequate teacher training, and the lack of teacher and administrator familiarity with the literature on children's learning, a parent who works with the district observes, "I think that Jeanne has a sense just that there's a lot more to be done. She's got a handle on things. I just don't think that she has the power, I mean, the energy or the know-how to actually act on it" (Parent interview, 8/92). Jeanne's creative, people-focused rather than organizational detail-oriented style of management may contribute to people's sense of the school's inability to draw on its potential to provide an academically challenging program for each child. On the other hand, the autocratic decision-making patterns in this school district and the nature of public schooling in general limit Jeanne's ability as principal to help teachers or the school provide what some of these community members and teachers desire, regardless of her management style.

For some people, Jeanne's main weakness is that she does not act like a real administrator. These critics base their expectations on traditional definitions of school leadership: principals should set goals, solve problems, and keep the school running smoothly at all times (Ortiz and Marshall, 1988; Yeakey et al., 1986). Parents' ideas of the principal's role rarely reflect more recent definitions of leadership emerging from studies of women in positions of power that emphasize a process of shared decision making and responsibility (Hurty, 1995; Irwin, 1995;

Regan and Brooks, 1995). One parent describes Jeanne's style as "leadership by nudging" and finds it an effective process for keeping everyone involved and engaged without imposing an agenda from above (Parent interview, 7/92). Others, however, believe that Jeanne lacks the training and personality to develop the organizational and management skills the school needs. Without these, she can not be a real school leader.

> I love Jeanne dearly. I'm not sure that she's an administrator. I think she has difficulty—her memory skills and so forth are horrible. . . . I think she's a very positive influence on the kids. As an administrator, I'm not sure what kind of feeling parents have for her as an administrator. I know everybody loved her as a teacher. And she's very pleasant to talk to—she always has something positive to say about your child. . . . If I had a problem I always felt comfortable going to her with the problem, but I didn't assume she'd be able to solve the problem. . . . It's a shame because she's a wonderful person. But I just don't think that's her place, I really don't. (Parent interview, 8/92)

Relationships with Teachers

Jeanne has developed the skills Blase and Kirby (1992) identify as leading teachers indirectly by providing them autonomy, involving them in decision making, setting expectations, and providing encouragement. Some teachers, especially new ones, would sometimes prefer more direct guidelines and more clearly delineated expectations. Over time, though, most Greenfield-Weston teachers have come to appreciate Jeanne's more indirect leadership as a style that allows them grow. They describe feeling good about working in a school where their work is valued and they can participate in decision making: "This is the nicest school for teachers to be able to teach. It's not the best, well run school, but as far as your own personal growth and feeling of—I guess even accomplishment—you're able to feel that feeling of accomplishment here in this building more so than in the other buildings" (Teacher interview, 6/92).

Jeanne continues to see herself as a good teacher, and she works to find ways to translate those skills into her principalship. She finds, though, that it is much easier to teach children than to teach other teachers: "You see, I can't really tell people about teaching; I have to show them. This job requires me to tell them about it and takes more out of me" (Interview, 11/91). She does enjoy working with teachers, however, and believes that she is good at it: "I like a certain part that's clearly me. Helping teachers figure out problems about kids I clearly like. I've always been good with the underdogs, kids, and I'm much more effective here. And I'm even effective with teachers who are considered excellent!" (Interview, 10/91). In a meeting with a new teacher, for example, she listens carefully to the teacher's concern about not being able to reach all of the children, not being able to accomplish all that she wants. Jeanne encourages her to develop a repertoire that includes several less teacher-directed strategies. This, she points out, relieves some of the pressure on the teacher to perform; it provides a way of engaging students of all levels in the work; and it contributes to a more child-centered classroom. Here Jeanne's role as counselor, listening to this teacher's concerns, blends into her role as teacher as she gives specific suggestions of strategies that might work. Like other women who have spent many years teaching before entering administration, Jeanne tends to focus on teaching and instruction, bringing her own classroom skills to her work as a principal (Shakeshaft, 1989; Marshall, 1985; Tibbetts, 1980). Jeanne believes that her actions and ideas also draw on her own experiences as a parent and a divorced woman who had to work through her own periods of "craziness":

> I think all these things happen for a reason. I'm sorry that sad things happen to other people but Darren [her son] not knowing how to read makes a hell of a lot of difference for a lot of kids where I am now. And losing that marriage makes a big difference, even in counseling teachers. (Interview, 11/91)

Despite their appreciation of Jeanne's work with them, some teachers, like some parents, raise concerns about Jeanne's nontraditional leadership style. One teacher describes how teachers' and parents' expectations of roles and of effective leadership influence how they see Jeanne and the school:

> I think that no matter what she's doing, somebody would be faulting her. And that there are sometimes when, maybe because she hasn't come across as a leader, that they've been able to find more faults or complain more. If she came across as more of a leader, maybe they would respect her a little more and not go after her at times about policies they don't like or things that are happening that they don't agree with. (Teacher interview, 12/91)

In the eyes of some teachers and parents, Jeanne's ability to "come across as a leader" may be compromised by her race. She herself once wondered if a school board evaluation of her that found her "disorganized" reflected racial stereotypes. To what extent do people believe that being an African American and being a school leader are as mutually exclusive as being a woman and a school leader? The few studies of African American women administrators examine how cultural differences and expectations go beyond the more polarized view of male versus female presented in other work (Walker, 1993; Doughty, 1980). One black woman educational leader in England described the challenge of working with people who have not had experience in working with "different kinds of managers." She not only had to consider the needs and expectations of others, she had to find ways to hold onto her own style and culture while developing strategies to communicate and act effectively. Another woman, describing the effort it took for her to achieve both career success and a cultural/black identity, said:

> It was as if to succeed they [other women administrators] had to forfeit their own cultural background—that was the price of success. So I was, if you like, out to prove that you could do both. You could become academically successful, you could go on to a professional career, and still maintain some sort of integrity towards your culture and working for your people. So I did a lot of reading that . . . had to do with my own cultural development. I didn't receive it in school, I didn't receive it in college; it was something I had to do off my own bat, and that has been a strong motivator towards helping me become the woman I am today. (Walker, 1993, p. 19)

Jeanne, too, works to maintain her own identity as she balances the expectations, demands, and perspectives of others. In developing a management style that is effective for her within the community, she sometimes has to resist the pressure to forego her own needs, goals, and interests.

Leadership in Action: Responses to Community Expectations

Jeanne's reactions to parents' concerns and their desire to be involved, and her interest in helping teachers and students grow and develop, leads to actions and responses that sometimes look defensive, sometimes facilitative, and sometimes indecisive. In each situation, she is actually trying to balance her own personal style, the expectations of others, and the demands of the particular situation. The steps she takes in response to parents' and teachers' growing concerns about discipline in the school the year of this study illustrate how she negotiates these various issues. For parents, the cafeteria was a key concern. They wanted to know why it seemed so chaotic, why children "were not being fed quickly and going outside." At Jeanne's suggestion, a group of parents sat in the cafeteria for several days, assessing the situation and coming up with a set of suggestions for improvement. One parent, in describing Jeanne's approach, explains that "an administrator, or a true manager, would have gone down and assessed the situation and put up a set of rules and, 'Done!'" (Parent interview, 8/92). Another parent elaborates, "What a 'normal' principal would have done would be to have them (students) all in a line and told the teachers that they should enforce all these rules and 'Here are the rules.' And Jeanne just never worked from that premise at all. . . . She used consensus" (Parent interview, 8/92). Again, when parents compare Jeanne to what they think of as a "normal" or "true" administrator, they find her approaches unusual, and sometimes (although not always) unsatisfactory. Perhaps what makes Jeanne's style so disconcerting to some is that she prefers to share power, deliberately involving parents in decision making rather than wielding it autocratically.

Some parents trace increasing disciplinary problems at school to permissive parenting practices at home (Parent interview, 8/92). Others feel that it is Jeanne's responsibility to address these problems since they occur in the school. For example, at a Home and School meeting called to discuss discipline in the fall (October 1991) some parents raise concerns about student rudeness to one another and the ways in which students interact and solve problems. Jeanne is shaken by this meeting; she feels attacked by the parents and is surprised by the vehemence of their concerns. Teachers, too, see discipline problems. Jeanne tries to emphasize with both groups the underlying goodness of the children and stresses the need for everyone to take responsibility for discipline and civility. Still, both groups continue to pressure her to take some definitive actions to change policy and practice in the school. This set of interactions with parents and teachers causes Jeanne to reassess her own values, actions, and leadership skills. Here, and elsewhere, she struggles with holding on to—or redefining—her sense of self as a leader as she tries to give members of the community what they demand.

> I think, two groups are saying that we need [attention to discipline]. And the principal is stubborn and saying, "I don't agree with you. I'm going to run this school my way." And, so, I have to listen to the community on that one. [But] I don't have to like it. I've never thought of it as a problem. I think that underneath these kids are wonderful. And, they have asked me, over and over, in subtle ways to . . . take a stand. Teachers have. And I say, "You know, it's your problem." When, in fact, if I see it, it's, I don't want to say that it's my problem but I can make a difference just by being the leader. So it's sort of like, the role of leadership—I mean—the, essence of leadership. I've never thought about that either. Maybe because I haven't thought about it, maybe because I never cared about it, but either one, I know have to think about it, because it matters. (Interview, 10/12//91)

Her concrete response over the course of the year is to involve students, parents, and teachers in different ways. She talks directly with students at monthly all school meetings about what they need to do to improve their behavior. She also devotes a part of each meeting to formally recognizing students who have exhibited positive behaviors. She holds several faculty meetings at which teachers discuss how to respond to certain disciplinary infractions. Although she makes it clear that she does not always agree with the teachers' decisions (e.g., she does not believe in pulling children out of their classrooms as punishment), she demonstrates that she supports their decision-making process and their choices. She also encourages the Parent Organization to form a "Discipline Committee," whose members would provide feedback and suggestions to the school. She does provide the more direct intervention and policy making that principals and teachers see as her responsibility as a school leader. She chooses to do so, however, through a process that engages all those involved in the definition and establishment of the policies and interventions.

Serving Others: Summary

Jeanne draws on her past experiences, personal and professional, in developing a style of leadership that feels comfortable to her and that serves the community and school within which she works. To some extent, her approach reflects literature that explains school leadership of the 1990s as leadership for empowerment and transformation (Beck and Murphy, 1993; Grundy, 1993; Sergiovanni, 1990). She also demonstrates a style described in the work on women school leaders, which suggests that women tend to focus on curriculum and instruction; on interpersonal relationships with students, teachers, and parents; and on participatory forms of leadership (Hurty, 1995; Irwin, 1995; Shakeshaft, 1989). In addition, race, class, personal background, and the context of the community within which Jeanne works help to frame the management style she develops over time. Parents and teachers expect Jeanne to exhibit traditional forms of leadership; she struggles to meet and challenge those expectations as she works to define the kind of leader she wants to be. School leadership is, then, a dynamic process—an evolving dance—rather than a unified or fixed concept. It emerges in the actions and interactions of the principal as she tries to meet the needs of the children, parents, and teachers with whom she works.

MEETING INSTITUTIONAL EXPECTATIONS: NEGOTIATING THE CULTURE OF SCHOOLING

The context within which Jeanne works involves more than the community relationships and roles she negotiates on a regular basis. It also includes the institutional structures and systems of belief within which she carries out her work. Schools have cultures with their own values, definitions of knowledge, behavioral norms, and language. These attributes of school culture are themselves rooted in the gendered forms of power and interaction that characterize the larger society (Marshall,

1993, 1988; Ballou, 1989; Shakeshaft, 1989). Both the individual school and the larger district impose a set of constraints on a principal's actions, limits that must be considered as she works to define her own style and carry out the work of the school. The section that follows illustrates how Jeanne negotiates these structures and norms as she implements a school-based management plan mandated by the district.

School-Based Management

In February 1991 the Boyerton-Greenfield School District adopted a School-Based Management Plan to be implemented during the 1991–1992 school year. The document outlining the plan for the school board uses language that echoes an early 1900s emphasis on the scientific management of schools, management meant to be implemented by competent, white men. The district defines school-based management as: "The application of modern business management theory to the school system. It attempts to place maximum responsibility for educational planning, accountability, and management of personnel and material resources with the staff in the individual school building" (Plan for School-Based Management, 1993).[4] The decision to move to school-based management, like the changes in school configuration described earlier in this chapter, grew out of a number of financial and demographic pressures. The district experienced declining enrollments from 1970 to 1986; starting in 1989 and continuing through the year of this study, enrollment began to climb. The tax base, meanwhile, was eroding and the district faced a projected need for major capital improvements and maintenance expenditures. The reorganization of grades and schools aimed to take advantage of existing space and provide equity in student-teacher ratios across the district without increasing (and ideally decreasing) expenditures. Although educational issues were considered in this reconfiguration, financial issues remained paramount. School-based management appeared to be a natural next step after the reorganization, since, in theory, it allowed each school to allocate its limited resources in ways that would best meet the needs of that school, staff, and community.

In Boyerton-Greenfield, "school-based management involves a balance of decision-making accountability between a school and the district. This means that policies, content and *what* will be included in instruction is established at the district level; strategies, processes, and *how* the instructional program will be delivered is determined at the school level" (Plan for School Based Management, 1993). A District Advisory Council consisting of representatives from each school, generally the principal and a teacher, would review areas of shared responsibility and control, acting in an advisory capacity to the superintendent. Each school was charged with forming a School Advisory Council comprised of elected representatives from the faculty with input from support staff, parents, and students. The School Advisory Council would be responsible for developing an annual plan containing specific strategies for accomplishing the school's goals. Under the initial plan, the schools were responsible for making decisions about and allocating funds for instructional staff, support staff, supplies, equipment, school-level staff development, special transportation, and textbooks. The district would allocate resources to each school based on the type or level of the school, student enrollment, and the type of instructional programs needed in the school.

What is striking about the description of school-based management found in district documents and meetings is the focus on the technical process of running a school. Paradoxically, school-based management, which requires a leader who can involve parents and teachers in making decisions that affect them and the children with whom they work, is framed here as an organizational plan that involves negotiating district hierarchies and managing budgets. There is an inherent contradiction between the bureaucratic culture of this district, whose language is used to describe school-based management, and the kind of personal, interactive, democratic leadership needed to make the process work. In a democracy, the group making the decisions takes responsibility for those decisions. But in the Boyerton-Greenfield district, the principal remains responsible (to central administration and the community) for decisions made democratically by the building staff, via the School Advisory Council. Jeanne is, therefore, in the awkward position of being told to—and wanting to—involve her staff in decision making, but at the same time knowing that she will have to answer for the decisions made. Jeanne works within this contradiction, negotiating the imposition of a plan from a hierarchical and fairly domineering central administration and implementing it in ways that reflect her own style and the actual demands of school-based management.

Being a Democratic Leader

At the Greenfield-Weston School during 1991–1992 (the year of the study), Jeanne and the teachers and parents in the school begin experimenting with what exactly school-based management means for their building and community. Some suggest that, in fact, Jeanne already runs the school in a manner much like that called for by school-based management, given her frequent attempts to communicate with teachers and parents and to engage them in decision-making in the school.

> I think [school-based management] will [work]. I think it will if it works in the district. And I think that's because we were doing it last year, even without the term. You know, I think the fact that we did go to vertical grouped classes and the other schools didn't, because we decided that it would work for us. It was fine, that the teachers had been making a lot of decisions. Or at least contributing to the decision-making process. (Teacher interview, 4/92)

Examples of Jeanne's collaborative approach occur throughout the year. One strategy she uses frequently is to delegate responsibilities to individuals and groups. This, she explains, is a way of managing that fits her sense of how the school staff can work together as a community. She is aware that this is not a risk-free approach; it requires trusting the people to whom you delegate work.

> It's that quality of supporting and caring for people that I like about the job. You can make it a family. I don't know how you do it though without risk. Somebody said to me, "Looks like you have so many pieces to pass out, you need somebody to do some of the work." And then that triggered something in me and said that I don't have to do it all myself. I can delegate a lot more. So I started passing out [jobs]. But then when you delegate, you better trust them. (Interview, 10/92)

Delegating is sometimes uncomfortable for the others involved, as well. Jeanne gives grade-level chairs responsibility for communicating with teachers, running grade level meetings, setting schedules, mentoring new teachers, and distributing supplies. The chairs sometimes feel that Jeanne asks them to address issues that go beyond the limits of their responsibilities, and they and other teachers wonder if Jeanne occasionally delegates responsibilities of her own that she wants to avoid. Their comments also suggest, however, that their relatively traditional conception of the role of the principal allows them to resist accepting delegated responsibility or participation in key situations.

> But yes, she does delegate and—I don't know if that's, I think it's sometimes that we don't want it. That we feel like we're dangling. But I think everyone is willing to rise to the challenge. And to tell her if it's too much of, "This is not how should be. No, Jeanne, you really need to do this. You should be the one to do this. You need to do this for us at this point in time." And we have asked her to do that. And she's listened. At times she might say, "Well I don't really want to." And we'll say, "But you have to. This is what you need to do. You're the principal." (Teacher interview, 12/91)

Jeanne herself has mixed feelings about teachers' desire for her to lead by controlling and directing, noting that "You have to be aware, you have to patrol what you can control" (Interview, 10/91). Implementing school-based management involves considering the existing culture of the school and its norms relating to acceptable roles and behaviors of principals and teachers.

The first actions Jeanne takes in the school to put school-based management into effect involve learning more about the school's budget and sharing that information with teachers. Her goal is to have teachers prioritize their own needs, primarily in terms of class size, teaching aides, equipment, and supplies, and see how their interests could be met within the constraints of the budget. In mid-October 1991, Jeanne begins preparing for a series of faculty meetings on resources by gathering up, reviewing, and organizing information on current school finances. She wants to be able to show teachers the total amount of money available, how aides are currently being used, what conferences have been requested, and so on. After providing that information, she intends to let the teachers make some decisions about how to spend the school's money.

The Greenfield-Weston faculty generally meets about once every week or two from 8:00–8:40 a.m. Jeanne plans three consecutive faculty meetings (Wednesday, Thursday, and Friday of one week) around the topic of resources in order to maintain some momentum in the discussions. She envisions stepping back into her role as a teacher to run each of these meetings "cooperative lessons style." On the morning of the first meeting Jeanne arrives at school early and sets up the library chairs in groups of three or four. As teachers arrive, she assigns them to a group and gives each teacher a letter. She tells them that she will model a cooperative learning lesson that they can then use in their classrooms. She also suggests that mentor-teachers could help some of the new teachers with this kind of lesson (there are five new teachers on the staff this year). She explains that the job of each person in the group is determined by the letter they now hold, and she uses a prepared poster on an easel to review the jobs of facilitator, encourager, recorder/reporter. Then she says that they are going to be a "textbook model of site-based management, but since there are no texts they could write one and share the money." When few teachers respond to her humor, she tells them, teasingly, that they can smile back at her. She reminds them that she knows they are a great group of teachers, and, poor as she is, if she could take her paycheck and give it to each of them, she would. She notes that she is not alone in her high estimation of the staff; colleges from all over the area ask for student placements in their school.

Jeanne explains that these meetings will focus on resources other than teachers. She flips to another page on the easel displaying the agenda for the three days:

Day 1. List and prioritize the elements need to support excellent teaching.

Day 2. Agree on the elements we lack; begin addressing how we acquire what we need.

Day 3. Finalize how we arrange and/or rearrange the available resources to get the things we need.

The groups work for about fifteen minutes on the first task as Jeanne circulates, often reminding people of their assigned cooperative group roles. Toward the end of the fifteen minutes, she reminds the teachers that they needed to prioritize their lists. Then she calls them back together and asks the group recorders to report their lists. She collects the lists in preparation for the next day's meeting (Field notes, 10/30/91).

The next morning Jeanne again arrives at school early and arranges the library chairs in groups. She tells me she is very anxious about the meeting; the previous night she went to sleep at 7:30, woke up at 4:00 a.m., and was at school by 6:00 a.m. She starts the meeting by reviewing group members' roles. She reports that, thanks to the secretary's analytic skills, she has a collated list of the priorities from the day before. The data show teachers evenly split between instructional aides and materials as their first and second priorities, with peer interaction and observation third, and professional conferences fourth. She gives them three minutes back in their groups to break the tie. When she calls them back to the full group, she praises them for the work done in their cooperative learning roles, singling out a few teachers as especially good encouragers. She points out that if they were doing this kind of cooperative lesson in their classes they would probably not monitor and then praise all three group roles at once. Upon polling the seven groups, she again finds that they are split three/four. She announces that instructional aides are the top priority and materials the second. A heated discussion ensues about the vote; some teachers maintain that the vote really means that both priorities are equally important; others point out that teachers in different grade levels or who teach special subjects (e.g., art or music) have different priorities than grade-level teachers.

At this point, Jeanne loses control of the agenda and, to some extent, of the meeting as well. Her carefully organized plan and sequence of activities begins to unravel as the teachers debate their priorities and the meaning of their votes. Jeanne abandons her group approach and asks teachers as individuals to vote for their top priority by standing up. Relinquishing her directing role, she says, "I honestly don't know what to do. It's 8:20. Should we keep meeting for the next several mornings around this to talk more or keep going? What's your pleasure?" Teachers continue the discussion until one teacher asks Jeanne to clarify the task for the day. She obliges by reading it from the posted agenda. One of the three male teachers in the building proposes, "Let's vote to move on—All in favor?" The majority of teachers raise their hands, and in response to that vote Jeanne moves the discussion on to a consideration of what teachers want in each of the prioritized areas and how to get it. She provides them with some statistics on student enrollment, amount of aide time available, and costs for aide time. The next step, she explains, is for them to decide who needs aide time and how they can get it while staying within the budgetary parameters and demands. She asks them to return to their groups to work on this task.

As the meeting ends, Jeanne remarks to the teachers, "What I think is great is this democratic process." As the teachers leave and she and I begin to straighten up the library she says, "I hate democracy. I told my boss I needed help on this helping teachers make decisions." She is clearly frustrated as she leaves but she does not have the time to reflect on what went right and wrong in the meeting. She is due to meet with parents of a child from another Boyerton-Greenfield elementary school who want to transfer their child to Greenfield-Weston and then with a disgruntled parent who questions her about a range of school programs (Field notes, 10/31/92).

In the third of the series of faculty meetings devoted to budgetary decision making, Jeanne reviews what has been accomplished thus far and reopens the discussion of how they might begin to get the teaching support they need while remaining within the existing budget. The teachers clearly have limited understanding of how much money is available and how it might be spent. In addition, they seem uncertain about whether they are discussing how to spend this year's budget or making plans for next year's. One teacher remarks that she is concerned about "this site-based management" because it could be divisive; it requires that people compromise and that they be supportive rather than critical of each other. Another teacher adds that they have to decide as a group how to spend the school's limited resources. Jeanne asks the teachers—partly as a challenge and partly in earnest— if they want her to make these decisions, since that would alleviate the need for them to judge each other's programs. The teachers continue to discuss how best to budget the extra money—for supplies, conferences, and the like. Overall, for the coming year, they seem to favor giving each teacher a small lump sum to spend as he or she sees fit. Jeanne ends this meeting by asking how many teachers want this dollar amount approach for next year; all hands go up. She says, as she dismisses the meeting, "I don't know where we're going next, but we're leaving the room now, and I'll get back to you on what's next" (Field notes, 11/1/91).

Jeanne envisions these three meetings as an opportunity to educate the faculty about budgetary issues in preparation for decision making under site-based management. She also hopes to generate conversation about priorities and goals that will help guide those same decisions. She discovers the multiple difficulties involved in presenting and clarifying a great deal of complicated information, of engaging people in conversations about conflicting needs and limited resources, and in facilitating a group conversation as a democratic leader. As she reflects on the process later in the year, she comments,

> I think it's cumbersome, it's in the way, it's a pain, you know. I could go in and get the work done. But I think it's excellent at the same time. I wouldn't really have it any other way, but the process—you know, I'm down to my last day of school [making last minute budget decisions]. And it makes—it helps define a part of my job I don't want to do—I have to be a sales person. And that means I have to know [the information] cold and have the articulation to convince. . . . So it's going to make me work harder when in fact I could have just done all this. (Interview, 6/92)

Jeanne discovers, unconsciously at this first set of meetings, how relinquishing some decision-making power and responsibilities can translate into giving up control over the structure and content of meetings. Over the course of the three meetings the cooperative learning approach and the more general, philosophical agenda gradually disappear as teachers question, challenge, and air their concerns about both the process and the content of the meetings. Jeanne also begins to see how her role will change. Site-based management will require her to have a more complete understanding of the budgetary aspects of running the school, for example. And despite her well-deserved reputation as a collaborative, participatory, democratic principal, sharing decision-making power challenges her normal modes of operating. Teachers describe the process of preparing for school-based management as somewhat of a "threat" for Jeanne and as "belabored and a pain in the neck, because we don't really know what site-based management is" (Teacher interview, 12/91).

In March, the school establishes its Advisory Council, consisting of teachers and parents.[5] According to Jeanne, the teachers have determined both the categories of representation (e.g., a teacher from each grade level, a new teacher, a special teacher, etc.) and the individuals who will represent them on the Council. (These decisions lead to some disaffection on the part of veteran teachers who feel left out of the action.) The Advisory Council meets regularly in the spring to develop a school plan that will set the number of classroom teachers at each grade level, the number of aides and how much time they will spend in each classroom, the schedules for lunch and special subjects, school goals, and to determine orders of supplies, books, furniture, and materials. Teachers on the Advisory Council, and those watching them, agree that formulating the school plan takes a great deal of time, both in meetings and in preparation for meetings. Overwhelmed by their tasks, the teachers on the council at one point tell Jeanne, "Jeanne, we don't want to make the decisions. We don't want to have all the discussions before the decisions are made. Why don't you come up with an idea and present it to us, and we will okay it or not okay it" (Teacher interview, 4/92). In response, Jeanne does take a more active role. Rather than just setting the agenda and asking the group to come up with a decision, she begins to present an idea or set of ideas for discussion and decision. For example, at a meeting in April, she passes out a page describing staff allocations for the following year and asks for questions, comments, and concerns. There are a few comments, but in general teachers think that the plan, which summarizes several meetings' worth of discussion, looks good.

Jeanne begins to find a balance between knowing when to provide answers, given that her voice might be heard as authoritative and definitive, and when to withhold her views in order to allow other voices to emerge and to make decisions with which she may not agree. Calls for democratic leadership rarely examine the tensions involved in implementing this practice in real school situations. And literature that suggests that women administrators tend to focus on interpersonal issues and use more collaborative approaches while men tend to be more "managerial" and directive oversimplify a complicated process. Regan (1990), who talks about integrating the "hard" and "soft" aspects of herself and her management style as a school principal, comes closest to capturing the image of Jeanne, who is working, although not perhaps consciously, on how to draw on a range of approaches to reach her goals within a particular institutional context.

Instituting democratic procedures in a school setting challenges the expectations that give principals the power to make and impose decisions. It also runs counter to institutional structures. Teachers have no common times to meet during the school day; they are not trained to undertake administrative decision making; and their jobs already include enough other responsibilities that they resist "opportunities" to learn the information necessary to participate in decision making. The institution itself constrains Jeanne's ability to translate the abstract technical processes of school-based management as described by the district into a real-life community undertaking built upon shared power and mutual commitments. In gendered terms, Jeanne can be described as drawing on the more collaborative, democratic, and interactive styles of leadership she prefers. She also sees these approaches as necessary for bringing about school-based management in a school culture that emphasizes hierarchy, control, specialization and circumscribed roles. Given her own personal management style, she is relatively successful. In order to be effective, however, she also has to negotiate her role with the central administration that required this process.

Negotiating with Central Administration

The Boyerton-Greenfield Board of Managers and the superintendent of schools imposed school-based management on the schools in this district; principals and teachers had little or no voice in the decision. While such an approach is not unusual, it does reveal the paradox of trying to implement a democratic model of management within a hierarchical, bureaucratic, and somewhat dictatorial system. As one teacher sarcastically points out: "School-based means when the administration wants you to do something, they're going to make you do it. When they don't want to have to put the responsibility to them they're going to say, 'Okay, site-based'" (Teacher interview, 6/92).

Jeanne has a relatively good relationship with the superintendent and assistant superintendent, both white men who have been in the system for many years. Although she does not always agree with the superintendent's decisions or his process of decision making, Jeanne feels he has been very encouraging; he gave her "her chance" and then provided the support she needed to survive her first few years. Jeanne, like the other two principals whose cases follow, is careful to do the work the central office asks of her. She is the only principal in the district to get an Advisory Council up and running the first year of the school-based management plan. Her success may have been based in part on the fact that she normally works more closely with her teachers than is typical of the other principals in the district. In addition, however, Jeanne is used to doing what she has been told. Her attitude, "They want some of that? I can give them some of that," serves as both a survival skill and a strategy for keeping the authorities, usually male, happy as she moves in her own directions. Jeanne does not find the heavy-handedness of the central administration particularly troublesome. She points out that the superintendent's management style is "the only one I've known for twenty-two years" and that this man believed in her and gave her the opportunity to do this job. And yet her own goals and her approach to achieving them differ from his in important ways.

Jeanne frequently asks the superintendent and assistant superintendent for advice and support, especially during the first few years of her administration, sometimes overtly referring to herself as the "rookie," the newest (and at this point the only female) principal in the district. During her five years as principal, Jeanne becomes more savvy about how to get what she and her school need and how to use and interpret advice from the central office. Jeanne describes using a process of listening to the superintendent, agreeing with him, remaining silent, and then using his input along with her own judgment to make a decision. On the other hand, she respects the superintendent enough to turn to him for advice, for example, about working with a new, difficult teacher and about her role as a principal. Both central administrators respect Jeanne and supported her candidacy for principal (though their motives were mixed, as noted earlier). Still, they manage to keep her in her place, making her ask for help in ways that emphasize her lack of experience or attributing problems to her style and approach. When she plays the role of supplicant, looking for advice and help, the superintendent responds benevolently. When her decisions conflict with his, he attributes her "mistake" to lack of experience and understanding. This interpretation has the dual effect of minimizing the definitive actions she takes and undermining her knowledge base. The superintendent's responses suggest that central administrators have an expectation about the role and place of principals, especially, perhaps, African American female principals, in the district's hierarchy.

The culture of power in this district has far-reaching implications. It imposes unacknowledged stress on Jeanne and shapes the way she perceives herself as a principal and acts within the role (Marshall and Mitchell, 1989; Ortiz, 1982). For example, at an Administrative Council Meeting (superintendent, assistant superintendent, and building principals) in the fall of 1991, just as the schools faced the implementation of the school-based management plan, the superintendent admits that he has left the principals "out on a limb" with the new program. He wants to hear how it is going, and he asks the principals if any of them want further training in site-based management. Jeanne identifies herself as needing further training, maybe in helping teachers in the decision-making process. Another principal remarks that they have been thrown into the idea cold and are bound to make mistakes. The superintendent asks again, "So what do you need?" One principal responds that he wants to "live the year" and see what happens. Jeanne says again that she wants training in helping teachers make decisions. She also points out that the district and the school each ask teachers to do many things, potentially overwhelming them. The teachers in her school, for example, have chosen to focus on whole language approaches this year; now they will have to learn about decision making as well. The superintendent says that he has heard no definitive call for more training. Jeanne repeats her request for board funding for training, and another principal suggests they visit schools already using site-based management effectively. Jeanne agrees that that is a good idea, as does the superintendent.

The superintendent repeatedly ignores Jeanne's request for help at this meeting. Perhaps he wants to see if others will raise similar concerns; perhaps he forces her to ask for training several times in order to emphasize his control and her lack of knowledge. Unlike her male colleagues, Jeanne is willing to take the risk to ask for help, perhaps drawing on her identities as "rookie" and outsider for courage. The superintendent, in turn, makes it clear in his control of the interaction that she lacks the power and position to make her voice heard. Only when a male colleague makes a suggestion does the superintendent respond.

Both the assistant superintendent and the superintendent give Jeanne advice during the year on how to become an effective site-based manager. Each, however, identify as problematic different (and nearly contrary) tendencies in her leadership style. The assistant superintendent worries that Jeanne may err on the side of delegating too much power, choosing to defer to teachers and parents "rather than to listen, and absorb, and then mull over and decide" (Administrative interview, 4/92). The superintendent, describing a process he himself never models in this district, suggests that she needs to let go of her authority:

> She made the mistake of the old long-term administrator. And that is, "I'll take what I need and I'll give you the rest." I told her she had to hold out her hand and say, "This is all I have. You may take it all but I need some back." And convince them that she needs it back, not just that she would take it first. (Administrator interview, 6/92)

The two central administrators' views of Jeanne's ability to carry out effective school-based management contradict one another; they disagree on the level of central decision-making power the principal should have and how she should work with others to get it. In addition, they themselves act much more autocratically, modeling a style of administration that conflicts with what they ask Jeanne and the other principals to do.

Jeanne's relationship with the central administrators continues to evolve, paralleling her balancing of collaboration and authority in the process of school-based management. At one point during the spring Jeanne uses the School Advisory Council to help her argue with the superintendent about allocation of special (e.g., music, art, physical education) teachers to the school. In the previous year Jeanne had "broke[n] the paradigm" in the district by finding additional work for her special teachers (who would otherwise only be part time). For example, her music teacher and art teacher both worked in the gifted program, making it possible for them to be full-time staff members at Greenfield-Weston. When the superintendent tells Jeanne that these now have to be counted as full-time positions and part of her regular staff allocation (normally special teachers were included in the district allocations), she is furious. She recalls that when she questioned him about the change, he explained, "'Well, I changed the rule because—I didn't change the rules I just wasn't prepared to tell you at the time, because I hadn't gotten all my pieces together'" (Interview, 3/92). The superintendent puts his own spin on the process, attributing the conflict about the special teachers to Jeanne's inexperience rather than to Jeanne's and the school's rather clever plan to best meet their needs within the district's guidelines. His interpretation seems to undermine Jeanne's attempts to take control of the process of school-based management. Jeanne, however, uses the Advisory Council to fight back. She takes the issue to them, knowing that they will argue that the school-based management guidelines talk about providing incentives to schools and giving schools authority over such decisions. "They send me back with words to say," Jeanne recounts. "And I change them around, you know, to make it so he, he's the psychology person because he's got to come out the winner and looking good. You've got to make him look like the hero" (Interview, 3/92).

As Jeanne learns to work within and, when necessary, around the system, she is aware of the danger inherent in adapting. She wonders if accommodating will change who she is and what she wants to do:

> Sometimes for me, it's been getting a little bit dangerous. I've been thinking, "Oh, I shouldn't wear this." Before I came to this job I didn't think like that. I appreciate hearing, or being reminded, even from myself, that [I'm] different. . . . It's important, focusing on the small stuff, you know, because you can be affected by what you do every day. (Interview, 9/91)

Despite her need to hold on to her own values and identity through this job, Jeanne feels constrained by the white male system that dominates in the district. For example, she remembers after the Administrative Council meeting described above, "I was about to let go and let my own language come through, but I controlled myself so I could be serious" (Field notes, 10/91)—and be taken seriously. Jeanne explains that her "own language" means "talking black." Experience has taught her that "letting go" and explicitly using that aspect of herself limits her effectiveness. Even when she speaks in "acceptable" terms (as, for example, when she asks three times at this same meeting for training in democratic decision making), other administrators ignore her voice. Jeanne says that she wants to be able to do what the other administrators (all white males) in the district do, but she certainly does not want to be the kind of leader she sees in them. When asked if she wants to become more like one of the other principals she bursts out, "No—oh my God! No! Oh! No! Maybe inadvertently in places I will become—have some things like him—but I don't want to be like any of them. . . . But there are things about them I think I have to be" (Interview, 10/91). Being an effective school leader, she has come to realize, means achieving a balance between giving the district and community what they want by learning to act in certain, demonstrably effective ways while at the same time holding onto her own ideals and identity.

Meeting Institutional Expectations: Summary

School and district cultures depend on normative definitions of power, leadership, interaction, and process that frame the work of a principal. People respond differently to these norms, depending on their own personal background and beliefs, their definitions of leadership and learning, and, in many cases like Jeanne's, their gender and race. The norms are grounded in an institution that has historically awarded power and privilege to white and male ways of defining roles and relationships. If the institution is to be maintained, these norms must also be upheld, even when the incumbents are neither white nor male. Jeanne, sometimes conscious of working within (or against) a system that does not necessarily recognize her strengths, her goals, or her way of interacting in the world, has to find ways to function effectively without losing her sense of who she is and wants to be. Not only is she asked to implement a policy, school-based management, that, itself, contradicts many of the traditions and norms of the system, but she must do so in ways that meet teachers' expectations, the structural exigencies of schools, and central administration definitions of appropriate procedure and style. She struggles with definitions of leadership, with finding a language through which she can communicate and still be herself, and with working within and around the structures, policies, and relationships dictated by the institution. Her principalship is an ongoing process of negotiating her place in the institutional context. The choices she makes and the actions she takes are constrained by the limits of the culture, but they are also a challenge to the status quo. Jeanne does not hesitate to use the principalship to push against normative boundaries when these constrain her ability to meet the needs of her school.

BALANCING CONTINUITY AND CHANGE:
NEGOTIATING WITHIN THE SYSTEM

As the complications within the shift to school-based management suggest, Jeanne's attempts to implement change at the Greenfield-Weston school encounter the barriers and paradoxes involved in trying to carry out change in any school (Sarason, 1971). Those calling for change, in this case the Board of Managers and the central administration, do not consider how mandated changes contradict existing school and interpersonal regularities. They also fail to recognize the repercussions involved in trying to change one part of a larger system. No one pays attention to gendered power structures, modes of interaction, and approaches to leadership that might help or hinder the process of change.

Jeanne, however, is not one to be limited to changes imposed from above; nor does she want to be constrained by the system's structures and norms, although she recognizes the need to work within them to accomplish her goals. During the course of the year, Jeanne develops a vision of a long-term change *she* wants to accomplish in the school, one which she hopes will have social repercussions as well. An evolving mentoring relationship with Alan, an African American boy, and her own personal and professional experiences prompt Jeanne to work toward making students and teachers in the school more aware of and responsive to the strengths and needs of all children in the school—and all people in the society. To achieve this goal, she has to balance the existing values, beliefs and needs of those with whom she works, the structural norms of the school, and her own vision of what can and should be happening.

Alan: The Catalyst for Change

Alan comes to Jeanne's attention in October, during one of her regular monthly meetings with a first-grade teacher. Having finished with some other issues she wanted to raise with Emily, Jeanne says, "So, tell me about your life." Emily launches into a description of an eight-year-old child in her class who repeated kindergarten, does not know his letters, and is "way behind." He was tested at one point but receives no special attention. Emily speaks very quickly and intensely, angry for the child who has fallen between the cracks and for herself because Alan takes up a disproportionate amount of her time in the classroom. Jeanne interrupts her along the way, at one point asking, "What do you like about this kid? What would you like to have happen?" A few minutes later she comments, "I don't even know if you like Alan."

When Emily finishes her story, Jeanne takes the floor. She suggests that Emily visit Alan's home, in part to dispel any inaccurate assumptions she may have about this boy. Describing the home life of another African American child whom she drives home every day, Jeanne notes, "I see a clean, orderly home devoid of literature. There's no chaos. I see his mother who just beams when I say he's doing well." She tells Emily that she is glad Emily discovered Alan, and she confesses that she is embarrassed because she is the principal and still she didn't know about this child. She is especially upset that she overlooked Alan because he is an "American black child and I lie awake at night thinking I'm going to save them." Jeanne offers Emily some help in the class and some suggestions for working with Alan for the moment. Toward the end of this mini-lecture, Jeanne says to Emily, "I hope he [Alan] is in your goals. American black males are dying in the street" (Field notes, 10/7/91).

Jeanne follows up on this conversation over the next several weeks. The reading teacher begins to work with Alan, and Jeanne herself tutors him regularly. The school psychologist carries out another core evaluation of Alan, and he and the teachers recommend that the child be transferred to another elementary school in the district where he would be in a self-contained special needs class. Jeanne overrides this decision, saying that they will keep him in the school and meet his needs at Greenfield-Weston. She herself continues to tutor him nearly every day throughout the school year. During the summer, Jeanne arranges for a parent who has close ties to the school to continue tutoring Alan while she is away. This parent and Jeanne have since helped Alan's mother enroll in a GED program to get her high school equivalency degree.

During an interview later in the year, Emily explains that Jeanne's decision made her angry. Jeanne, she says, did not consider this child's low level of functioning. "She didn't see his test score and didn't take into account his age. She just looked at his disadvantaged background and the fact that he's black and therefore made special considerations for him." Emily also points out that there is a larger black population in the other elementary school that might have provided more of a community for Alan than exists at Greenfield-Weston. On the other hand, Emily could see Jeanne's side, too. She acknowledges that since Alan now seems to be succeeding, "Maybe she was really right. . . . Somebody once said, fair is not always equal. So maybe she's right. Maybe by going out and giving these kids something extra to help them, but it seems unfair that so much energy goes to this small group" (Interview, 4/92).

Jeanne's work with Alan proves to be a catalyst for school change. In particular, two ideas grow out of this experience, ideas that reflect the vision Jeanne has of the school as a place that can serve all students in exciting and challenging ways. First, Jeanne begins to think about ways to increase the enrollment of minority students at the school. Her goal is to make the school a more supportive community for the African American (and other minority) children and a more diverse community for all of the children at Greenfield-Weston. In the fall of 1992 (the year after this study) she gathers together a group of parents and professionals to talk about the possibility of developing a tuition-free program through which minority students outside of the district could attend the school. The group opposes this idea, but continues to work with Jeanne to develop multicultural curriculum and new approaches that would better serve the needs of the majority and minority students attending the school.

Second, Jeanne starts to consider how to better meet the needs of students identified as requiring special education. She has begun with a small summer tutoring program for Alan and a few other students. Her aim is to expand the summer program into a full-year school for special needs students *and* any children who need or want support in their learning. She is interested, as well, in examining Greenfield-Weston's special education program and its classroom process to see how to better meet the children's needs. In the process of working with Alan, Jeanne begins to develop her own personal goals for the school and a possible set of programs to meet them. These goals center on meeting needs of students and teachers (but students first) and developing a school community that is diverse, supportive, and focused on growth.

Commitment and Resistance to Change

Although Jeanne's attention to this individual child and her decision to work directly with him may reflect a style more typical of women principals than of men, it also illustrates her growing interest in acting on her concern for African American children in the school. Like many women principals, Jeanne's lengthy tenure as a teacher contributes to her concern for individual children, in this case Alan, and, perhaps, to her sense that his needs could and should be met by the classroom teacher (Shakeshaft, 1989; Prolman, 1983; Charters and Jovick, 1981). A principal whose chief area of concern is building management might have agreed to send Alan to another school in the district to take advantage of an effective program. He or she would also have been more likely to use and uphold the existing administrative process by which that decision was made. Jeanne, again reflecting women's approaches in general, focuses less on immediate effectiveness or traditional rules in this decision and more on the experience of the individual child and her goal of developing and maintaining a diverse and supportive community in the school.

In order to keep Alan at the school, however, Jeanne has to "pull rank," overriding the decision made by Alan's teacher and the school counselors and challenging the existing structures and guidelines about serving the needs of special education students. Some studies suggest that women administrators tend to collaborate with teachers and involve them in a process of democratic decision making (Eagly et al., 1992; Charters and Jovick, 1981). While Jeanne certainly involves Emily in the process of determining Alan's program, she alone decides that he will remain in the school and that she will tutor him. Her unilateral decision making is reflected elsewhere in the school (although it is certainly balanced by her work to develop a strong school-based management program that involves teachers in all aspects of decision making). One area in which she consistently tends to act more independently is in the work she does with individual minority children and in promoting multicultural awareness throughout the school. In these areas, she resists the expectations and norms that define her role as a woman principal and that dictate the appropriate procedures for running the school.

Jeanne's efforts to achieve her goals expand beyond her work with Alan. For instance, over several consecutive months, Jeanne asks all the students to memorize Langston Hughs poems for the school's monthly meeting. Some teachers and administrators are comfortable with Jeanne's looking out for individual minority students and emphasizing multicultural issues, seeing it both as natural for her and as beneficial to the school. Parents, too, often see Jeanne's approaches as valuable and seem to appreciate her openness about her goals. They approve of her attention to individual African American kids and applaud her push for a more diverse curriculum.

> But people are so happy that she's black, just because we really would like a more diverse group. . . . I think she's very conscious of trying to make the kids of Greenfield more aware of things than if she weren't principal—but we all like that, too. (Parent interview, 6/92)

> I think she really does care. She—as a minority and a woman, both minorities—she is more sensitive to the diversity of the school and wants to iron out any problems that may arise due to that. Although the school is really not that diverse . . . she's very sensitive to that. (Parent interview, 8/92)

Parents note, however, that not everyone agrees with this view, because it leads to Jeanne treating children unequally. As a black woman she may be seen as taking a political stance if she provides extra support to black children. Some may see this stance as appropriate but others may see it as overstepping the boundaries of her roles as woman and as principal.

With race, I do see her being an advocate for children who are of some minority. Some people might be offended by that; I'm most certainly not. I think she's very up front about it. I think some people just chalk it off as Jeanne's cause. I think it does affect decisions, like Alan. I'm not sure that would have been the same decision if that was a nice little white child from a prominent family in town. (Parent interview, 7/92)

Jeanne's attention to African American students in the school and to a multicultural curriculum clearly makes some teachers and parents uncomfortable. The notion that a principal should treat all children equally stems from teacher and parent expectations of principals and from their sense that women principals will "mother" the children in their care. Principals and mothers should not have favorites.

I've never seen her mothering the poor white kids, the way she would a poor black one. I don't know that that's bad at all. But going to the home, bringing them here, it's wonderful that a principal would do that. But I haven't seen her do it for other kids. . . . It doesn't seem right. Maybe it is uncomfortable—it's embarrassing, and I'm not sure why. To hear her gleam about teaching Alan—any kid would want tutoring. . . . And I think the more global picture is that she's right, we've got to do something. We've got to do something. But I'm not sure she should do it in the school where she's the principal. I think it sets up all kinds of social conflicts for the child. (Teacher interview, 3/92)

Race complicates the expectations others may have for Jeanne as a principal, especially as a woman principal. Mothering, when used in reference to a black woman, may reflect a stereotype—that of the nurturing black mother or caretaker (Grant, 1984; Lightfoot, 1980). Even acceptance of Jeanne's behavior, may, then, hinge on others' expectations of black women in our society.

Certainly it's a wonderful thing for kids to be educated in this school, with this wonderful picture of a black woman who is talented and warm and generous and giving. I've heard parents who were upset that she paid attention to black kids; I think it's a subtle bit of racism on their part. I hope to hell she's paying attention to black kids . . . because I think she cares very much about their being valued. I would be very surprised to see, though, that she doesn't pay attention to other needy kids. I don't know if there's any child who would need help that Jeanne would not find a way of connecting to and saying, "I care." (Administrator interview, 4/92)

Jeanne becomes aware of some of the teachers' discomfort with her championing of African American children. Although she has no intention of giving up her more direct approach to these issues, she does choose to use a "female" approach to address their concerns, one that emphasizes communication, interpersonal interactions, and participation (Shakeshaft, 1989; Charters and Jovick, 1981). At a faculty meeting she raises with teachers her concern that they might not bring black children to her attention because she might think they are prejudiced or because she might act on her own without listening to their views. It is not at this point a topic for discussion, but more an opening of the issue, with Jeanne acknowledging her prior actions and saying that perhaps it is a problem in her own perception of the issues. Her willingness to raise the topic reflects her investment in open and congenial interpersonal relationships with these teachers. It is through such relationships that she runs the school. Even in one of the areas where she tends to be less collaborative in her style, she is at least aware of the responses of others and thinks about how to include them in a conversation about her decisions. It is not clear that this overture leads to further conversations or adequately addresses teachers' discomfort, however. Jeanne may have raised these issues less as a conversation opener and more as a conscious or unconscious move by which she lets people know that she recognizes their discomfort but wants to keep it under control.

As of the 1991–1992 school year, Jeanne had lived and worked in the Greenfield-Weston district for twenty-five years. She has made a commitment to the school district and finds a comfortable home in this predominantly white community. As a principal, however, she challenges the system, the community, and her teachers over the issue of working with black children. Her determination to serve the black children in the Greenfield-Weston schools intensifies during the five years of her principalship, as she finds more ways to use her position to make a difference. After five years of a more indirect style of leadership, Jeanne has gathered the resources and strategies she needs to take a more directive stance on an issue of importance to her as a school leader. Her determination to act comes from her own background—both her experience as an African American woman and her experience as an abused child:

> Whenever I go back to an American black community like home, to my family, or to another school, somewhere where I see the community, my psyche cannot stand it. It is the abuse I suffered there that prevents me from going back there. So, I will never be able to manage that. Never. But I can do something here. I can do something, not only for the American black kids that come here, which I'm just beginning to, after being here [five] years. . . . But I can also do something for the rest of the population. (Interview, 9/91)

By the end of the year of the study, Jeanne feels even more strongly that she has a particular role to play as a black principal in the community. She becomes increasingly aware of race as a part of her actions and goals over the course of her five years as principal and begins to act on the issues rather than accepting her race as a given or her role as that of a symbolic model or figurehead. She finally, after several years of talking about it, arranges a trip to Africa; she begins listening to a black radio station; and she becomes more actively involved in her church. Explaining that her father was a spiritual man and that she believes that all things happen in one's life for a reason she says, "There's something happening, I don't quite know what, and it's happening for some reason, you know, spiritual things outside of my control. I've never had to face race issues except for myself and the kids I was limited to teaching. But now I'm facing it, with these kids and the issues here and my concern about them. . . . I think something of significance is happening" (Interview, 6/92).

Balancing Continuity and Change: Summary

Jeanne's personal and professional background and her consciousness of her racial identity and role as an African American woman principal in a predominantly white community influence the choices she makes about Alan and her subsequent school goals. The changes she institutes during this one year are small; they involve a single child and the content of school assemblies. Nevertheless, they are clear statements about her goals and expectations, and they face the scrutiny and resistance of the school community. Unlike Ming Lo and his wife (see chapter 1), Jeanne has her eyes open when she chooses to focus on multiculturalism and meeting the needs of African American children in the school, and she has years of personal experience in dealing with people's responses to these choices. Both the content of her goals and the processes she uses to begin to implement them reflect how issues of race and gender intersect as she makes use of her role as a principal to contribute to school and social change. She knows that such change will be slow and will require attention to how people feel about volatile issues of equality and race; she recognizes their needs for continuity within the school structure. She also knows that such change requires risk taking. She will have to challenge that structure, and she is willing to do so because of her commitment to the issues. Her own outsider status may allow her to see and question the norms and systems that often limit the possibility of change.

SUMMARY

Race, gender, and level of experience make a difference in Jeanne's selection as principal and her actions and choices around school-based management, Alan, and multiculturalism. Administrators', teachers', and community members' perceptions of Jeanne as African American, female, and more of a teacher than a manager also influence her interactions with people, their expectations of her work, and their understanding of her actions and ideas. Others' examination of and responses to Jeanne's level of organization and management, her decisions about individual children, and her curricular choices, depend on the lenses they use to see and evaluate her work. She, in turn, struggles to be effective both in traditional ways and ways that seem true to herself.

When Jeanne talks about balancing her own personal style and her own goals with the demands of the school and district, she is aware of the constraints of the system on her approach to leadership and conscious of finding ways to meet expectations without losing her sense of self. Consciously and unconsciously, she seems to be looking for ways to resist, to change how she runs her school and to shape what that school will look like. Not all of her actions can be classified as those of a female administrator or as acts of resistance against a white, male system. Some are the result of her own personal experiences, her teaching background, her personality; others stem from gender, race, and class influences on her life and work and from responses to the reactions and perceptions of others in the multiple contexts within which she operates. What she wants for the children with whom she works is the same understanding she is developing as a principal. She hopes they will realize that the ordinary struggles and achievements of their daily lives are themselves the rewards.

> How did I get to be this principal? It's bewildering, you know. I don't know how the hell I got to be a principal. When I talk to people about how I came along—I look back and I think it was very ordinary and it was an escape from other things. But in fact, it was doing all the things that got me to be here. And it never occurred to me that it was a rich path. And yet it was very rich. And I've been looking over a rainbow trying to figure out, you know, how to have a rich life beyond and it's right here. So now I want people to know, "Kids, that what you're doing right now is, is rich and right." (Interview, 10/93)[6]

CHAPTER 4

Handling It Graciously

Eve and Bob Cohen, parents of Emily, a second-grader, and Josh, a prospective kindergartner, enter the office and hug and kiss Ann Becker, head of the lower school at Pepperdine. Eve hands Ann a bakery box, saying it's to provide energy because they know how busy she is. Ann introduces me and everyone sits down. Bob starts, saying that they have had a good day—he's on vacation this week, so they took the day to get a tour of the middle and upper school and had a chance to chat with the headmaster while they were up there. They have some questions about Josh, who is visiting the kindergarten. He turned five last September and is in a very structured preschool. He can already read and do math. The person who tested him for his kindergarten application said he was an unusual child; Bob wonders if he belongs in kindergarten or first grade.

Eve interjects, saying that she has to talk about curriculum, even though Bob doesn't want her to. She goes on for quite a long time, with some interjections from Ann and her husband, about Josh's preschool, about the curriculum in the kindergarten and first grade at Pepperdine, and about her daughter who is now in second grade at Pepperdine and doing well (despite her earlier difficulties and the lack of intervention from the school). Eve says she knows her kids: they need structure, they need guidance. She doesn't want Josh to be bored, to regress, to become a wild boy in Ann's office because he isn't being challenged. At one point Ann explains that by third grade, most of the academic differences among kids even out; Eve and Bob really needed to consider the whole child, including social and emotional development. Josh might be ready to do third-grade work, but there is other growth that needs to occur. At another point Ann mentions that she visited another school today where the kids did worksheets all the time, but she wondered about the social and emotional growth of the kids.[1] Bob comments that Ann is echoing what others have told him—better to put Josh in kindergarten. Eve again questions the curriculum, asking what he'll get in kindergarten and first grade. If they do put him in kindergarten, what will be done for him to assure he isn't bored?

Ann recommends that they make an appointment to observe in a kindergarten and a first-grade class and to talk to Sue Green, the reading teacher, about the curriculum. Bob and Eve agree and plan to meet with Ann again after they get all the information/feedback from Josh's visit today. Ann notices people outside her door and realizes she is fifteen minutes late for a meeting with the Pre-K teachers, the psychologist, and a parent. She and the Cohens hastily say good-by. (Field notes, 2/2/94)

Ann Becker had been head of the Pepperdine Lower School for five years when she agreed to participate in this study.[2] The conversation described above, with parents Bob and Eve Cohen, captures some of the interpersonal and curricular issues Ann copes with every day. Pepperdine is a Pre-K–12 academically oriented private school, located in a predominantly white, upper-middle-class neighborhood and serving students from a number of similar communities. As head of the lower school, Ann fills the role of public relations manager with current and prospective parents, working to market the school as unique, academically strong, and committed to meeting the needs of individual students. At the same time she is responsible for meeting ongoing student and teacher needs and the demands of a new headmaster who wants to shape the school in new ways. Although this is not an impossible combination of tasks, it threatens to become so for Ann. Throughout the year of the study she struggles to maintain her positive sense of self as a principal in the face of escalating expectations. As someone who is used to pleasing her superiors and succeeding in her work, Ann finds it a challenge to perform well in the changing school context in which she works, despite one teacher's comment that, "I think she's handling it very graciously" (Teacher interview, 11/93). In some respects, Ann's experiences becoming a principal, defining herself in that role, and balancing her own style and standards against the expectations of others and the constraints of the institution echo Jeanne Price's (see chapter 3); in other respects, Ann's path differs sharply from Jeanne's and from the general pattern described in the literature (see chapter 1). Using the four themes introduced in chapter 1 as a framework, this chapter explores some of the ways in which gender, age, personal and professional background, and community and institutional contexts affect Ann's actions and effectiveness as a principal.

Overview of the Themes

Ann, like Jeanne, took her first steps toward *becoming a principal* as a result of being "pushed" by a district administrator. Once she made the move, however, she embraced administration with an enthusiasm not always represented in prior descriptions of women principals (see, e.g., Ozga, 1993; Pavan, 1991; Marshall and Mitchell, 1989). The role provided her with a focus and purpose that previously had been missing from her life; it also led her to redefine her personal goals and priorities. In her administrative positions in the United States and overseas, Ann develops a leadership style that emphasizes the organizational aspects of management. Unlike Jeanne, who focuses on community and relationship, Ann chooses to limit interpersonal connections in order to focus on administration and organization.

At Pepperdine, Ann *serves a community* of parents whose class and educational background differ from her own. In looking for ways to feel competent and confident, Ann often draws on her own standards of professional behavior and appearance. Like Jeanne, however, Ann finds that parents and teachers hold contradictory expectations for her as a woman principal. Some parents and teachers, even as they equate femininity with weakness and leadership with authority, want a woman head who is warm and empathetic rather than coolly confident and organized. Ann's relatively impersonal, often unilateral decisions sometimes make others uncomfortable. Because Ann tends to define the needs of students, teachers, and parents in administrative terms, she focuses on actions necessary to assure the smooth operation of the school. Had she been a man, her constituents might have been more likely to perceive Ann's strong managerial style as a personal and institutional asset (see, e.g., Bloom and Munro, 1995; Pavan, 1991; Yeakey, 1986).

With the arrival of a new headmaster in 1992, Ann finds it increasingly difficult to *meet institutional expectations* at Pepperdine. She feels undermined personally and professionally by the new head, whose agenda for change involves Ann in responsibilities beyond her existing areas of expertise. For the first time in her experience, she finds herself unable to satisfy those in power. In Jeanne's case, the institutional context and Jeanne's personal style allow her to respond with some flexibility to the demands of the hierarchy. In contrast, Ann's actions and experience seem constrained by Pepperdine's administrative structure and by her own personal and professional background. Both Ann's age and her gender contribute to this dynamic and complicate the negotiations that ensue over if and when she should leave Pepperdine.

In the year of the study, as Ann *balances continuity and change*, she gives priority to maintaining the status quo. Ann sees the headmaster's proposed changes, which include a major overhaul of the K–12 curriculum and policies to promote diversity and multiculturalism, as unwieldy and problematic. Her desire to keep all aspects of the school working smoothly and her lack of training in curriculum contribute to her emphasis on stability rather than change. Ann equates her effectiveness as a principal with her ability to control the daily operations of the lower school. She uses her superior skills in organization and administrative management to facilitate the work of her faculty and keep the parent community well informed. Having served the system successfully as a relatively traditional manager, Ann finds it difficult to initiate, pursue, or respond to changes that demand skills she does not value or has not developed.[3]

Ann struggles to balance her strengths and experience with the changing demands of the context within which she works. She has, in the past, managed to function successfully within the system and maintain a sense of her own skills and contributions. In this case, however, the negotiation process falters, as conflicting expectations and styles overwhelm the balance.

BECOMING A PRINCIPAL:
NEGOTIATING THE PERSONAL CONTEXT

Access and Entry

Like many other women principals, Ann did not achieve her position as the result of a carefully determined career plan. In fact, she did not initially choose the field of education. Ann grew up, the third of four children, in a small midwestern town. Her father, educated through the eighth grade, was originally a barber; later he started a small oil delivery business. Her mother was a country schoolteacher who "always made us feel that school was important" (Interview, 8/93). Ann decided early on that she wanted to be a doctor; she wanted to help people, to be like the small-town family doctor who had cared for the people in her community.

> And you know, it sounds really trite and corny, that you want to help people. That was one of the things I had to say at [my medical school interview]. You know, this guy just probing, "When did you first want to be a doctor?" "Well, I don't know, when I was a little kid." . . . Our family doctor was the doctor that delivered me. I lived in one of these little towns, and Doctor Parker was this tall, handsome, gray-haired gentleman. Later I worked in his office when I was in school, in college. And I'm sure that played some role, in wanting to be like somebody. There was nobody in my family that was a doctor, so it was probably some of the prestige that went with it, but it was not the money. I was not out there to make lots of money. (Interview, 8/93)

Her parents did not explicitly deter her—in fact, Ann's father was committed to sending his children to college. Still, Ann knew that her family lacked the "money and influence" that would have been the prerequisites for any young woman to attend medical school in the 1940s.

In college, Ann majored in biology and enrolled in a medical technical program, financing her undergraduate education by working in a lab. Even though she knew that her gender and class background would limit her chances of getting into medical school, Ann gave it a try:

> So in my junior year, I started thinking about medical school again because my roommate was the governor's daughter and her mother knew the head of the medical school at the state university. So through her I was at least given the opportunity to be tested. And do you know what they did? In those days they would—they put me through three days of testing, the Rorschach being one of them. I'll never forget Rorschach. And the conclusion was—they had a file like that big on me when they finished—"You're intelligent enough to go to medical school, but you're a female and we'll flunk you out in the first year." There was no quota for women, no nothing. Well, if I had known then what I know now about the schools in the east and the women's colleges and that sort of thing, or had anybody again in a counseling role—but the end of it was that I didn't get into the state university [medical school]. (Interview, 8/93)

Following college, Ann worked in the state Department of Health, in a clinic that conducted polio research, and as a researcher at the Kresge Eye Institute. She married in 1950. When her children were born (three girls, in 1953, 1954, and 1956), the family moved to a more rural area, and she stopped working.

Only when her children entered school did Ann become involved in education as a potential career. At the urging of her children's school principal (a woman), she began working as a substitute teacher. When her youngest child was in third grade, she returned to the campus of a local state university and worked part time toward her elementary teacher certification. In 1966, at the age of forty, Ann started teaching fourth grade (full time) in the same district's elementary school. Ann points out that because she was older than most of her teaching colleagues, she quickly earned respect and responsibility. Within a year she became a head teacher, standing in for the principal when needed.[4]

In 1980, at age fifty-four and with fourteen years of experience teaching elementary school, Ann was "pushed" into her first administrative position.

> I had a good reputation for teaching, and we did a lot of committee work and everything you know. And so . . . in 1978, one of the principals went out on a short term medical leave and they posted the interim job—and I was given it. My [male] principal just pushed me into it and said, "You're going to go and interview for that," so I was

only there the last two months of school. And the [male] superintendent said to me, "Now you're going to get the next school so you get
a masters in administration and get certified for administration." So
while I was teaching I went back and forth to the state school which
was an hour and a half away and in '80 I finished a masters in administration and was certified in that. And then that next fall, I was given
my first elementary school. (Interview, 8/93)

The presence of predominantly male gatekeepers and the lack of
mentors tend to reduce women's chances of becoming principals. Nevertheless, women point to the role of encouragement from superordinates
as a major factor in their career movement (see, e.g., Ozga, 1993; Pavan,
1991; Yeakey et al., 1986). In Ann's and Jeanne's cases, we see why; each
seemed to lack the ambition, the sense of self as an educational leader,
and the opportunities for hands on practice that might have propelled her
into administration. Each of the three women in this study had a male
superior who encouraged her to consider school leadership. Even given
this support, however, Ann's initial entry into the position seems to have
happened to her rather than occurring as a result of her own choices or
actions. She, like Jeanne, did not purposefully prepare for the transition
into administration during her years as a teacher. Both of these women
assumed their first principalship at the urging of another. And, like many
women, Ann's graduate training occurred after she took her first position
rather than as part of a preplanned route into administration. As Pavan
(1991) suggests, "most (women) recognized that they were on the path
long after they had taken the first step or walked many miles" (p. 10).

Ann's age (fifty-four when she became a principal) also set her apart.
Because they tend to enter administration later, and in less consistent patterns than do men, women principals lack the experience of an age
cohort moving through the ranks at the same time. Thus these women
often do not have the personal and professional support that would be
provided by such peers; they also have fewer models to emulate (Grant,
1989; Ball and Goodson, 1985). Ann may have been unusually conscious
of her age because she entered teaching later than many other women.
Being older than her faculty and staff and having no peer group for support become important to Ann in her work at Pepperdine during the year
of the study. Both gender and age influence the interactions Ann has with
others, shaping expectations others have of her, affecting her perceptions
of herself as a principal, and influencing how she chooses to respond to
the headmaster, who is male and younger than she.

Not many years after Ann became a full-time principal, her marriage dissolved. In part, this resulted from the large amount of time and
energy she chose to put into her work. In retrospect, she explains that
she married because "there was nothing else in my life."

> You know, I have no idea why I ever got married because I just wanted a career. I never wanted children. I dearly love my children, but I don't know why I stayed married so long and just felt so unchallenged. So once I started teaching, that just filled the gap. And I felt very very responsible for my children. And then, I must have just grown up at a time when you just didn't get divorced unless something was really, really wrong. (Interview, 8/93)

Her work as principal fulfilled Ann in ways marriage and motherhood had not. It challenged her, introduced her to new and interesting people, and gave her a sense of competence, of making a contribution, that had been lacking in her life. She happily let the work take over much of her time, energy, and commitment. In May 1984, at the age of fifty-eight and after four years of work as a school principal, Ann divorced.

Ann's discovery of a new kind of power in her position as an administrator; her opportunity to identify with others, women and men, in independent and influential positions; and her growing independence as her own children matured into adulthood acted as the catalysts she needed to change her life. Although Ann herself does not connect her experience to larger social movements, her personal and professional changes occurred in the late 1970s and 1980s, at a time when the women's movement gave women greater economic opportunity, provided more cultural support, and supplied a language that helped them describe and act on their needs and skills. Ann recognizes how class and gender affected her chances of going to medical school in the 1940s, but she does not perceive the influence of the historical context on her later career decisions. Still, generational and gender-related factors seem to have affected the choices she made to enter administration, continue in it, and leave her marriage in the early 1980s.

Taking on the Role

In the fall of 1984, divorced and in her late fifties, Ann took a position as head of the lower school in an international school in Turkey. She made a conscious decision to cut herself off from the relationships and places that had previously defined her. Although she admits that she has occasionally regretted this decision, she saw it as a part of her new self-definition and dedication to being a good principal. Relationships often became secondary to doing her job well.

> I wish it had been possible to maybe keep in touch a little bit more closely with a lot of the good friends that I had in Indian River. But it's, when you're not living someplace, reality is that it's just impossible to maintain lots of friendships when you don't see people. (Interview, 2/94)

After three years in Turkey, Ann took another lower school headship in an American school in the Philippines. Both schools hired her because of her organizational skills and her no-nonsense approach to administration. In each case, she explains, the school she took over had been both physically and administratively neglected; her job was to "clean it up." Ann lived and worked in the American community in each country, and she feels that her perspectives broadened and changed during her time overseas. Ann's descriptions of her stays in both Turkey and the Philippines suggest, however, that she spent little time learning these nations' culture, language, or politics. Rather, she focused on becoming a good administrator, someone who could facilitate the work of the teachers and children in her school.

Pepperdine recruited Ann from the Philippines, in part because she had the reputation of an administrator who could straighten up a school that had been allowed to drift. Teachers describe her predecessor at Pepperdine's lower school as a student-centered principal who lacked the organizational skills seen as necessary to run the school effectively. Parents and teachers agree that Pepperdine hired Ann to "organize," "clean up," "shape up," and "pull together the lower school." During her first three years in the school, Ann focused on organization. She made schedules, got her office staff running smoothly, arranged for parent communication on a regular basis, developed systems to keep better track of student placement and special needs, and hired many new teachers. In designing and implementing these administrative changes, Ann used the skills and experience she had developed during her previous principalships, especially at the two international sites. At all three schools, her leadership responsibilities centered on creating and maintaining orderly, site-based operations in institutions that had been in administrative disarray before her arrival.

Ann loves the work of the principalship. At Pepperdine, as at the other schools she has led, she feels she can and does make a real difference. Early on in her career as principal, she realized that she most liked the managerial aspects of the job, organizing facilities and people so that a school runs well. She recognizes, though, that this managerial approach does not always mesh with others' expectations of the role of a woman principal.

> I have to tell you that I liked—I wouldn't describe it as liking power. I liked managing. It was a real challenge to see how organized I could get things without being insufferable. I've always been told when I left a school that I left it in perfect condition. The people that have followed me—I have had contact with them later—and they said, "Gosh, I've never come into a place like this." Now, it doesn't mean that there isn't room for change because I think that each personality has things,

things that are important. But I've always come into places where there was very little organization, where there didn't seem to be rhyme or reason—the schedules, all the other stuff like that, the office being run well. I think everybody here, I think, would say that I take care of anything they ask me about. I see to it that their needs are met. Some of them probably think that I should be warmer. They don't, they don't understand that I can't open myself up to them. I open myself up as much as I can. They like to know where I've been in the summertime. They like to know what I'm doing, and when I can, I tell them. But I try not to be any more emotional than I can possibly be because it just doesn't work. (Interview, 8/93)

To what extent does Ann's assumption of an organizational rather than interpersonal approach to the principalship stem from a need to adapt to male power structures and expectations and to what extent is it part of her own personal style? How did the mandates she received, to "clean up" disorganized schools, influence the skills she developed and her understanding of what a good leader should be? All of these variables appear to have affected her actions and style of leadership. Ann seems to unconsciously recognize the strength of institutional norms as she considers what actions are appropriate in her role. She also sees her own personality affecting her leadership style. And although she does not consciously accept gender as a determinant of her behavior, she sometimes uses gendered norms as she reflects on her own actions. For example, Ann struggles with controlling her emotions and feelings, in part because she considers them out of place in the role she plays in the school, in part because as an individual she needs to feel in control. She also associates some of the need to downplay emotions to the fact that she is a woman.

> I think that women have earned, fairly or unfairly, the rap of being too emotional. I don't believe that's true at all. I believe [if] you're a lot more feeling, if your emotions spill out, so what. But some of that [need to control emotions] is just me. Like, when I had my own classroom, if anybody could have criticized me for anything, it was that I didn't baby the kids. I understood them, and I tried to coax them along, and with my own children, if you fell down or something, you picked yourself up and you didn't make a big deal about it. It's kind of that sort of a thing. . . . But probably the emotional stuff is a little bit more with me. If my emotions get out of control, it's really hard for me. But I'm certainly a very feeling person, and I try to keep it tucked underneath. (Interview, 8/93)

Her own personal needs *and* the demands associated with being principal of a school in need of organizational attention may have prompted Ann to adopt an accepted, male-normed management style

(Regan, 1990; Marshall and Mitchell, 1989). In addition, Ann recognizes that some parent, teacher, and administrator expectations challenge the idea of a woman in a school leadership role. Ann uses "impressions management" (Marshall and Mitchell, 1989) as a way of balancing some of these conflicts, drawing on expected gendered behaviors to help both herself and others accept her as a woman manager. For example, Ann's approach to appearance differs from Jeanne's. Jeanne is sometimes reminded by others that her clothing might influence others' perceptions of her. She generally chooses, however, to use dress and appearance as a way of asserting her individuality rather than as a way of helping people accept her as either a traditional administrator or a female administrator. Her clothes include African woven vests and her hair styles have varied from close cropped to dreadlocks. By contrast, Ann deliberately uses appearance to convey the message that she is both female and in charge. When she first became a principal she "bought a ton of suits"; in both overseas schools she was known for being stylish.

> And you know, I've been accused—I've had one teacher tell me that I expected everybody to be in suits. Well, you've seen me lately out of suits rather than in suits. And I think that maybe during the time when I first started this that I was always in heels and stuff like that. And it means a lot to me, the way somebody looks. I think it does matter— you don't have to have expensive clothes or anything—but you can look neat. (Interview, 2/94)

Dressing in suits and heels, Ann explains, "increases my self-confidence" (Field notes, 10/93). Her attention to dress allows Ann to look like the manager she wants to be—and is. One of the lower school teachers observes that Ann's style of dress is professional rather than feminine, which allows her to function in both the male and female "worlds."

> She's not a real feminine fluff person, she's very professional, and turned out and immaculate, but you never see her in ruffles and fifteen bracelets and big girl shoes. She presents herself in a very tailored—so she could kind of float back and forth into a man's world or a female world, just on her appearance. You know, she's not going to relate to—women wouldn't necessarily relate to her because of her extreme femininity, nor would men necessarily relate to her because of her extreme tailored, professional look. She's very innocuous in that way. She can just float. (Teacher interview, 12/93)

Becoming a Principal: Summary

Ann has little difficulty assuming the role of principal, as both she and the schools that hired her define it. She so enjoys the work of her first principalship that it replaces much of her personal life. Even as a more experienced administrator, as she balances retaining friendship with pursuing professional commitment, and becoming professional with maintaining traditional femininity, she consistently chooses to work toward being as effective as possible as a principal. She believes in the need for authority and hierarchy in schools, and she seems comfortable with her role in the middle, simultaneously addressing needs of community members, teachers, and the school administration. Unlike Jeanne, who frequently questions definitions of leadership and her own actions as principal, Ann has a clear, unwavering perspective on what a principal should look like, how she should behave, and what responsibilities she should take on.

SERVING OTHERS: DEFINING LEADERSHIP IN THE COMMUNITY CONTEXT

Ann's leadership style grows out of a convergence of several factors: the crisis conditions of the schools she is hired to lead, her interest and skill in management and organization, her desire to control and monitor details, and her concern with professionalism and appropriateness. Her strengths lay in developing and maintaining an environment that she assumes will allow teachers to do their jobs effectively. Unlike the women managers depicted in much of the literature, and despite her fourteen years of teaching experience, Ann does not see her role at the lower school as including leadership in curriculum and instruction. She concentrates instead on facilitating teachers' abilities to carry out these, and other classroom responsibilities, themselves. Perhaps because her first several administrative jobs called on her organizational skills, and perhaps because she has had little success in her past attempts to mix personal and professional relationships, Ann focuses on organization rather than people in her work with both parents and teachers at Pepperdine. Her age, her traditional professional style, and her improvements in the school's day-to-day operations over time help her win acceptance among members of both constituencies. Still, issues of class in the community context and differences in expectations regarding how women should act in the role of principal complicate Ann's negotiation of a management style.

Leadership in the Community

> Pepperdine School is a PreK–12 coeducational day school committed to educational excellence and dedicated to developing in each student a love of learning and a compassionate participation in the world.

Through a strong college preparatory curriculum in the humanities and the sciences, the School encourages curiosity, creativity, and respect for intellectual effort. Pepperdine upholds and promotes moral integrity, a sense of personal achievement and worth, and concern for others at school and in the larger community. (School mission statement, 1993)

The Pepperdine School was founded in 1894. In 1993–1994, the year of the study, it served approximately six hundred students, divided into lower, middle and upper school divisions.[5] The lower school's 210 students occupy a separate campus about two blocks from the middle and upper school buildings. The lower school facilities, which consist of a modern school building and two large houses, provide space for one Pre-K class, two kindergartens, three first grades, two each of second, third, and fourth grade, and three fifth grades. Each class contains 12–15 students. Children admitted to the Pre-K and kindergarten classes typically come from other nursery schools or preschools. Many, like Josh in the initial vignette, come from fairly academically oriented settings. While Ann and the teachers emphasize a developmental approach in the early elementary grades, the school also requires test scores and reading screening as part of the admissions process. Most children entering kindergarten (especially the boys) are six rather than five and adept at initial school tasks. Competition from the many other private schools in this area results in Pepperdine having to work hard to attract academically able students to fill its classes. Teachers and administrators acknowledge the ongoing dilemma that results from a commitment to meeting individual needs *and* the financial necessity of filling each class. Full enrollment might involve accepting and meeting the needs of students who require academic and learning support that Pepperdine's staff cannot adequately provide.

Although the school provides some financial aid, most lower school families pay the $8,000–$10,000 annual tuition. The majority of Pepperdine's families are headed by white, upper-class professionals. Often both parents work, or the mother has a professional degree, held a job until the children were born, and now chooses to stay at home. Teachers and administrators, and the parents themselves, describe the clientele of the school as both supportive and demanding. Parents are involved in their children's education; they believe that the tuition they pay gives them the right to intervene in their children's schooling when they feel it is necessary.

And sometimes I think right or wrong, and it's not really a very nice way to be, but I think we tend, when we go to an independent school and we pay all this money, to sometimes [say], "I pay all this money and I'm—!" And so I think we're a little less shy than maybe some people about going and saying what we think or what we want or what we hope it to be or want it to be. And I mean, I think we as parents can be maybe selfish in that respect. And I think that's tough to deal with, you know because it's not the best quality in a person. (Parent interview, 5/94)

The school accepts the need to be accountable to parents and, in return, expects both financial and other support from those whom it serves.[6]

Ann describes feeling somewhat out of place in the community served by Pepperdine. Despite the fact that "her" families respect her, Ann comments on her awareness that she grew up in relative poverty, raised by parents who had much less education than many of the parents with whom she now works. Ann also believes that her age makes her different from the people she serves. She observes that she faces not only differences in class and family background but also generational differences in the types of expectations parents hold for their children. She explains that while she can find her way around in the community served by Pepperdine, she does not really feel at home in it.

> I'm very aware a lot of times that I grew up almost poor and didn't know it. I grew up in a family where my father was not educated, my mother was a country school teacher. . . . My families never make me feel anything other than just respected in all. Because most of them just have so much money, they just think everybody does. And it's old money; most of them didn't earn it, somebody else did. But I find in general that it's just such a—and I can kind of take it for granted now—that here on the East Coast there's so much history and so many schools and universities and things that I used to just hear about but not have any connection with. And so I have gotten used to it, and I guess it's partly that I can find my way around, but it is definitely not my world. . . . Anybody from the Midwest will tell you the same thing if they've ever lived in the Midwest. We're open, friendly, and generally middle class, and I don't consider that a put down at all. . . . Like, for my generation, it was not too uncommon that my parents were not both college educated. I mean, I could have come from educated parents, but it was not that unusual. Like you know, my peer group in Michigan, lots of them came from farm families, and more that sort of thing—small towns, not lawyers and doctors and all of the rest of this. So it's just been very interesting for me. I don't have a lot of—I don't have any really personal contact with people [in this community] because I don't socialize with them. I only go to these stupid cocktail parties in the fall where I get into some of these huge homes where I see this other side of people. (Interview, 2/94)

Some of Ann's emphasis on appropriate dress, behavior, and demeanor—for herself and her teachers—reflects her need to find a respected place in this previously unknown culture. She gains confidence by closely adhering to what she considers the hallmarks of professionalism. For example, she frequently comments on the dress (appropriate or not) of the teacher candidates she interviews during the year of the study, and she is candid about her own deliberate efforts to dress the part of a private school head. Attention to appearances is also an important facet of control. Ann insists that chairs come off the tops of desks first thing in the morning in classrooms because it looks better, and she reminds students in a chorus concert that they must have "uniform uniforms" for the concert, including black shoes. Given the community in which she works and her own background, being in control and maintaining self-esteem are closely related. Mastering appearances addresses both needs as Ann copes with a class culture different from her own. Ann's success in managing impressions helps ensure that she is accepted as an effective administrator *and* contributes to her feelings of confidence and competence in this community.

As Ann goes about communicating with parents, keeping them happy as clients and maintaining the regular functioning of the lower school, her straightforward managerial style earns approval from some people and complaints from others. Some parents, even those who have gone over her head to the headmaster of the school, speak highly of her ability to work with them to best meet their child's needs. These parents appreciate Ann's candid approach even if it challenges their own views. They describe a directness untainted by political maneuvering or attempts to exert power for its own sake, a frankness meant to serve them and their children:

> I think that, I think that on appearances, she looks like she might be very set in her ways, very straightforward, with a one-dimensional idea of how things ought to run. But as soon as she starts to speak to you, you really get a different perception. She's not only very, just very polite and warm, which she would have to be in her position, but just, when you're speaking to her, she encourages you to let her know how you really feel about things and to make you comfortable. . . . The other thing about Ann—she's not a politician. She's a good person and she wants the best for the children in the school. But she's not going to tell you what you want to hear just to play the role of a politician. And I think that there have been issues like that with parents who wanted her to take a particular stand because it fit in with what they needed at that time. When she didn't do it, they perceived her as uncooperative or unapproachable or whatever, but I've not encountered that. Not that Ann hasn't said, "I don't think that that's the way to go." The way she handles it, she does tell me when she disagrees with something or she thinks that something that I'm considering for my son, for example, is not in his best interest, but she doesn't tell me in a way that I feel attacked or anything like that. (Parent interview, 5/94)

In phone conversations with disgruntled or questioning parents and in conferences with parents and teachers, Ann appears poised and, for the most part willing to listen, to explain, and to support, even at times when she knows she is dealing with rumor, with parents obsessing about the achievement of their child, and with demands for services the school does not provide. For example, one afternoon Ann spends twenty minutes on the phone talking to a parent who is agonizing over whether or not to send her child to Pepperdine or to a competing all-girls' school. Ann describes what Pepperdine has to offer, but acknowledges that what matters most is "the fit" for each child. She also responds sympathetically to the apparent conflict between the two parents over which school might be best for their daughter. She arranges for the parents to visit some classrooms and warmly tells the mother, "Once you resolve and make a decision then you just stick to it" (Field notes, 2/15/94).

Not everyone evaluates Ann's style positively. Some describe her as cold or distant in her dealings with parents, defensive when approached with a complaint, and unwilling to respond or act on parental demands and requests. Some parents feel blocked by her and go instead to the headmaster; others say they use humor and directness to challenge Ann's resistance or to get her to reconsider a decision they do not like.

> I think she's, her only weakness as far as I'm concerned is she's, it's hard for her to listen to criticism. I think that's her. She tends to be defensive, but eventually, you get through to her. But I think for the more timid or the more easily intimidated, that must be a lot harder. I mean, I'll do it—I'll try it direct, which is my most prominent style, then I'll try it with a sense of humor, then I'll try it with, you know, and I'll finally get my point across. (Parent interview, 6/94)

Paradoxically, lower school parents criticize Ann for demonstrating the same skills and attributes that Greenfield-Weston parents criticize Jeanne for lacking. Being a "real administrator" does not ensure women principals the same support that would be given to their male counterparts. Women administrators suffer from contradictory expectations about what constitutes an effective principal and what characterizes a woman in that role. A good administrator is direct and authoritative; a good woman administrator should be warm and understanding. These are not necessarily mutually exclusive expectations; the parent, quoted earlier, appreciates Ann for being both direct and warm. In this parent's mind, Ann meets both sets of expectations. Such success is hard won, however. Women in administration must learn to cope with the tension between people's traditional beliefs about how one leads a school and how one interacts as a woman. Both in her work with parents and with teachers, Ann continually negotiates these contradictory expectations as she develops a management style that fits who she is and the community context within which she works.

Relationships with Teachers

When she was hired, the original headmaster gave Ann free reign in the lower school and a charge to get things "under control." Being given such a mandate might cause any new administrator some interpersonal problems with her existing staff. In addition, Ann brings to her work a personal style that does not radiate warmth or invite close relationships with her colleagues. She describes experiences in each of her prior principalships in which, when she developed or kept friendships with teachers in her school, both she and the teachers suffered. In her first United States principalship, when one woman with whom she had taught came to work in her school, the outcome was unexpectedly negative. "What she wanted was out of line and I had to tell her, 'You're a good teacher and I'm glad you're here, but I can't let you do the things you want to do.' And [another teacher friend] almost hated me from the time I got the administrative job, and yet, she didn't want it and I don't understand why she hated me. And those two people were very close to me" (Interview, 8/93). A teacher with whom she became friendly in the Philippines was ostracized by her peers for socializing with an administrator. These, and other personal and professional experiences, taught Ann to be somewhat wary of opening up to others: "I'm very human and I'm very warm, but I can't get as involved as some people would like me to because it just doesn't work. They're always pressing me about that" (Interview, 8/93).

Several teachers left Pepperdine during Ann's first three years as the head of the school. Ann acknowledges that they may not have liked her much, but, she explains, they left of their own accord.

> And thank heavens for me, the people that really were not effective and that I would have recommended not renew[ing their contracts], decided to leave. And I am most grateful they found jobs. And they left, for all intents and purposes, on a friendly note. Like I can see them outside of school now and its fine. I'm sure they didn't like me much. . . . But anyways, so we started to pull things together. (Interview, 6/93)

Others suggest, however, that Ann forced certain teachers to leave, or made them uncomfortable enough to make that choice themselves. Teacher morale was low in those years; people worried about keeping their jobs. Some teachers comment that Ann's temper, or her potential or actual displeasure, also made relationships tense. At one point in the first two years, a teacher told Ann that her colleagues believed that one of the fourth-grade teachers reported to Ann on the actions of her fellow teachers. Other teachers also describe the "spy system" they thought was in effect. When the new headmaster arrived, at the beginning of Ann's fourth year, he found what he describes as a lower school atmosphere lacking in trust and warmth.

> When I came in, that group—the lower school faculty—was a group that made it clear that she was not somebody that they could trust. They didn't like her, they didn't respect her. And I tried to weigh those things, because she had had to do some difficult things here at the school. But she has a very hard time listening and hearing, and a very hard time giving back in a way that is—that exudes any kind of warmth. (Interview, 5/94)

Mark Rubin's arrival initially did little to improve morale. The many new demands he placed on all of the administrators in his first year created tensions and pressures that seemed to make Ann, and consequently her lower school teachers, more uncomfortable. In addition, Mark asked teachers to come in and talk to him about what they did and did not like about the school—and about Ann. In turn, he clearly described to Ann the problems he saw. Rubin's demands and expectations, and his own leadership style, made Ann's fourth year as head of the lower school more difficult than the prior years.

It upsets Ann when Mark encourages her faculty (or parents) to talk to him rather than directly to her. She maintains, and some of her teachers confirm, that she functions best when people speak out and are up front with her; she can not understand why some teachers might not be comfortable with this approach.

> If you can't handle something, be up front and honest. If you have a question, for heaven's sake come and ask me. Don't stew inside until you're really upset by the whole thing. Talk to your parents in a compassionate but up front way and you won't have so much trouble. And when you see something, take care of it. If you need me I'll be there. But I don't know what it is. I've found this all over. They [the teachers] are terribly insecure people. (Interview, 6/93)

Jeanne and Ann differ significantly in their views of what constitutes the best environment for learning, what responsibilities the principal has for maintaining and promoting that environment, and what approaches work most effectively for involving teachers in the work of the school. Jeanne tends to ignore or delegate decision-making responsibilities. When pushed, by parents or district mandates, she reluctantly assumes organizational control at Greenfield-Weston. When she has a particular goal in sight, she becomes more directive and actively involved in engaging faculty and parents in her vision. Her teachers recognize the "chaos" that sometimes results from this approach, but they applaud the freedom and opportunities to learn that accompany Jeanne's style.

In contrast to Jeanne, Ann wants and needs to be in control, to be respected, and to be consulted. She cares very much about her faculty, and she demonstrates that care by making sure everything runs according to plan. This, she explains, makes it possible for teachers to do their jobs well.

> What makes a good principal? Well, I'll tell you. I think that for different people, different things. Basically, I think it's somebody that is willing to take the responsibility day-in and day-out for keeping a school in pretty good shape. And that means that it's organized enough so that things run smoothly, so that you're not always plugging up the dike. And so that teachers have what they need when they need it, and so that they know what's expected of them. And you—I think [you] have to protect them sometimes from [those] higher up. (Interview, 2/94)

Ann, however, sometimes gives the teachers mixed messages; she expects them to follow her guidelines, take care of business, and still be willing to question and raise concerns. Ann seems unaware that her own calls for openness and honesty and her work to keep the school running smoothly frequently appear contradictory to teachers. In addition, some of her actions do not encourage people to approach her freely. For example, she has held teachers' contracts (rather than immediately rehiring them in the spring) without clearly explaining why; she sometimes loses her temper or responds curtly to teachers; she appears uncaring and unresponsive about her faculty's personal and professional needs; and she is frequently unwilling to share her own feelings and needs with others. Ann's commitment to "shaping up" the school, her understanding of the principalship, and her more general interpersonal style and need for control contributed to her sometimes distant and problematic relationships with the faculty during her first four years at Pepperdine.

A distinct change occurs in teachers' views of Ann's style in the fifth year of her principalship, the year of this study. During this year, they consistently describe her as more supportive, warmer, more human, and more willing to share their and her own feelings. The teachers attribute this shift to several factors: Ann seems increasingly comfortable with the teachers, perhaps because she hired many of them; she now shares with the teachers more of her concerns and feelings about the pressure she is experiencing from Mark, making herself more open and honest (and perhaps more vulnerable and sympathetic) in their eyes; and she may be considering leaving the school.

> But I think last year Ann—I guess she probably went through a lot with Mark coming and everything. It seems like this year she's more

honest with us as a faculty about what she's doing and how the power comes down, and I have—I just feel more respect for it, knowing what she does. I always like that, when the administration tells you what kind of work they do. . . . And Ann's doing a little more of that this year. I find her very responsive when I have anything to say or I need something. (Teacher interview, 1/94)

I think she's getting better, you know, she's mellowing out. I think she feels most of her teachers are in one building—before that wasn't true. Most of the teachers who are here now were hired by her. The teachers who weren't, like me, she's come, most of us, she's gotten to know well. And I think she feels that she is in control, so she's loosening up. You can see it happening. She's more honest with us and she's more open about what she thinks, and she's less worried about things going wrong. (Teacher interview, 5/94)

Thus, when Ann takes on a more traditionally female style of interacting, one that involves a more personal and responsive approach and that allows her weaknesses to show, teachers become more comfortable with her and more accepting of her in the role of principal.

When teachers and parents describe Ann's early years at Pepperdine, they comment on her comparatively impersonal approach and note that Ann's style seems neither feminine nor female. She does not meet people's expectations of women in general, and of a woman administrator in particular. Even during the year of the study, one teacher describes Ann as a "very masculine woman" although she "plays up to men" (Teacher interview, 3/94). Another explains that Ann is "not a warm female," but rather "a colder, walled-up female" (Teacher interview, 6/94). Although some parents and teachers characterize certain female traits as negative, the perceived lack of these same traits may be even more problematic. Being a female female implies being fluffy, unprofessional, and prone to tears, not the defining characteristics of a principal; yet when Ann does not fulfill these expectations, there is some discomfort in people's descriptions of her professionalism and behaviors. When, during her fifth year, Ann interacts more personally with her staff, they see this change as positive, and they welcome it. Ann's more personable approach contributes to a greater sense of community in the lower school, perhaps in part because now her style more fully matches teachers' and parents' expectations of how a female principal should behave.

Serving the Community: Summary

Ann has served the school well in the capacity in which she was hired—to organize and "clean it up." During the year of the study, everyone describes the lower school as well run, organized, and a comfortable place to work. Ann focuses on creating a school environment within which she believes teachers can and should work efficiently and effectively. She describes this as her way of taking care of teachers, students, and parents. This approach blurs distinctions some researchers make between male and female or authoritative and caring management styles; care and empowerment can, perhaps, be achieved through authority and assumption of power. Parents and teachers, however, feel more comfortable with Ann when she exhibits the personal openness, warmth, and responsiveness traditionally expected of women. Perhaps they would have preferred this approach in a male principal as well, but in Ann's case the tension prompted by the perceived misfit between her professional, managerial style and her gender seems salient to those with whom she works. In developing an administrative style, Ann negotiates definitions of leadership within an upper-class community whose parents are actively involved in their children's education and who make many demands on the school; with teachers and parents whose expectations of women administrators involve inherent contradictions; and within her own personal and professional history. Ann's experiences suggest that leadership cannot be satisfactorily understood as a single construct. Instead, it is better formulated as a dynamic process of construction and revision in response to many factors, including cultural expectations regarding gender-appropriate behavior, community expectations and interactions, and the formal and informal practices that characterize an administrator's institutional environment.

MEETING INSTITUTIONAL EXPECTATIONS:
NEGOTIATING THE CULTURE OF SCHOOLING

As she begins her fifth year at Pepperdine, Ann has worked for fourteen years as a school administrator and feels successful and competent in her role. Her experiences at the lower school have been mixed, but she has accomplished the job she was initially hired to do. Under her leadership, the lower school operates in a positive, predictable, and orderly fashion. Beginning in her fourth year, with the arrival of a new headmaster and in response to an increasingly competitive private school market, however, Pepperdine begins to change. The skills demanded of all three division heads by the new administration and the school include curricular leadership; an ability to help teachers develop their knowledge and skills; an understanding of issues of diversity and multiculturalism; and an ability to continue to market the school successfully. While Ann appears to be effective in the latter, the former three are not her strengths. The story that dominates the year of the study, 1993–1994, is the ongoing struggle between Ann and the new headmaster over when Ann should retire from the lower school. This conflict arises, in part, because of differences in management styles, age, and role expectations. Ann and Mark Rubin's difficult interactions also reflect tensions in the gendered negotiation of power and authority between a principal and her central administrator, in this case the school head.

Responding to Demands from Above

Ann was hired by the former head of Pepperdine, George Godwin, described by many as a warm, nonconfrontational, caring man who epitomized the old independent school headmaster. Some felt the school drifted a bit under his headship, but others saw him as the linchpin of the place, the unifying factor that gave the school its focus. Lower school teachers point out that they rarely saw Godwin; he never appeared in their classes and seldom called all-school gatherings that might connect them to the upper school. As described above, Godwin gave his division heads a free hand in running their sections of the school.

Mark Rubin became headmaster of Pepperdine in 1992, having taught in both public and private schools. Mark, in his late thirties, came to Pepperdine with his wife (a former English teacher who eventually taught in Pepperdine's upper school) and two small children. He had just received a doctorate in education from a prestigious university. This was his first headship, and those who hired him were excited about his energy, his commitment to communication, and his vision for the school community. By the time this study began, Mark had his advocates and his critics among the Pepperdine community. Parents and teachers comment on his dedication to pulling the three divisions of the school together, developing a strong financial program, marketing the school well, and remaining open to hearing everyone's voice. People appreciate his directness and his willingness to make decisions.

The problematic aspects of Mark's style evolve out of some of the same elements that contribute to his strengths. First, his lack of experience, especially in the independent school sector, sometimes leads him to make decisions that alienate people. He tends not to consider prior views of the school or indicate a thoughtful understanding of how to work effectively with people. One teacher explains that while Mark is "the kind of person who knows that a good headmaster listens, is understanding, has an open door," he does not have "a gut level understanding of that," nor does he have the experience to make it happen (Teacher interview, 2/94). The contrast between Ann's years of teaching and administrative work in a range of settings and Mark's lack of experience strikes some as a source of tension. "If I were Ann and I were someone with her years of experience and a woman in this field, I would feel a lot of resentment with having someone come in, tell me things that they think are right but you know are not" (Teacher interview, 4/94).

Mark's concern with parents' "perceptions" contributes positively to the school's marketing efforts and helps him remain open to parents. Teachers, however, find this aspect of Mark's leadership problematic. They often charge that, because he does not know the reality of what they do in their classrooms, he lets parental perceptions govern his decisions. For example, at the first lower school faculty meeting of the 1993–1994 year, Mark tells the teachers that some parents have complained that they do not know their children's homework assignments. Mark describes a new policy he would like the lower school to implement, one in which each teacher leaves her homework assignment with the school secretary at the end of the day so parents can call in for it as needed. Teachers point out to Mark that his policy contradicts the lessons of student responsibility they are trying to teach, and they outline for him the many ways they address this issue in their classrooms. The policy also conflicts with the realities of the school schedule; the secretary leaves at 4:00 p.m., long before most parents sit down to do homework with their children. Mark's decision to impose this policy on the basis of some parental complaints suggests to teachers that he cares more about pleasing a few parents than investigating what really happens in the lower school.[7]

Admirers applaud Mark's strong decision-making style as necessary to move the school along on some needed changes. Critics describe Mark as impulsive, arguing that his decisions reflect his lack of experience, his dependence on perception, and his personal style. Despite his emphasis on communication, for example, Mark promises parents certain teachers for their children without consulting either Ann or the teachers (who work together to develop balanced class lists). He rehires teachers, hires classroom aides, and changes the parameters of teachers' positions without talking to Ann or other division heads. And he hands down decisions about issues as relatively minor as dress code and as major as the number of sections at each grade level without first discussing them with any of the people affected by them. Mark's impulsiveness leads some lower school teachers to distrust him; they feel they never know what he might decide next. Even his administrative colleagues express some reservations, although they believe that Mark will continue to grow in the job: "The way I like to describe Mark, although I think he's getting better at this, is that he often solves a problem before he finds it. And it's going to come with age and experience where he's going to work a little bit more. But he always wants to have the answers" (Administrator interview, 4/94).

    Mark's desire to have the answers results in his use of the kind of control that can disempower those who experience it. Ann, who also needs to feel in control but who has usually done so by adhering to the rules and attending to all of the details, finds the new headmaster difficult to work with. Mark's goals include getting Pepperdine on a more financially sound and balanced budget, coordinating the work of the three divisions of the school (lower, middle, and upper schools), improving public relations with existing and prospective parents, clarifying and publicizing the school's mission, and examining and addressing issues of diversity. He approaches these tasks with a range of strategies. He holds frequent meetings with the division heads; he reconstitutes the curriculum committees charged with the goal of articulating the K–12 curriculum; and he uses his own presence and voice across the school's three divisions to encourage communication and continuity. Ann struggles to find time to attend all of the meetings and accomplish all of the tasks Mark requires, worrying that responding to these demands detracts from her ability to run her school effectively.

> I'll tell you, I don't honestly know how I'm going to put everything on the calendar that he tells me I'm going to do. He tells me I'm going to be in the upper school and the middle school once a week; I'm going to evaluate all the teachers with lots of observations; I'll be active in admissions talking to parents like I have been ever since I came here—I like doing that, I can be interrupted anytime that anybody chooses—and then I'll be directing arrivals in the morning and dismissal traffic at night. And just hope that you can just get everything done. So it's going to be, well, he's putting a lot of pressure on us. (Interview, 8/93)

Ann also dislikes Mark's interference in decisions traditionally left to the head of the lower school.

    By the year of the study, Mark's second year as headmaster, Ann feels burdened and resentful. She still has not been able to figure out how to please or respond to Mark. Strategies that have worked in past situations fail, leaving her unsure how to be successful and competent as a principal.

> You know how I honestly feel? I think I'm a very conscientious person, and I've told him, "I don't know how I can give you any more. You've squeezed just about everything out of me that you possibly can." I feel that in a way it's a challenge, and I'm going to prove to him that I can do it. But in another way—you know because I told you I'd be honest with you since you know how old I am—it makes me feel that he's taking some of the fun out of the job. Now, I've never worked like this before. I've worked now for two superintendents in Illinois, one in Turkey, one in the Philippines, and this is my second one here. And I don't feel that I need to be told so much or lectured to quite so much.

But on the other hand, I have to flip it over and say that this job—he has to learn—[but] he questions my professional ability. Now, in all fairness, this is the world of the young. However, I feel that in a job like mine, there's a lot that comes with experience. (Interview, 8/93)

Ann's attention to propriety, to doing what the boss (especially the male boss) asks her to do and doing it well, stems in part from her sense that playing by these rules allows a woman to succeed in a man's profession. She is used to having male superintendents and school heads, and used to responding to their authority. For the most part, she accepts the hierarchy of educational institutions. Even as she asserts that women need to be independent and abandon their more "female tactics," she herself needs to please her male superior in order to feel both liked and competent. Now, though, she finds herself unable to do so. "I have never worked for someone who I really felt didn't like me" she remarks (Field notes, 2/94), and later comments on feeling incompetent for the first time in her career. Ann's tendency to equate approval with competence contributes to her conflict with Mark. Part of her wants to do what he asks of her, to gain his approval. As more and more of Mark's demands conflict with her management style, or call for skills outside her areas of proficiency, or undermine her ability to communicate openly with him, however, Ann's chances of pleasing Mark decrease. In turn, her sense of authority falters, making her feel resentful and, at times, incompetent.

Gender issues contribute to Ann's discomfort. While the institution itself emphasizes the hierarchical and idiosyncratic power of the headship, it also uses gender as a way of maintaining traditional status and control (Marshall and Mitchell, 1989; Ortiz, 1982). Mark, for example, often kisses women (including Ann) in public and is very open in saying—both to Ann to others—that he "adore[s]" her. Some people at the school, including Ann, regard this behavior as inappropriate and unprofessional: "I think he's got to realize . . . it's sort of condescending to kiss a woman in public. It's like, he's not going to do it to the males, you know" (Teacher interview, 5/94). Yet neither Ann nor the teachers who comment on it feel able to challenge Mark's behavior in this or other areas of disagreement. Gender and power merge here, constraining Ann's sense of control at the school.

Responding to institutional and central administration demands in a relatively small private school takes on a more personal and idiosyncratic dimension than responding to those same demands in Jeanne's public school district. The culture of the private school and the acceptable actions and interactions in it reflect both the historical and philosophical roots of the school and the person and style of the headmaster. Private schools have fewer bureaucratic layers than do public schools,

and there is no union; teachers and administrators can be hired, repri-
manded, and fired at will and are quite aware of their vulnerability.
Even without the bureaucracy, private school culture constrains the people who work in it because administrators continue to wield power
within a clear hierarchy. The negotiating that a principal needs to do—
finding ways to meet the demands of the central administration while
maintaining a coherent and confident sense of herself as a leader—
remains the same. The issues of power and hierarchy, exacerbated in
Ann's situation by gender and age, impact a principal's effectiveness and
her experience of herself as a person and a professional. For Ann, this
negotiation of power at both the individual and institutional levels coa-
lesces around the question of her possible retirement from Pepperdine.

Negotiating Retirement

In August 1993, when Ann returns from her summer vacation, she meets
with Mark to discuss her annual evaluation. She describes the meeting
as follows:

> Well, when I had a meeting with Mark, I'd just gotten back from a
> vacation—I'd only been back one day—and he and I were to have a
> meeting to finish my evaluation. I had to write a self-evaluation. Before
> he even got into anything, he said to me, now he said, "How do you
> think that two more years here will be?" I don't know what prompted
> this, I really don't. But this is his style. I said, "Oh, probably okay." I
> said, "I told you once I would not do any more than three more." "But
> yeah," he said, "then you could really make next year, a year from
> now, the best year of your life." That's for me to decide, not him. And
> he said, "Then in a year from now you could, we'll hire somebody, and
> you could train that person for a year to take your job." He said, "Do
> you see anybody from inside moving up?" "No," I said, "I truly
> don't." I said, "Do you?" He said, "No, but there are a lot of people
> that would like your job." . . . So, what I'm looking at right now, this
> is two years. And I'm going to start, as soon as I have a minute to
> breathe, I'm going to start looking at something that I can do overseas,
> either interim principalships or working with the Peace Corps, or
> there's a thing called Mercy Ship. I'm going—I want to do something
> that's useful, and that hopefully some of my skills that I've learned
> along the way will come into play. (Interview, 8/93)

Mark's perspective, explained to me in July 1993 and to Ann at meetings in August and November, is that Ann does not have the educational
or interpersonal skills needed by the lower school at this point in its
growth and development. While she has provided the school with stability and organization, they now need someone to address issues of curriculum, staff development, and diversity.

Mark also mentions, both to me and to Ann, that "sooner or later someone [is] going to ask her her age" (Field notes, 11/93). Only two or three people at Pepperdine (including Mark) know that Ann is sixty-seven, although others speculate about it *because* she keeps it a secret. Ann's sensitivity to her age comes from several sources. She shares little of her personal life with her professional colleagues; secrecy about her age fits this pattern of emotional protection or interpersonal distance. In addition, she frequently mentions her age when she talks about her general competence, her physical ability to keep up with younger friends and teachers, and her ability to do a good job as principal. She once told a teacher, "Anybody over fifty-five has no value, and I'm over fifty-five" (Teacher interview, 11/93). To me, she confides, "I don't want anybody—now, I'm probably overzealous with this—feeling sorry for me because I'm older, telling me I can't do something because I'm older" (Interview, 8/93). At this point in her life, Ann's age contributes a great deal to her sense of who she is, how she assumes others see her, and to her self-esteem. By deliberately referring to her age during his conversations with Ann about retiring, Mark capitalizes on a weak spot in her confidence. Given Ann's sensitivity about her age and her unwillingness to challenge her boss, she does not point out to him that her age is not directly relevant to her performance as head of the lower school.

In the eyes of some of her colleagues, Ann's age gives her added skills and experiences that enhance her ability to do her job: "I appreciate her being a little bit older than us, too. I think she has that on her side. You know, she's been through a lot of different phases in her lifetime, so she can—she has more perspective than the rest of us" (Teacher interview, 1/94). While others, Mark included, say that her age is insignificant, they note that perhaps if she was younger they would press her to change. Mark concedes that their relative ages may be affecting their interactions and influencing his desire to help her leave Pepperdine "with dignity."

In October 1993, Ann receives her formal letter of evaluation for the 1992–1993 year, which she is asked to sign and return. She chooses not to sign it, given the last paragraph, which states that she will leave after next year. The letter itself provides a mixed review of Ann's performance and some suggestions for change.[8] In evaluating Ann's performance, Mark compliments her for her attention to detail and organization, for running the school so well, and for coping with the year that involved getting used to working with a new head. He calls her ability to "dot all the i's and cross all the t's" impressive, but he also points out that such thoroughness has drawbacks; when things do not go as she has planned she gets annoyed. He compliments her on her work with parents, especially in the admissions process, but then points out that some parents do not see her as responsive in a crisis; she is sometimes perceived as defensive rather than willing to listen. Mark calls on her to be able to respond to parents effectively in all realms. He notes and praises her warm relationship with students and the knowledge she has of each child. In the letter, Mark describes teachers as the hardest group for Ann to work with. He points out that some faculty members are afraid of her, perhaps because she had to "clean house" during her first several years at Pepperdine. He also comments that Ann needs to address curricular issues in the lower school, helping teachers coordinate content and process across grade levels and between the divisions.

Ann's response to the letter focuses exclusively on her concern about the last paragraph, in which Mark states that they have agreed Ann will retire at the end of the 1994–1995 school year. Ann recalls that he "lay that on her" when they returned in August and that it was a complete surprise. She is not sure she ever really agreed to it. She admits that part of her resistance to stepping down comes from her discomfort with the idea of getting older; she realizes that aging is something she just does not want to face. She also questions what she wants to do next or where she wants to be (Field notes, 10/93). Ann does not refer to any of the other issues Mark raises in the letter, despite the seriousness of the concerns and the areas in which he asks her to improve during the coming year.

Ann and Mark meet in November to discuss her decision not to sign the letter as he has written it. He agrees to remove the final paragraph, but he points out that they did have a conversation and agreement about her departure date. Ann describes how her "stomach had turned over" at this meeting. "I don't like being pushed into a corner. Mark doesn't know what he does to a person inside." Echoing Jeanne's stance when maneuvered into an uncomfortable position by the central administration, Ann insists that she will carry on: "I've got enough pride so that no one could push me to do less than my best" (Field notes, 11/93). For both Jeanne and Ann, the goal is to hold onto their own pride, values, and sense of what is best for the school and themselves, even as they work to respond acceptably to the problematic demands of those with more power in the institution.

The question of when Ann might leave Pepperdine prompts speculation among teachers at the lower school. Some say they would not be surprised if she left after this year, 1993–1994, given the pressure from the head and her interest in overseas work. Others imagine that she will retire in the next couple of years. They attribute Ann's possible departure to her obvious desire to travel and try new things, to the apparent difficulties she has working with Mark, to her clear successes at the school, and to her age.

I think she's ready. I think she sees—my guess is like two more years. This year and next. And I think she sees that this is a time when things are going really well for her, and she'll leave here being liked—and I don't mean that in the meaningless, surface sense of the word, but really appreciated. She really has gotten to know this place, really tried to do what's best for it, and I think done a lot to structure this place in a way it needed to be structured. And I think she can leave now, pass it along, feeling proud of what she's done. So I have a feeling, I really feel—and I also don't think she wants to be his—I don't think she wants to work with Mark. I think she's just tired of dealing with that. I can't blame her. (Teacher interview, 5/94)

Between November and April, Ann and Mark do not speak directly about if and when she might leave as lower school head. Their relationship and interactions go up and down during these months. Ann occasionally refers to leaving, sometimes jokingly, sometimes seriously. In November, for example, she comments several times that she wants to take care of a number of things at the school before she leaves, implying that the prospect of leaving gives her the extra push she might need to accomplish certain tasks. In December she receives and completes the Peace Corps application and sends it in. In February, after several run-ins with Mark, she talks about leaving during the current year: "The more sensible part of me says to hang in for another year, but I have never worked before for someone I have no respect for" (Field notes, 2/94). In thinking about her 1994 summer travel plans, Ann remarks that she needs to consider the timing of her departure from Pepperdine carefully, since she will not be able to travel the summer she plans to leave. She also explains that Mark's son would be in the preschool class in the lower school next year: "Another reason to leave!" (Field notes, 2/94). But she remains conflicted about the idea and the process.

Oh, every once in a while, I'll laugh and say to [my secretary], "Well, let's see Gina. Maybe next year better be my last year!" I'm really not [settled on it], but I don't think—I'm smart enough to know that he has not forgotten that he wants me to leave, and I am not going to announce it early. I am not going to do all these things with a big fanfare. But I think that in another year, this school would be in pretty good shape because we would see kind of how our population is growing. And a lot will depend on how he is willing to do a search. I have no idea what I want to do, you know, I really don't. And I haven't had much time to think about it. (Interview, 2/94)

In April, Ann receives her contract letter—as do all of the school's teachers and administrators. In the letter Mark thanks her for all of her work for the school and says that they will make this final year a good one. Ann writes a response on the bottom of the letter saying she would like to hear his reasons for asking her to leave. She tells Mark that she wants to be involved in her career decisions, that she works best in an open and honest environment, and that she would like to leave in June 1996 rather than in a year (i.e., in June 1995) as his letter specifies.

In May, when Ann and Mark meet to discuss her response to the contract letter, Mark is angry. "He told me to 'announce my retirement or else,'" Ann recounts. She feels threatened, frustrated and "ready to punch Mark" during this discussion; she cries when she leaves the meeting, although she "could have kicked herself for doing that" (Field notes, 5/94). For someone who tries to keep her emotions in check, Ann's current situation is intolerable; she feels out of control both personally and professionally. Resolving matters is not easy, however. Ann says she is "old school enough to do what my boss tells me," but she needs to feel that she has control over such a major decision in her life. She also continues to resist the notion of retiring because it makes her focus on her age, and, she explains, she is looking forward to working with several new teachers she has just hired. In addition, Mark pressures her to say that she is retiring rather than allowing her to tell the truth, that he has asked her to leave. This struggle over her departure epitomizes Ann's attempts to balance personal needs and values, professional goals, school processes, and the authority of the headmaster.

During June 1994, Ann concentrates on ending the school year but continues to think about her conversations with Mark and how best to respond. She talks about looking for a permanent place to live—a home base, as she calls it—in Atlanta, where one of her daughters and her former husband live: "Thinking about Atlanta, whether I do it or not, has made it a lot easier to live with the inevitable" (Field notes, 6/94). While "working through her anger" (Field notes, 6/94), Ann stays busy hiring teachers, drafting next year's schedules, closing up the school, and developing a mentor program for new teachers. She vows not to confront Mark, acknowledging, "that's never been something I was good at" (Field notes, 6/94). Still, she makes no plans to announce her resignation. While she considers plans for next year and the year after, she continues to resist the notion of being pushed out.

By July 1994, Ann has come up with a clear stance.

> Well, I'm just going to say to him, "Mark, I sincerely believe that you have the right to do anything you want to do. You have the right to make a decision, you have a right to work, to bring change here. But any decision that you make, I think you should be comfortable with and take full responsibility for it. I am not going to lie. So therefore I am not going to announce retirement or that I'm, or that I'm going to leave, because that was not my decision. So I'm not going to resign, I'm not going to retire. But if you want to move me out, that's OK. But

you're going to have to tell people that you're doing it because you want a change and you feel that a change is needed in the lower school. And I promise you I will keep it from being ugly. I'm not going to let anybody trap me into conversations." But I am not going to support his method of making his decision. (Interview, 7/94)

She admits that had he not pushed her to it, she might have chosen to leave in the next year or two anyway, since she does not really enjoy working with Mark. At times, she slips and talks in relatively positive terms about next year being her last: "I think it will be sort of fun to work with Gina, my secretary, to make sure even more than we have right now that everything is in order as much as I can have it be so that if next year is my last year, and it wouldn't be bad if it was, that things are in running order" (Interview, 7/94). Her mixed feelings come from several sources: a sense of being ready to leave, an awareness of the difficulties involved in continuing to work with Mark, trying to fulfill his requirements and the needs of the school, and a desire not to have the confrontation implied in the above quote. For Ann, the conflict between the demands of the institution and her own personal style and needs has become unresolvable.

In fact, by the time everyone returns to school in the fall of 1994, Ann has decided to resign. She never has the conversation with Mark that challenges him to live with his own decisions. She explains that maintaining such a hard line "would have had negative vibes to it; I'm not sure what I would have to gain except some satisfaction" (Telephone conversation, 10/94). In the end, Ann prefers to "handle it graciously" rather than engage in an explicit and potentially ugly confrontation with Mark. In late October, she announces her resignation, effective June 1995, to her faculty. On November 2, 1994, she sends the following letter to the lower school staff and parents:

Dear Colleagues,

When a person truly enjoys the position in which she/he is employed, it is difficult to determine the perfect time for a change.

I'm in my sixth year as Lower School Head at Pepperdine and I've felt great satisfaction and challenge in this role. However, I know that the time is right for a change which will allow me to move on and become involved in service programs here and abroad. After 14 years as a teacher and 15 years as an administrator I'm certain that my talents and skills can be used in developing countries.

I've had the "itchy feet" syndrome for quite some time and knew that I'd recognize the right time to pack my bags and explore the world. That time will be June 1995. It is only fair to announce my intentions early to allow Mark the time to conduct a "search" for my successor.

Farewells and separations are difficult for many of us, so please know that I'll carry on as usual until the school year ends.

My best to you,
Ann Becker

Mark includes a letter of his own in with Ann's to the parents. His letter reads:

Dear Lower School Parents:

Ann Becker's decision to leave Pepperdine was not an easy one. I know that it caused her a great deal of consternation and concern. Her decision was made after careful thought and consideration. As she said in her letter, determining the perfect time for a change is not easy. While I respect and understand her decision and will support her in it, it is with regret that I accept her resignation.

For the past six years, Ann has put everything into the job. She has overseen the Lower School with wisdom and compassion and has taken a division that was in flux and created a sense of stability and growth. Ann has played an instrumental role in making the three divisions into one cohesive school. Personally, I have grown to rely on her a great deal and will miss her immensely.

We are proud of the job she has done and grateful that Ann is leaving the Lower School in such a healthy condition. Of course, those who know her and her passion for travel will appreciate Ann's decision to pursue her interest in service programs. Her capacity to observe a variety of cultures and understand them will make her successful in this endeavor. She will make a difference to all of the schools with which she works in much the same way she has for us. Our loss will be their gain. It is my hope that she will find a way to continue to work with Pepperdine in some capacity.

I know you join me in wishing her the very best. Ann will continue in her role as Head of the Lower School until the end of this academic year, and I know that she will continue to do a superb job. Her leadership is important to Pepperdine.

Warmest regards,
Mark Rubin

Meeting Institutional Expectations: Summary

Ann had been hired by George Godwin, the former head of Pepperdine, to organize a faltering lower school. Under Godwin's headship, the institution gave Ann little guidance, provided no evaluation, and exercised minimal control over her work. Under Mark Rubin's vision and style, however, the culture of the school shifts and becomes more focused. While Pepperdine has always been a place that emphasized the idiosyncratic power of administrators, that control becomes more overt and centralized as Mark works to make the school a more cohesive community. The power he wields is the authority found in the hierarchy and culture of most schools, private or public (Marshall, 1993, 1988; Ballou, 1989; Shakeshaft, 1989). Within this hierarchy, the position of middle manager, one that in educational institutions involves assuming a great deal of responsibility while being granted only a limited amount of power, is one which all principals, but women principals in particular, must negotiate.

Within this culture of power, Ann and Mark debate Ann's departure from Pepperdine. Ann sidesteps Mark's attempts to be direct about the issue, perceiving his ultimatum as a challenge to her competence, her authority, and her identity. She also avoids his efforts to be personally warm or caring; this reflects both a general interpersonal pattern for her and her sense of what constitutes appropriate behavior in their respective positions. Ann and Mark are not completely honest in their dealings with one another; both attempt to protect themselves and the other from the kind of confrontation that would challenge deeply held beliefs about professionalism, education, leadership, self, and other. Ann's decision to leave Pepperdine probably serves the best interests of the school, and, perhaps, her own best interests as well. The negotiations that characterize Ann's decisions about retiring illustrate the influence of institutional power, self-concept, and school culture on the process of the principalship.

BALANCING CONTINUITY AND CHANGE:
NEGOTIATING WITHIN THE SYSTEM

Of the three principals in this study, Ann most resists change. Given her somewhat tenuous situation at Pepperdine, she may experience calls for change as indictments of her effectiveness as lower school head. In addition, her management style focuses on developing and maintaining effective organizational routines rather than on initiating change; she creates an environment within which others can, if they choose, make changes within a given structure. During the year of the study, the school grapples with possible curricular changes and continuing attempts to diversify its student body. Ann's responses to these issues demonstrate that a principal's beliefs and actions can reinforce the status quo or contribute to the process of change in her school. Although Ann never deliberately blocks change, she does so unconsciously by supporting established practices and adhering to existing school routines. Much as Ann finds it difficult to challenge the culture of power in the school on her own behalf, she finds it uncomfortable to delve into areas that would require a change in behaviors, roles, or routines in the operation of the school.[9]

Curricular Change

Several years before Mark Rubin arrived as headmaster, an external accreditation report recommended that Pepperdine focus on articulating its K–12 curriculum. The school responded by forming curriculum committees. During the year of the study, teachers describe the school's lack of curriculum structure as providing freedom but also as causing concern.

> One of the curses that I have about this school is—the curriculum has been basically in a state of flux. For the first three years that I was here, I taught a different social studies curriculum every year, and that is not good. Same thing with spelling. We've had a different spelling program every year. Same thing with some of this decoding [in reading]. It's just, it's too much in flux, too much, "Hey this is a new idea, let's try it," which is great, but we need some consistency here. And I think that's what we're all trying to aim for at the school. (Teacher interview, 11/93)

Mark makes curriculum issues a high priority during his first several years as head. He re-forms committees in each subject area, charging members to analyze, describe, and modify what should be taught at each grade level. Mark's push for curriculum clarification and development leads Ann to pay closer attention to curriculum in the lower school and to talk more about it with parents and teachers. She lacks some of the skills and knowledge to do so effectively, however. When asked to name her strengths as a principal, Ann always describes herself as a manager first, someone with less training and experience in curriculum and staff development. Sometimes, she dismisses her lack of experience in nonadministrative areas, noting that a principal could and should not be expected to do everything. In fact, she argues, leadership for curriculum development should come from teachers. If no such development occurs, the problem lies with the teachers, not the principal.

> Look, [there are] all kinds of theories on this with administrators. Like most times you hear, and I believe it's true, that an administrator just

simply cannot be everything. You can't do all of the evaluations, all of the this, all of the that, the physical plant, the hiring, the discipline, *and* curriculum. And I don't think that the principal or head should be the leader of curriculum. I think it should come from the teachers. And this is what they've tried to do [at Pepperdine] but the leadership has simply not been there. . . . But you know, another thing, this is also a direct result of Pepperdine having hired teachers, noncertified, nonelementary teachers. And they just sort of move along [doing what is easiest for them]. And when you have really, really bright kids with no problems that's one thing. But curriculum is a definite weakness and there is not leadership on it. (Interview, 2/94)

At other times Ann speaks almost wistfully about her lack of training in curriculum development: "I always wish that I had time to sort of back up and maybe do more work in curriculum. Not that I don't understand it, but just that if I'd had a little more background in how to work with a faculty and get the curriculum in place, that would have been helpful" (Interview, 2/94). While it is difficult for many educators to find time for professional development, Ann does not attempt to develop her own knowledge in this area, even when under pressure as she is during this year. She reads no professional journals or newspapers and attends no professional meetings that would contribute to her ability to work with faculty or give her more familiarity with the content or processes for teaching elementary reading, math, science, or social studies.

In response to Mark's request for more information about lower school curriculum in the year before the study, Ann asked teachers to submit their lesson plans to her on a weekly basis. The faculty viewed this request with distaste and eventually chose to ignore it. Because Ann, herself, had little investment in knowing the content being taught or the methods teachers used, she let the matter drop instead of confronting teachers with their unwillingness to turn in plans. The failure of this strategy also allowed her to believe in the impracticality of Mark's idea that she monitor curriculum. In February of the year of the study, Ann tries a slightly different tack. She asks teachers to make charts or calendars of what they are covering in each subject each week. Once again, few teachers respond and Ann, in a behavior uncharacteristic in most areas of her administration, again ignores their resistance. This lack of teacher response may have had little effect on Ann's ability to address curricular issues; even if teachers had completed the charts, they would have provided Ann with sketchy information about content and little or no insight into goals, sequences, and processes. Somewhat more effective is Ann's deliberate efforts, as she makes her informal rounds of classrooms, to pay closer attention to what is being taught. Although she does gather useful information this way, it is piecemeal at best.

Teachers see Ann's lack of expertise in curriculum as understandable, perhaps, but problematic.

> I think that she would benefit from knowing more about education. I think she really trusts other people a little bit too much. I think that there are things that, things that I was teaching in my class that really came out when she was checking our planbooks. It kind of backfired on her because there were things I was putting in there like, "Cuisenaire rods for spatial skills," and she would come up to me and say, "What are Cuisenaire rods and what are spatial skills?" And that concerned me. She's looking over my curriculum, she's reading my reports. I really felt like, "Wait, that's one of the NCTM [National Council of Teachers of Mathematics] standards. She should know that word." And things with reading. I think there's some things with reading that she really counts on Sue for and that I would like to see her become more familiar with on her own. . . . I think, I really think that she would—I think she'd be more effective if she knew a little bit more. Not knew what was going on, but knew more curriculum issues. I think that puts her at a real disadvantage because it makes her depend on other people. (Teacher interview, 11/93)

Others point out that parents sometimes get a run-around when they asked Ann for curriculum information (as happens with Eve and Bob Cohen in the opening vignette). Since Ann does not know the curriculum, in part because a clearly defined curriculum does not exist at Pepperdine but also because she has not gathered the information, she responds with stock phrases about meeting the developmental needs of children and refers parents to teachers and to Sue Green, the reading teacher. Teachers suggest that this strategy leaves some parents feeling ill-at-ease about the quality of education the school provides.

Ann's lack of engagement in curricular issues is illustrated by a problem that develops over the reading curriculum in the lower school during the year of the study. Parents like Eve and Bob Cohen insist that their children be challenged. Increasingly, parents focus on reading; they want to know that their children will learn to read (perhaps in kindergarten), and that they will read well. Prospective and current parents, meeting with Mark or Ann, inquire in detail about the lower school's reading program; they want to know exactly what it includes and how it will be individualized to meet the specific needs of their children. Some parents express concerns about a new primary teacher who they feel might not be doing what is needed in reading. At Mark's request, Ann meets twice with the first-grade teachers in January and February 1994 to talk about their reading and math curricula. Although Mark has indicated that he will join them in these discussions, he does not attend either meeting. His failure to appear reinforces lower school teachers' perceptions that Mark neither knows or cares about what they really do in their classrooms. Ann, on the other hand, describes Mark's interest and potential involvement as feeling like an "invasion" (Field notes, 2/15/94).

During these two meetings, Ann asks the teachers to describe to her some of what they do in reading, and she follows up with questions about particular activities and units. At one point she explains that this is "all new to her," because her own children had used basal readers (Field notes, 2/15/94). Her questions and comments suggest that she has little or no general understanding about recent shifts in reading instruction or knowledge of more specific reading strategies or programs. Ann recommends that the teachers provide more information to parents. She suggests the possibility of a teacher-written newsletter or a series of parent-education meetings aimed at informing parents about the content of core subjects like reading and math and explaining how teachers teach these subjects. Later, Ann reports to Mark that she has "spent a great deal of time with K and 1 teachers talking about how we do things and she is satisfied with the program" (Field notes, 3/2/94). Teachers may have increased their communication with individual parents as a result of these meetings, but neither they nor Ann initiate a newsletter or try to set up parent education meetings. Concern over the reading curriculum in the primary grades seems to dissipate, at least temporarily.

Another administrator at Pepperdine points out that Ann might have responded differently to this challenge. Curricular leadership does not necessarily mean knowing everything about an issue, but could involve structuring teacher time and providing information so that development occurs.

> See, I don't see myself as an expert in curriculum either, but I think, for instance, we're talking about writing mechanics [in my division], and we have to do something, and I don't know what to do about writing mechanics, but I think I know enough to point people in the direction to find out what we need to do.

This administrator suggests that the questions about the reading program provide Ann with a perfect opportunity to approach Mark for support for teacher training and development.

> I said [to Ann], "Look, if he wants the reading program to improve, use it as an opportunity. Say, 'This is what I need to improve the reading program: I need to bring in a speaker, I need to send my people to workshops, I need money to do this, I need money to do that.'" I said, "If he wants it better, seize the moment and go for it!" (Administrator interview, 4/94)

Ann, however, seems comfortable with her minimal understanding of classroom curriculum in the lower school and does not follow up on the suggestion to provide teachers with opportunities to learn and grow in those areas. She sometimes appears to go on the defensive rather than the offensive when faced with a problem in this (and other) areas of her administration. Rather than actively participating in a schoolwide initiative to examine and address curricular needs or capitalizing on opportunities to make changes in this area, Ann emphasizes the status quo, letting the natural regularities of the school structure overwhelm any chance for change.[10]

Moving Toward Diversity

In the two years preceding the study, Pepperdine began a tentative, informal analysis of their acceptance of and support for diversity. Some teachers and administrators had grown concerned about this issue for educational and social reasons. They argue that Pepperdine needs to address larger community and curricular issues involved in making the school a more diverse place for its majority and minority students and staff. Their goals include hiring a more racially and ethnically diverse staff, providing academic support for underprepared students, and addressing what some describe as an "unwelcoming" school culture for those who are not white and upper class. Another (perhaps more salient) incentive to examine the question of diversity came from the National Association of Independent Schools' offer to undertake a multicultural assessment of affiliated schools, such as Pepperdine. A school that passes this assessment can list that fact in its brochure, which serves as a valuable marketing tool.

Many at the school understand diversity narrowly, as an admissions issue focusing on race; diversity means admitting more African American students. Many also equate African American students with lower academic skills, deprived cultural backgrounds, and financial aid. Teachers and parents frequently couch these equations in the language of school tradition, standards, and community.

> I think diversity is an important issue. I think, I think certainly America is very diverse. I think our school can be more diverse. You know, but I watch carefully when I see little notes from the board or something like that because sometimes diversity—I'm not sure if they're looking for diversity in academics because I think Pepperdine has a standard and has the, not only the right to keep it, but it needs to keep it, its standards. And I think sometimes, I'm not sure sometimes how admissions, not admissions itself, but why some students are here, except for possibly diversity. And I don't know how right that is. I think there are a lot of diverse, very bright, and able students that would do very well at Pepperdine and contribute to Pepperdine. But sometimes I feel that there are students who are here

because they add some diversity. Maybe they aren't able—they're not able to handle it academically—and that's just not fair. (Teacher interview, 12/93)

Mark Rubin wants to continue the process of examining and beginning to act on issues of diversity. He thinks of diversity as being both a marketing issue and an educational one that will require long term commitment and a great deal of work.

I think it's going to happen by the nature of the independent school today—that it's not possible to house this school with kids who are just from this community or the accompanying neighborhood. On top of which I happen to think from an educational perspective it's essential that this school not be filled with students who are only from this area. So it's also a personal conviction that way. I think historically when you look at diversity, one of the issues has been that as a minority of any kind comes into a community, "successful diversity"—in quotes—has referred to the assimilation of the minority into the majority. I don't happen to believe that. I happen to believe successful diversity isn't a numbers issue, or isn't assimilation. It talks about integration in a more sort of complete manner, where people in the community really learn from, through, and about each other, in such a way that the culture of the school actually shifts. That takes a long time. (Interview, 5/94)

Ann falls into the group of people who tend to equate skin color, academic success, class status, and financial need. She understands the need for the school to address issues of diversity primarily as a marketing issue—Pepperdine must diversify its student body (and staff) because all of its competitors have begun to do so. But as far as she is concerned, diversity has brought to her lower school a handful of African American children, many of whom seem to be both financially and academically needy. Diversity has, therefore, created another set of problems for her, as head. She seems reluctant to diversify the student body if it means, as she sees it, admitting students who bring financial and academic challenges to the school, the teachers, and the administration.

I don't think that we probably will ever get rid of Peter [an African American student who has been in frequent behavioral and academic trouble in the lower school] because of diversity. You know, it's just one of these things. And now they want to bring in his little brother, and I have no idea what this little kid is like. But this is where I believe that we have not done a very good job with admissions and financial aid because the heads are never asked for their opinion as to who should come in under that. And I think that's wrong. I think that we have to deal with it, and I think there should be a review every year, and that you should have something to say about the renewal of that contract and the amount of financial aid. . . . I think it can be based on need. But I think that if they are not doing well and do not bring something to the school that that should be a part of the consideration. It's just perpetuating, from kindergarten on, a thirteen-year commitment. I think it's crazy. And I'd rather go out and recruit smart students of color that want to be in our school. (Interview, 2/94)

Ann is aware of cultural differences between students of color from the city and the white students from the suburban communities who populate the school. She tends to see those differences as individual or group deficits, not as values or attributes to which the school should respond or as differences from which the school could benefit.

They're trying to coax them [students of color] into the school. But, you see, the children that come from the inner city who are streetwise would never associate with this kind of thing. Bringing them into a school like this means that they must be pretty well balanced, because their friends are not drawn from their neighborhood. And because being streetwise is not exactly a plus in these private schools. (Interview, 1991)[11]

Despite her own sense of being an outsider in this community, Ann projects a definite sense of "otherness" on those she does not know. Perhaps she does so as a protection against having to learn about them; perhaps this is her way of defending her own identity at Pepperdine and in the larger society.

The slow progress on issues of diversity and multiculturalism at Pepperdine does not occur solely because of Ann. Diversity is a schoolwide issue that will require extended conversation and planning throughout the school. In addition, some teachers and parents share Ann's views and contribute to the resistance to change. But Ann's personal background and her tendency to focus on running an efficient school prevent her from recognizing or responding to the complex concerns and changes involved in diversifying Pepperdine. She helps to reinforce the status quo by emphasizing the existing values, structures, and attitudes of the school in her actions and interactions with others.

Balancing Continuity and Change: Summary

Change is hard to come by in a school that must respond to parental perceptions and demands, must constantly recruit new clients, and must work within a history of teacher and administrator autonomy. It is easier to maintain existing norms and structures, especially in a community that has prospered under those conditions. The culture of this school, like the culture of most schools, consists of norms and attitudes that may resist change or subsume the attempts at change that do occur. Individual principals may be in a position to challenge these norms, but they may, like Ann, prefer to maintain a structure and culture that has been effective for them in the past. Even when the school's culture begins to work against her, Ann seems unable to envision how to question, challenge, and change the institution and its processes.

Ann's resistance to change, her desire to preserve the culture she knows, may be traced to several sources. She has learned to function comfortably and successfully in the male-dominated hierarchy of schools by focusing on doing what she is told to do, by developing and maintaining organizational structures that make her school run smoothly, and by trying to please her paying constituents. With this approach, she reflects the more "male" style of leadership found in the literature on gender and management (see, e.g., Shakeshaft, 1989; Gross and Trask, 1976). In addition, although Ann is marginally conscious of her own outsider status, given her gender, her age, and her class background, she does not draw on that knowledge to question the system within which she works. She neither consciously nor unconsciously resists the social structures that constrain her. Instead, she focuses on adapting to them. This process of adaptation makes her less willing to recognize the need for change and less able to take the risks necessary to bring it about.

SUMMARY

Ann's entry into the principalship provides her with the experience of being in control and making a contribution, much as she had once hoped to be able to do as a doctor. Her strength as an administrator rests in her ability to organize a school environment in ways that, from her perspective, allow others to do their jobs well. Meeting students' needs is always her ultimate goal. She deliberately takes an unemotional, businesslike approach to her job, although she knows that some of her constituents would prefer that she demonstrate a more comfortable and conventionally feminine interpersonal style. Ann tends to hold back her emotions and limit the involvement of colleagues in her personal life, both to protect herself and to help project a professional image needed to succeed as an older woman in the hierarchy of school administration. She does, repeatedly, handle things graciously.

Ann's unquestioning acceptance of the system and cultural norms of schooling serves as both a survival strategy and as a way of achieving a sense of confidence and competence in her social world. Until her last two years at Pepperdine, she had been applauded and appreciated for her work. When, with the arrival of Mark Rubin as headmaster, expectations for her performance begin to shift and the demands of the job change, Ann has difficulty adjusting. She has chosen to be a part of the system and succeeds by playing according to its rules, but she lacks a sense of how that system really affects her life. She seems unwilling and unable either to change or to challenge the structures that have previously defined her and contributed to her success. Like other women administrators, she interprets her job experiences in personal terms only. She does not recognize how the conflicting expectations of her as a woman and as a school leader and the shifting cultural and educational frameworks within the school shape her professional life.

Ann's case lends support to the notion that women administrators who are more cognizant of their role within the larger system might be more able to contribute to school change. It seems possible that some of the characteristics attributed to women in leadership roles (characteristics Ann did not usually demonstrate), such as attention to interpersonal relationships and the use of democratic and empowering leadership practices, might allow principals to be more responsive and flexible when changes occur, and, perhaps, more able to initiate change. Consciousness of her position both within and yet outside of the system may provide a perspective that allows a principal to adapt to external expectations and demands and still maintain an internal vision or stance that empowers her to challenge institutional norms. Even if that internal vision is more personal than political, it may still be a kind of resistance that enhances the possibility for school change. Ann's negotiation of the system, influenced by her personal background, her gender, her age, and the community and institution within which she works, seems to have been limited by her style and perspective within it.

CHAPTER 5

Playing the Referee

Ellen Fried, principal of Fieldcrest Elementary School, and I go into the staffing meeting in which she, teachers, and learning specialists will discuss this week's caseload of special needs children. She has brought an Entemann's coffee cake and cuts herself a piece to go with her coffee. The first child discussed is Mike Olansky; present are Mike's teacher, Emily; Faye, the school social worker; Alison, the school psychologist; and Donna, the reading specialist. Ellen takes notes. Emily explains that Mike is unable to work independently and is disruptive. Ellen comments that he cannot sit still—something she's noticed for years. She asks if he is verbally disrespectful; Emily says sometimes. Alison asks if anyone was talking ADD [Attention Deficit Disorder]. Ellen says, "I sure did as I read his record." Faye says last year was a hard year for him. Ellen says, "One thing that makes it difficult is the difficult mom. She is someone who complains a lot—about the bus stop, about teachers who hit, which is fallacious. She had a terrible marriage and she is out of it now. She lives with a guy she calls her fiancee, but she let down her hair at one point and said, 'Miss Fried, I'm not going to marry him,' not after the terrible experience she had with marriage. Last year when the teacher called [the mother] always seemed to be asleep or tired, on edge. We wondered if she was on medication. She seems better this year—she calls and says, 'I know you'll look into it'; she's tried not to get too worked up about it. . . . She's less supportive of Mike than the two girls." Emily says she had the sister last year and never talked to the mother. Ellen says they gave Mike to Emily because she had a good relationship with the mother and daughter. Emily says she's talked to the mother six times this year.

Ellen reads the special teachers' reports, including a reading report. She asks Emily if her class is participating in the Reading Buddies program and says it might be good for Mike. She also suggests they test his eyes and ears; parents like to hear you've checked all this out. Alison says it sounds like she needs to observe. Ellen says her standard line this year—they have heard it before—is to

*collect samples of his work and put it in a folder for the occupa-
tional therapist. She says that actually the mother's fears about
him dropping out are well founded. She asks if he gets Chapter 1
support.[1] Donna says she sees Mike but just three days a week.
Ellen says, "That kind of help works for some kids. Let me read
back what I have—check eyes and ears, reading buddy, Alison will
observe, stuff to occupational therapist. I think this mother will be
supportive. When we talk to the mom we have to give her some
ways to deal with Mike positively, especially when he has trouble. . . . We can't just look at the product but have to watch him
in class—how he gets to the product. I wonder if we could get him
an extra gym class if he did a certain amount of work. If he's
ADD—we should sound like we practice what we preach." Ellen
points out that the gym teacher didn't put down any needs Mike
had so it wouldn't be like asking her to take this wretch. Or maybe
he could help out with lower grade gym classes. She says they will
get together again on Mike on November 30th before conferences
with parents. (Field notes, 11/9/93)*

Ellen Fried is in her eighth year as principal of Fieldcrest Elementary
School, a public school in a working- and lower-class community. In this
vignette, she demonstrates her attention to detail, her knowledge of the
children and families in the school, and her need and ability to be
involved in decisions affecting students and teachers. Each week, she and
the appropriate school specialists and teachers have a "staffing meeting"
to discuss individual students who have academic and other problems at
school. In the community served by Fieldcrest, the problems are serious
and broad ranging, and, according to both teachers and parents, have
become more prevalent and severe over the last decade. During the past
eight years, Ellen has developed administrative systems for addressing
these problems, has become a known and accepted advocate for children,
and has worked with, and when necessary around, teachers, parents, and
the central administration to improve the academic program at the
school. Not one to see herself as limited by abstract issues such as gender
roles or district requirements, Ellen works to support and manage the
educational development of the teachers and students in her school. At
one point during the year of the study, she describes herself as "playing
the referee," referring to her role in negotiating teacher-parent and
teacher-teacher interactions (Field notes, 3/30/94). The metaphor captures her work as principal; she stands on the playing field, both in control of the play but also subject to the rules of the game and the interactions of others. Ellen's case provides insight into a principal's negotiation
of the multiple contexts within which she works.

Overview of the Themes

For Ellen, *becoming a principal* involved balancing her enjoyment of teaching with concerns about teachers' status. Teaching, in particular elementary school teaching, is "women's work" and therefore less prestigious than other occupations (including school administration).[2] Ellen wanted to be in a position in which she would make a difference and be recognized for her contribution, and she explored a number of options on her path to the principalship. As she moved into administration, Ellen developed an energetic and relatively authoritative style that allowed her to find her niche as a principal in the same school system in which she had worked as a teacher, as a reading specialist, and as an assistant principal. Like Ann, Ellen pays careful attention to organization and management; like Jeanne, she attends to individuals in ways which make them feel known and cared for.

Because Fieldcrest Elementary School draws its students from increasingly troubled lower-class families, *serving others* means that Ellen has to find ways to meet the needs of the school's children, parents, and teachers while neither imposing nor relinquishing her own values. She also has to negotiate with teachers, determining how to provide educational direction while giving them the voice and independence they want. Both parents and teachers respect Ellen's strengths and appreciate her firmness and sensitivity to their needs. At times, however, they also question her authority or the extent of her control. Like Ann and Jeanne, Ellen has to juggle the roles of woman and principal and the occasionally conflicting expectations her constituents associate with those two positions.

Ellen works within a district that is male-dominated and traditional in both persons and style. In order to *meet institutional demands,* in this case implementing a district-mandated math curriculum, Ellen has to balance teachers' resistance and their need for personal and professional support with the central administration's commitment to a rigid and very different kind of curriculum. In the process, Ellen deliberately maintains a cordial relationship with the district math supervisor even as she coaches him in how to implement the new program in her school. She also continues to negotiate her place and voice among a cohort of administrators who respect her and yet subtly undermine her through the use of sexist comments and behavior.

Ellen is an expert at *balancing continuity and change.* She works comfortably and effectively within the system's structures and still finds ways to challenge it to improve the educational experience of students and teachers. This section of the chapter focuses on how Ellen carefully gathers evidence to dismiss an incompetent veteran teacher. She insists on input and assistance from the district administration to ensure that the case will be strong, the outcome satisfactory and the treatment of the teacher legal and humane. Like Jeanne, Ellen chooses an issue about which she feels strongly, and pursues the relevant change needed to improve teaching and learning. While she describes feeling uncomfortable about challenging her superiors and perhaps acting outside of the expected behavioral norms of a woman in administration, Ellen remains committed to her goal of ensuring the best possible educational experience for the children in her school.

Ellen's story is one of strength, of achieving a balance between her own goals and the constraints of the system. She finds ways to work with teachers, parents, and administrators that allow her to be successful in the system even when her actions differ from those of other district administrators. She does not aim to change the larger system within which she works, and she remains relatively unaware of the institutional and social structures that frame and sometimes constrain her actions. The process of speaking with her own voice and holding on to her own values sometimes challenges Ellen, but she maintains a leadership style that emphasizes serving all of her constituents. Her strong skills in administration and interpersonal relationships help her avoid some problems and successfully resolve many others. By her eighth year as principal, Ellen has the personal and professional confidence to take on the difficult process of dismissing an incompetent teacher. As she works for change, she demonstrates her knowledge of school culture and her ability to use various approaches to reach her goal. Her case therefore provides an unusually clear lens through which to view the dynamic process of leadership.

BECOMING A PRINCIPAL:
NEGOTIATING THE PERSONAL CONTEXT

Access and Entry

Unlike Jeanne or Ann, Ellen always assumed that she would be a teacher.

> I think down deep that's sort of what I thought I was going to [do]. I think because it was familiar and I liked school and it was safe, you know. I toyed with other things, but I didn't really—I had a girlfriend from college and we went to graduate school together. She went to law school, and I was mesmerized by that. I mean we were both history majors. I guess I could have gone. It never occurred to me, it really just didn't. (Interview, 8/93)

Ellen grew up in a suburban middle class community, one of three children in a fairly close family. Her father worked as an auditor for a large insurance company and her mother returned to work as a secretary once Ellen and her brother and sister were older. Ellen remembers having wonderful teachers and enjoying school, singling out her sixth-grade teacher (who was "very bright" and very strict), and her student teaching supervisor as the greatest influences on her own decision to go into teaching. She chose a nearby state university that would allow her to be a liberal arts major and receive elementary certification, rather than going to a school in which she would have been an education major. This decision illustrates Ellen's recurring consciousness of position and status in the field of education: "I had a real snob thing: I thought maybe I wanted to teach, but I didn't want that title" (Interview, 8/93).

Ellen decided she would teach for a year and return to graduate school, perhaps in higher education administration. But her first job, teaching sixth grade in a middle school, convinced her to remain in public education. She enjoyed teaching and gravitated toward upper elementary and middle school grades, in part because she liked this age student and, in part because she saw elementary school teaching as less prestigious. Ellen does not consciously connect issues of status and gender. She does, however, juxtapose the two in ways that mirror historical and current notions of women as subordinate in elementary schools (Ortiz and Marshall, 1988; Connell, 1985).

> I was . . . in a middle school, which was really what I wanted. I didn't want to be in elementary school, and I was able to do that, and I loved it there. . . . I have this thing about not wanting to be in a totally female environment, and I thought that that would be the case in an elementary school. I also didn't feel like I connected—I wanted to be with older kids. And I thought it would be, I think that underneath it—I wouldn't feel this way now—that there was sort of more status attached, it was more exciting to me. I think that—I don't know if I thought it consciously, but I think I must have. (Interview, 8/93)

Ellen left her first middle school position after one year and went to graduate school in education, this time further from home. Like most women teachers, she had no plans to get an advanced degree in public school administration. She chose her graduate program because it recognized her teacher certification and consequently allowed her to take electives in the graduate school of arts and sciences. Her undergraduate history major had given her both elementary and history certification; she planned to take more history courses and prepare herself for the possibility of a secondary social studies position. At the beginning of the second semester, however, she broke her foot and was unable to get up the three flights of stairs to her history classes.

> I made it up [to the history office] to register, and . . . I looked at the reading list, and I said, "You know what, I don't think I can do this—carrying all these books up and down." And I had a bad break—I was on crutches for three months, so I just—it was bad. So, I went and looked in the catalogue and I saw what was on [the first floor]—this is really true! My reading supervisor freaked out years later 'cause I really came to love what I did. I looked in the catalogue, and I had taken this [reading] diagnosis course which I kind of liked. I had to talk my way into it in the fall semester because I wasn't in their program. And I saw that the [reading] courses were all on the ground floor. And I'd had the dean of the school for a science methods course, and we kind of got along—I got to know her. And she said, "Oh, yeah, that would work out," and she gave me a key to the elevator. (Interview, 8/93)

In 1972, Ellen graduated with a master's degree in elementary education. She then taught fifth grade for three years in the Edgemont School District. During this time, Ellen continued to take courses, paid for by the school district, to complete her certification as a reading specialist. This is a typical pathway for women who pursue further study in education, because it allows them to continue to work in a classroom with students (Mitchell and Winn, 1989; Shakeshaft, 1989; Prolman, 1983). In 1975, in the middle of her fourth year in the district, Ellen became the reading specialist for two elementary schools. She had no immediate plans to move out of the classroom until a colleague's departure created an easy vacuum to fill. Once in her first reading position, though, Ellen began to demonstrate some of the initiative and skill that would characterize her future work. She wrote a proposal that resulted in the district funding another reading specialist position; this allowed her to work full time in one school rather than dividing her time between two.

When the district decided to open two middle schools in 1981, Ellen chose to move into one as a reading specialist. She loved this position, not only because she worked with older children but also because she acquired a professional peer group. The middle school had a cohort of reading specialists who worked together, a contrast to the solitary position of an elementary school reading teacher. In her new position, Ellen assisted teachers in their lesson and unit planning; did classroom teaching, including demonstration lessons in science and social studies; and carried out individual and group work with children needing additional reading support.

Ellen had more than six years experience as a reading specialist before she began to pursue administrative positions. Unlike Jeanne and Ann, however, Ellen had at this point begun to consider the possibility of becoming a principal. She continued to take advantage of her district's willingness to pay for university coursework, and she completed her principal's certificate in 1979. When asked to be a summer school principal in the district in 1980 and 1981, she accepted (although she doubted if she was prepared for the job and explains that she depended on assistant principals with more experience for support). Despite these preparations, Ellen, like Jeanne and Ann, describes her move in to full-time administration as the result of a "push" from a mentor. In 1984, the (male) principal of the middle school in which she worked as a reading specialist, insisted that Ellen take a newly created assistant principalship. She hesitated when offered this opportunity, again questioning her own readiness:

> I said, "I don't really know if this is the best time for me, I don't know if I can, if this is the right time, if I'll be able to handle this," you know. And I was a little overwhelmed, you know, the discipline, and just the whole bigness of the school. And he said, "You can't afford to turn this down. This is too good of an opportunity." (Interview, 8/95)

Despite her hesitations, Ellen accepted the position of assistant principal at the middle school. After she had worked on curriculum, supervision, and discipline as the assistant principal with the sixth-grade classes for a year and a half, her principal deliberately changed Ellen's responsibilities, moving her to the seventh grade at the beginning of the next year. She protested the move, but the principal explained that the shift was necessary for her "preparation" as a principal. Each year, he changed the parameters of her job, providing her with the opportunity to work with all of the grade levels and departments at the school.

Ellen's path into the principalship differs from Jeanne's and Ann's, in some ways reflecting a more traditionally male pattern of career development. Like the other two principals, Ellen had no intention of becoming a principal when she entered teaching, and she, too, needed encouragement from others to consider administration. However, given her mentors' help and her own initiative, Ellen prepared for the role, gradually beginning to see it as a possibility, practicing administrative skills and roles, and then actively pursuing positions. When asked if, as an assistant principal, she had wanted to become a principal, Ellen responds,

> I guess I thought that was the general idea. I don't think I was, I guess I was, I was going through the motions. Like I was, like I wanted to go to that Harvard principals' thing [a training program for principals sponsored by the Principals' Center at the Harvard Graduate School of Education], and I was sending resumes out. But I don't think I could quite see my—but I was always like that. I could never quite see myself in the next place. (Interview, 8/93)

It may be that Ellen had difficulty imagining herself in the role because, like many women (even those aspiring to the principalship), she may have consciously or unconsciously felt she lacked the traits needed to be a school leader (Pavan, 1991; Weber et al., 1981; Biklen, 1980). Each time someone prodded her to move on Ellen resisted. She describes herself as never feeling ready, as less prepared than she should be, a reaction that seems to be common for women considering administration.

Despite her hesitations, Ellen continued to move along a path that would take her to a principalship. During her three years as an assistant principal, she attended a summer principals' institute at Harvard. This experience boosted her confidence and interest, and she began more actively seeking principalships. Ellen interviewed in school districts near her home as well as some in neighboring states, sending out more than sixty resumes over two years. She points out that her single status pushed her to look further than she might have otherwise:

> I think I also actively looked because of my personal life. I felt like I didn't have anything totally keeping me here, and maybe—I sort of extended my search not because I was totally emotionally ready to do it, but I thought I should. Like I was closing doors if I didn't do it. And so, I pushed myself a little bit. . . . Well, I think the fact that I was single, you know, that was really the driving force—that I didn't, you know, I always felt like maybe I should do a little more and try things since I wasn't tied down. But that can be a burden because just because you're not married doesn't mean you really want to fly around and do exciting things. In a lot of ways I'm sort of a homebody. I like to travel, but I think day to day I'm kind of a homebody sort of. (Interview 8/93)

The literature tends to focus on women's efforts to balance home (usually marriage and parenthood) commitments with the timing of their interest and entry into administration. Ellen's experience suggests that these issues are salient for women regardless of marital status.

In 1986, Ellen's search resulted in a principalship in her home district, Edgemont, at Fieldcrest Elementary School. At the time of the study, eight years later, Ellen is one of two female principals in a group of six elementary, two middle school, and one high school principals in Edgemont. Teachers and parents frequently use the term "old boys' network" to describe the process of hiring and promotion in the district. Even Ellen, who tends to underplay the role of gender in her professional life, suggests on several occasions that men and women seem to be judged differently when evaluated for positions. She notes that several of the new, young male principals in the district have less experience but more confidence than she had as a new principal. She is also aware that, during November of the year of the study, some of the male principals collaborate to guarantee that their candidate is hired for one of the two new assistant principal positions available to four of the elementary schools (Field notes, 12/9/94).[3] A senior administrator in the district, when asked about hiring, explains that the district looks at who applies and picks the best candidates. He acknowledges, however, that often fewer women apply, and that those hired do not stay in their positions for long. Perhaps most importantly, he also remarks that people hire people with whom they feel comfortable, who are similar to themselves: "I know when I hired people, I know I looked for people I knew I'd be compatible with. At least, I thought I would be" (Interview, 10/93).

These reflections about the role of gender in hiring in this district parallel the literature on gender in administration that suggests that fewer women apply and that both conscious and unconscious gatekeeping occurs in the hiring process (Bell and Chase, 1993; Edson, 1988, 1981; Marshall, 1984; Stockard and Johnson, 1981; Wheatley, 1981; Clement, 1980). Ellen was not aware of any barriers to her hiring when she became principal of Fieldcrest; her more male-normed career path may have made her an acceptable candidate in a fairly traditional district. She had learned the norms and behaviors of an administrator in this institutional structure during her years as a reading specialist, summer school principal, and assistant principal, and she was both comfortable and ready to work within that framework.

Taking on the Role

When Ellen began as principal of Fieldcrest Elementary School she was pleased that her new job kept her in her old district but somewhat anxious about the responsibilities to come. She succeeded a man who had been the school principal for many years, and she was the school's first female principal. In addition, she brought a very different work style to the building, combining a take-charge approach with high expectations and a willingness to provide her staff with a great deal of support. But Ellen soon felt comfortable in her role.

> Well, first of all, I had been an assistant principal for two and a half years, and some of my colleagues had no assistant principal experience. And I had also been a summer school principal for two summers back like in my early thirties—that was like six years before I came here. So I think I was pretty prepared. And the principal who came before me, he left good notebooks. So that wasn't, I was—at the thought of doing it, I was overwhelmed, but I have to tell you that, when I came here, it really wasn't that hard. (Interview, 7/93)

Management and organizational responsibilities came easily for Ellen, as they had for Ann, in part because of her prior experience and training in administration. Unlike Ann, however, who focused almost entirely on management, Ellen's background in reading and her own interests in the larger field of education spurred her to take on new projects. During her eight years as principal, Ellen has continued to educate herself, for example by attending inservice programs and professional meetings and reading education books and journals on her own. More than either of the other two principals, Ellen consistently looks for ways outside of her daily work to be professionally stimulated and engaged; in fact, her desire for intellectual engagement is a key reason she agreed to be a part of this project.

Ellen moved quickly through an "induction" or "survival and control" phase of her principalship into a phase of stability, growth, and leadership (Kremer-Hayon and Fessler, 1992; Parkay et al., 1992). The only challenge she experienced in her first year came from a teacher who had been at Fieldcrest for many years prior to her arrival. As Ellen saw it, this teacher contested Ellen's right to make decisions and run the school. The teacher recalls their conflict differently: "Everyone else thought she was wonderful, wonderful to start with. But I think it [the friction between Ellen and me] was because I was the most experienced teacher here, and she resented that" (Teacher interview, 4/94). The teacher complained to the union that Ellen overstepped her position. For example, Ellen insisted on being present at parent-teacher conferences that the teacher believed should have been private. In return, Ellen sent this teacher an eight-point memo at the end of the year outlining her expectations. In this way, Ellen demonstrated her willingness to respond when confronted, and to use her administrative position to maintain control over what happened in her school.

During the first five years of her principalship, Ellen involved the school in two big projects: the physical renovation of the school site in 1987–1988 and preparation for the National Elementary School Recognition Program in 1989–1990. Each undertaking challenged and engaged her skills and brought the community together. Although Ellen did not initiate the school renovation project, she closely supervised it. She helped to determine classroom space and design, building configuration, and the details of finalizing and furnishing the space. Each week, she attended construction team meetings, much to the contractors' surprise.

> And then, once we broke ground, I would go every week to the construction manager's meeting where there were forty guys and me. And they would be polite and my boss used to laugh at me. And he used to say, "They don't know that you could, like, swear them under the table." It was a learning experience. (Interview, 7/93)

Now when she gives newcomers or visitors a tour of the facilities, Ellen proudly describes the work that was done, pointing out changes and improvements that resulted from the renovations. Teachers had lived out of boxes and in make-shift rooms for part of a year, but all agree that the results were worth it. Sharing the hardships and inconvenience seems to have been a bonding experience, bringing the teachers together first in their discomfort and later in pride.

The second big project involved doing the self-study and writing necessary to be considered for a National Excellence Award under the National Elementary School Recognition Program.[4] Because she was not sure if the school fit the application guidelines, Ellen first studied the relevant test scores herself, without telling anyone, so that no one would be disappointed if the school was not eligible to apply.

> The Excellence thing initially was my idea, because you have to come in on improvement of statistics. You have to be at 75% achievement level—this is how it was then—in math and reading, which . . . forget it. We weren't near. . . . But [instead of meeting these criteria] you can show improvement. It has to be [gains of] 15% over three years and we had that, and we had more than that in math. So I spent just hours and hours taking all the old data. The other irony is that, a couple years later, in an effort to cut back and not overtest these kids—and also the expense and the time—we don't do it [test] at every grade level. So that's like the section of time that we also had the data available. So anyway, it took hours and hours to figure that out, and I didn't tell anyone that I was going to do that, because I thought if it doesn't work, it would just be a real bummer. (Interview, 7/93)

When asked why she chose to take on such a big project, she explains, "It's hard to remember, you know. Well, first of all because I thought it would be very thrilling for the school. I think it was like a personal challenge to myself. I like doing that kind of stuff. I mean, some people aren't into that. I kind of like that stuff" (Interview, 7/93). Ellen was very pleased when the news came that the school had been awarded a Blue Ribbon in 1990. Teachers and parents shared in the pride that came with the recognition, especially for a school that had long been considered to be on the wrong side of town.

In the years following the Excellence report, the cohesiveness of the school community began to give way, according to Ellen and her teachers. They associate this fragmentation with several factors, including some of Ellen's actions, increases in school size and student demands, and shifts in teacher alliances. A few teachers explain that Ellen seems more content when she has a big project to work on. Without a major challenge to occupy her time and attention, they say, she sometimes makes demands on teachers that feel like unnecessary interference. Others describe this period after the National Excellence Award as a stage in Ellen's principalship when she exerted a fair amount of control and authority.

> I think she went out of control a bit. I don't know what was happening in her own personal life, but she just pulled too tight, tried to take too much control. She became too autocratic, and that whole thing, and that went on for several years, and there was really a lot of unhappiness and unrest. People were very disgruntled with her. And then she's kind of let go recently, and I think it's been her most productive years and the school's most productive years. (Teacher interview, 2/94)

Ellen is aware of some of the issues and changes in her own leadership style over the years. She describes herself as having become so comfortable in the school and in her role as principal that she is more direct in her approach to leadership, less willing to use a process-oriented approach that takes more of everyone's time and results in the same decision she would have made herself.[5] She balances this shift away from shared decision making with a willingness to delegate tasks and responsibilities to others, including her new assistant principal who arrives in January 1994. During the year of the study, Ellen's consciousness of easing up somewhat on her engagement and control is heightened by the illness and death of her mother. This family crisis demands a great deal of her time, physically and emotionally, and distances her from the school in some ways. As she pulls back on the time, if not the commitment, she gives to her job, Ellen sees that both she and the school can mange under those circumstances.

> I always felt, number one, that I could only do this job in extraordinary amounts of time, and I felt that if I did it in less time the effects would be disastrous. Like in other words I spent so much time on the job it was hard for me to envision being able to do it in less time. And I guess I also—it's like a little bit of an ego thing. You think well, if you did it in less time it just couldn't be as good. I don't know if that's keyed into—like, they can't do it—I don't think in a conscious way, but like in an unconscious way—it runs better if I'm doing it. And I think 'cause of my personal circumstances I absolutely spend much less time doing schoolwork . . . but in my estimation, to tell you the truth, I don't know that it's made that much of a difference. And I think I've learned a really good personal lesson: that you can walk out the door at four o'clock and things go on without you. (Interview, 1/94)

Ellen traces some of her shifts in style to her own chronological and personal development. When she started the principalship at Fieldcrest, Ellen was thirty-seven years old. She remembers identifying, at the time, with the young faculty. When she turned forty, though, she began feeling less like one of the faculty; she explained that she "felt like she wore

40 on her chest" (Field notes, 12/15/93). When she now tells people she is forty-five, she says they look startled, perhaps reminding her that she is in middle age. For Ellen, as for Jeanne, age and experience combine in ways that allow a movement from a more collaborative to a more directive, and at times controlling, style of leadership.

> The good news is that I feel very comfortable here and I feel a part of things. I don't think anyone is indispensable, believe me. . . . But, I feel needed, you know. I feel like I, in some small way, make a difference. So, that's good, and I feel more sure of the decisions that I make about things, you know, and I have, I think, more long-term perspective. But I'm so comfortable sometimes that I say to my secretary, "I talk to people like I talk to my sister." You have to watch that sometimes, you know. I've lost my temper probably more in the last two or three years than I ever did in the first three years. I just didn't do that. (Interview, 7/93)

Studies of career development tend to ignore this interaction between gender, years of experience and chronological age. Women may begin their principalships more collaboratively and gradually take on a more authoritative stance as they become more comfortable in their leadership role. This process does not just involve adapting to male norms; it includes developing and finding a voice that reflects who and where they are. Experience seems to provide women in their middle years with an authority that young men may assume is theirs (by virtue of their position) from the start of their work in administration.

Becoming a Principal: Summary

Ellen's easy assumption of the role of the principal is a much more active process than the socialization described by Marshall (1985) in which women administrators learn to adapt to male norms and expectations. Perhaps because she is socialized into the system earlier, Ellen experiences less tension in taking on the position than do Jeanne and Ann. But she is not just passively molded by the institution or the role. She draws on personal skills and professional interests as she develops and acts upon plans and projects for her school, balancing her district's gendered expectations and practices against her own confidence and skill in the field of education. Ellen continues to find the role of principal a comfortable one, even as that role changes for her over time as she negotiates school, district, and personal demands and expectations.

SERVING OTHERS: DEFINING LEADERSHIP IN THE COMMUNITY CONTEXT

Like Ann and Jeanne, Ellen is different in several salient ways from many of the families and teachers in the community in which she works.

Some believe these differences create tensions in Ellen's relationship to the community, but others find that Ellen's ability to listen, respond, and act appropriately far outweigh the differences that exist. Like both Ann and Jeanne, Ellen experiences the conflicts involved in being female and a principal. Her actions sometimes challenge and sometimes reinforce the frequently contradictory expectations people have of those two roles. In learning to combine her personal style with the authoritative norms of the principalship and the interpersonal demands involved in working with parents and teachers, Ellen arrives at a balance that is comfortable for her and acceptable to those with whom she works. She has the administrative and management skills that Jeanne strives to develop, and the interpersonal skills that Ann infrequently practices for fear they might undermine her authority and professionalism. Women leaders not only need to find a balance that satisfies themselves; they must also negotiate one that allows them to be effective in the structures within which they choose to work. Definitions of women's leadership styles often tend to minimize these contextual and interpersonal constraints, focusing instead on more abstract conceptions of female leaders (see, e.g., Hurty, 1995; Irwin, 1995; Astin and Leland, 1991).

Leadership in the Community

During the 1993–1994 academic year, the Edgemont School District served 9,977 children. Fieldcrest Elementary School, with 737 children, was the third largest of the district's six elementary schools. In 1993–1994, the Fieldcrest's student body was 86% Caucasian, 8.5% African American, 3.9% Asian, and 1.4% Hispanic. Most of the children came from low-middle to low-income families.[6] The school had 27 regular classroom teachers, 9 special subject teachers, 4 Chapter 1 teachers, 2 resource room teachers, 1 reading teacher, 1 part-time social worker, and 1 psychologist.

Although the reputation of the school had improved during the eight years preceding this study, one parent points out that "they have always called Fieldcrest the armpit of Edgemont" (Parent interview, 5/94). Others note that people both within and outside of the district tend to conflate the community and the school, giving the latter a bad reputation: "I think people just think that because it's a lower income— and it's not even that it's a lower income—it's just, I don't know. They just think that we can't be as good, and that really bothers me, especially because it's my kids that they think aren't as good" (Parent interview, 5/94). Fieldcrest parents, however, carefully distinguish between the community and the school. Acknowledging the community's reputation as "a rough neighborhood" and "a tough little piece of the world," one mother explains why she switched her child from Catholic school to Fieldcrest: "I asked a few parents what they thought about it, and they all said it was wonderful. And this one women just got this look on her face, and she said, 'It's not the school, it's just the area.' And that's pretty much how I feel [too]" (Parent interview, 5/94).

When parents, teachers, and administrators talk about the community served by Fieldcrest, they emphasize the transience, the dysfunctional and fragmented families, and the increasing neediness of the school-aged children.

> I think some of it is that I'm finding that I'm not getting, our parents aren't as, as cooperative in working with the children. I see that difference. Probably I think they're also coming just more limited, with limited experiences also. You'll find with a lot of these students they're not children who leave this area and really have a wide range of experiences traveling or even going down into [the city] and going to a museum. Or even where parents just speak to them and carrying on day-to-day conversations, "How was school? What did you do? What did you think of that movie?" You don't get that. And so I've seen the children come in needing more and more. (Teacher interview, 2/94)

They also point out that the school population has continued to grow, stretching the school's physical, financial, and educational resources and demanding greater amounts of emotional energy from the faculty and staff as they work to serve the children well.[7] The increasing size of the student body makes it more complicated for Ellen to interact informally with the children as she has in the past; working on projects or having lunch with groups of students is harder to arrange. Similarly, Ellen's personal challenge to learn the names of as many of the school's students' becomes much more difficult; each year she finds it harder to know all of her students.

Many of the changes in the community and the school clientele result from social and economic trends that have hit lower- and working-class families harder than the middle class. Because Ellen comes from a more middle-class background, some teachers, especially those who themselves come from Edgemont, feel that she has difficulty relating to the community and its needs. Because she has not "lived the experiences," they argue, she can not understand and respond to the racial, social, and economic problems in the area served by Fieldcrest. These critics assume Ellen would prefer to work in a wealthier district.

> I think she would be better suited at another place. She didn't come from a place like this. A down to earth, meat and potatoes person with an empathy for troubles and lifestyle would be better—someone who came from here and succeeded. She's an adult, she's compassionate,

but she doesn't understand, hasn't lived it. She's floored by drugs, car accidents—things that have happened in my own family. She hasn't had enough of those kinds of experiences. (Teacher interview, 11/93)

Another difference between Ellen and much of the community is religion. Ellen is Jewish and there are few Jewish families (or teachers) in the school or district. Although few colleagues or community people comment on this as an issue unless asked to do so, in a few instances religious differences create some tensions. For example, during the year of the study, Ellen experiences what she calls her first "fight" with her Home and School officers in her eight years as principal—over whether or not they can run a holiday store in December. When the officers approach Ellen for permission, she requests some time to consider her answer. She talks separately to the president of the organization, asking her if she would be put in a difficult position should Ellen deny the holiday store request. Later, Ellen tells the group that she does not want the school involved in celebrating *any* religious holidays, reiterating a stance she has held since early in her principalship. She suggests that if the group wants to expand the school store in order to give children more experience buying and selling, she would be happy to support such a change. The group makes no fuss about Ellen's decision, but some of them say later that they find her "inflexible." "She decides what she decides and that's it. And it's not as though you sit down and—she does try to validate your feelings, but I've heard her talking to other parents about, like, she'll say, 'Well I understand what you're saying, but.' She's not really that understanding" (Parent interview, 5/94).

Despite differences in class and religious background, parents generally laud Ellen for her ability to listen and respond. She skillfully sees their needs for both empathy and direction, and she provides both. Teachers, parents and administrators agree that Ellen is largely responsible for improving the school's reputation even as the larger community has become more troubled.

Their scores were always low, they lacked direction, it was a struggling building, and it was like that until she took it over. And she has turned that place around. Very, very seldom do we get any problems from there because she handles those. The community really likes and supports its school now whereas before it didn't. And that's directly attributable to her. I mean, she works long hours with those people, and she cares about them, and they I think have grown to know it now. At first they were a little bit leery I think. They'd never had a woman principal before over there, for one thing. And that's not an easy section of town. But she showed them that this 5 foot 3 or 2 or whatever she is can stand right up to 'em and take 'em on, and she did. That building has turned around. That's one of our most successful stories in terms of our elementary ed. Others kind of maintain their status, but she has really turned Fieldcrest around. Now, she will tell you her staff has turned Fieldcrest around, but she's hired most of her staff and she's trained most of her staff the way she runs it, so. (Administrator interview, 11/93)

Parents also acknowledge Ellen's responsiveness to their concerns about their own children. Even when faced with a difficult parent, she usually manages to listen and act in ways that leave the parent feeling heard and respected. As a result, parents of current (and former) students seem comfortable seeking out Ellen to discuss their children with her. She is able, in most cases, to allow both teachers and parents to be heard and supported while making her own position clear. In short, she is adept at "playing the referee." When Ellen's constituents use the word "leader" to describe her, they typically do so in conjunction with references to her firmness and directness, qualities that fit traditional definitions of leadership. At the same time, they describe Ellen as responsive, using the language of care frequently associated with female leadership styles (see, e.g., Shakeshaft, 1989).

> I think she's really good with parents. I think she's ready to listen to a parent's problem and try to understand, even if the situation is such that the child or whatever, the parent or whatever has broken school rules, or is not in agreement with her own views of how life should be and so on. She's really very open, I think. But she's also a very firm leader who will say—I used that word again—firm principal, let's put it that way, who will say, "This is my school. We do have these rules, and while your child is here we expect—or while you're here—we expect that you're not going to be drunk or you're not going to be high or whatever. And what we want ultimately, what you want and what I want is the best for your child, so let's work on this together." So I find her really good. She can stand her ground against the worst of them. And she can be also really responsive to the ones who are the most needy. (Teacher interview, 10/93)

Observations during the year of the study support a view of Ellen as someone who can see, understand, and respond to the community's issues without passing judgment on the families and their experiences. She demonstrates substantial knowledge of children's families and their needs, as is illustrated in the vignette that starts this chapter. Ellen frequently addresses the range of problems her students face, for instance, by using discretionary funds in her school budget to buy shoes for several children and to support a child's continued in-school violin lessons. She talks with parents about their concerns, including problems that arise as children wait for buses in the neighborhood, about home situations, and about their children's academic work and social relations.

Ellen responds calmly to a range of challenges. For example, listening over the phone to the story of a mother who had just been evicted from her apartment, Ellen offers both empathy and constructive advice. She acknowledges that this is not an easy topic to discuss, she urges the mother to "find someplace temporary so the kids can come to school," and she promises to clear this arrangement with the truant officer, sparing the mother the pain of having to explain her situation to another school official. On another occasion, she very firmly tells a mother who is being investigated by Child and Youth Services for neglecting her children that she *must* pick her kindergartner up from school each day herself rather than depending on the child's older brother. Here, as in other instances, the overall emphasis is ensuring the welfare—and the education—of the children. For Ellen, the bottom line is what best serves the children's needs.

Parents occasionally comment that, as a woman, Ellen is especially sensitive to their needs, more responsive, and more able to work with children than a male principal might be. Mothers sometimes attribute her understanding of them and their children to motherhood, not realizing that Ellen has no children of her own: "Maybe [parents] feel more comfortable with saying things to her differently probably than they would to a man because she might understand more things. It's mainly being as a mother" (Parent interview, 5/94). Teachers, too, point out that Ellen's gender influences her relationships with parents in the community. They note that Ellen uses her gender to surprise parents with her strength, to establish relationships with mothers, and to say things that would not have been accepted from a male principal. For example, in a community that has fairly traditional gender-role expectations, only a female principal has a chance of not causing offense when telling a mother that her children's clothes need washing.

> I think she's wonderful with parents. I think that she can get away with saying what we would like to say oftentimes to parents, in her communication with parents. And they perceive it not as a threat for the most part. I mean, I know there's been isolated incidents, but I don't think for the most part that it's perceived as that. She is the authority, and she's very fair to a lot of the parents. A lot of them are her girlfriends—she has so much contact with them. (Teacher interview, 12/93)

Ellen thus uses her gender—to be a "girlfriend" and to be empathetic and responsive—while at the same time demonstrating the ability to take a stand, make unilateral decisions as needed, and be an authority figure. Sometimes parents find such actions surprising, or see them as indicating a lack of flexibility or understanding, perhaps because occasionally Ellen's actions do not match their expectations of how a woman, even a woman principal, should respond. But Ellen is respected, in part, because she does accept and use the traditional power of the principalship, while she is liked because she attends to the interpersonal relationships that make her an acceptable woman. She has found a balance that works for her and for most of the parents, functioning within the existing norms in ways that allowed her to be herself and be effective.

Relationships with Teachers

Ellen's relationships with her staff reflect a balancing of many of the same factors that characterize her interactions with members of the community. Among the faculty, though, some individuals interpret her firm leadership as a need to control the school, the curriculum, and the teachers. Still, the faculty agree that Ellen's primary goal is to improve the education of the children in the school. No one attributes to her a desire for control or power for its own sake.

Some aspects of the school environment that are beyond Ellen's control influence Fieldcrest teachers' daily experiences and their responses to her requests and decisions. An increase in the severity of children's problems and the number of students who need additional support make classrooms more stressful places and make it more difficult for teachers to feel successful. The growth in the sheer number of students adversely affects the school climate as well. One teacher sums up the frustrations of many as she points out, "There are lines everywhere and we're all waiting in line!" (Interview, 1/94). Larger classes undermine teachers' efforts to reach all of their students, and, despite the fact that Fieldcrest receives more Chapter 1, special education, and psychologist support than any other Edgemont elementary school, teachers often cite the inadequacy of support services for their—and their students'—needs. In this environment, any requests from Ellen to examine the reading program, to monitor another area of curriculum, or to serve on a committee seem burdensome.

Like some parents, some Fieldcrest teachers think that religious differences occasionally affect Ellen's relationship with the faculty. Ellen, the teachers, and the parents all agree that Ellen's decisions regarding how the school should celebrate the December holidays might have been the same, regardless of her religion. Still, her Jewishness seems to influence how teachers respond to her or interpret her actions. According to some teachers, Edgemont's policy stating the acceptable religious content of December celebrations is more strictly enforced at Fieldcrest than at other schools in the district. On the other hand, a minority of the faculty believe that Ellen has not gone far enough in minimizing religious celebrations and rituals. Ellen, while conscious of this tension, tends to downplay its importance, sometimes joking with the school's Jewish social worker about the small number of Jewish employees in the district. A few times during the year of the study she does refer to inequities stemming from religious differences. For example, Jewish teachers and administrators must take personal or unpaid days off if they wish to celebrate the Jewish holidays. She also describes how the district's response to a series of incidents with a neo-Nazi group at the high school (several years earlier) was to hush it up rather than address it openly as a potential learning situation for all of the students and families.

Teachers point out that how much control Ellen exerts has varied over the years in which she has been principal. After the school renovation and National Excellence Award projects, she seemed too controlling. The clearest example of Ellen's exercise of authority that left some teachers unhappy and, perhaps, less trusting of Ellen, is a decision she made three years before the study to shift five teachers' grade levels. In retrospect, Ellen explains that she asked the teachers to move for two reasons: she believes that change stimulates growth, and she judged that particular individuals would be more effective working with different grade-level partners.

> First of all I felt things had been the same way for too long. I was going into my fifth year, people had been in those places for four years, but some of them had been there before I came. I felt like Ann needed to be with older kids, and I also felt we needed someone strong in content in fourth. I felt like Elizabeth just needed a change, and . . . you know, this is funny, but sometimes I used to think she was a little impatient in fourth grade, and sort of tired of it. But I somehow kind of hoped that being with younger kids, you know, they're so—they're nurturing back. And it's funny, last year she had kind of a trying class, although she liked it—I guess it's her third year in second—but this year she has the kind of typical second-grade kids that you think of when you think of second. And she says to me, "Oh my God, they're so affectionate, they're adorable." It is nice; it's nice for her. And then so I moved Jeanne and Patty to fourth—Patty was the one I felt the most guilty about, 'cause she'd only been in second grade for two years, and I thought that was really premature. But I told her she was really the only person I felt that could smooth out the group. And who else? And then I took Rebecca out of first. That was a big thing; that was horrible for her, really [because she had been there], well, like sixteen years. And she really ran the show down there, and I just felt that if I didn't get her out of there, that other people wouldn't have a chance to have some leadership. And I also felt that, not that she wasn't good with first-graders, but I felt like she had sort of the temperament and the skills and the content to really benefit older kids but still teach them like they were younger. Which is really the need in our school,

because they might be third-grade age, but some of them are reading on the first-grade level. . . . I just instinctively felt maybe she was at a point where she was better to work with older kids. But I never totally articulated that, 'cause I didn't know how to express it myself. I just told her, which is true, I felt she had a lot to offer. I also told her that I felt that if I didn't move her, she'd never move herself. And not that there was necessarily anything wrong with staying in a grade level for thirty years, but I just didn't want to see her do it, and I was making that decision. (Interview, 1/94)

Despite Ellen's rationale, many teachers, both those directly involved in the change and others, cite this action as one that contributed to a growing sense of distance and discontent in the faculty, and to the development of cliques and a lack of trust that disrupted a prior sense of community.[8] Teachers concede that Ellen made the decision she felt best served the school; nevertheless, they remain unhappy about the personal repercussions of Ellen's decision and the authoritative way in she made and implemented it.

I don't challenge her right to make that decision. It was the only thing done in the years she has been here that violated trust and affected morale. I hope she learned from it. It wasn't worth discussing it with her. I told her I would act professionally, do what I was asked to do. She has a philosophy that I don't agree with that change is good for change's sake, and that's not appropriate for everybody. I resented the fact that changing me could be interpreted as maybe I was getting stale because I wasn't. I was a pawn in the shift, not a reason for it—it was convenient to move me. . . . She always puts the school first. I didn't like the decision for me, but if I really saw it in the best interest of the school I could understand it. All her other decisions before and after were in the best interest of the school, put the school first. But I don't think it did help the school—and this is three years later. (Teacher interview, 11/93)

Some individuals attribute the distancing and fragmentation that has occurred in the faculty less to Ellen's actions and more to the changing school population and to the overall nature of group dynamics and personalities. In their view, fluctuations in relationships occur naturally in any workplace. If anything, some teachers see Ellen's style as holding the school together during a difficult time.

The principal sets the tone for the school. The morale is higher with her even at a low point than it was with any of the other principals. She confronts the issues if something is bothering her. If she left and someone less capable came in, teachers would retrench even more. We're in the trenches now . . . maybe the exception was before and this is more normal. When I talk to people in other schools, I hear that this is not

> unique, with the cliques. When you have a situation in a school where the principal is not a strong leader then teachers had to support each other. She is the school right now. (Teacher interview, 11/93)

This period of "retrenchment" may also, however, reflect a real change in Ellen's leadership. In order to keep a sense of momentum and development after the effects of the renovation and the National Excellence Award had faded, she exerted a level of control and authority that left teachers feeling less empowered and less connected to her and to one another. Others mention that the former principal's lack of leadership forced them to work together; in contrast, as the teacher above suggests, Ellen's strength and directness allow people to drift apart.

Ellen is aware of the morale issue in the school. Her concern and the steps she has taken to address the problem exemplify the interpersonal and professional approaches she often combines in her work. Ellen accepts some of the staff groups as a given, and she deliberately avoids, during the year of the study, letting the cliques teachers describe bother her or get in the way of her working and personal relationships with the faculty. Still, she finds the cliques troubling: "I mean I guess I'm the type that if I had ten kids I'd want them all at the dinner table together. So I don't know if that says more about me. . . . I think the part of it that bothers me, apart from the social end of it, is I do think that it inhibits certain people making exchanges professionally" (Interview, 1/94). At the beginning of the year of the study Ellen appoints a senior, well-respected teacher to the social committee rather than waiting for volunteers.[9] Although this move is, itself, autocratic, Ellen hopes that with this teacher as chair, the committee, and the events it sponsors, will acquire a peer-based legitimacy and strength that will help to bring the staff together. Ellen also addresses morale and communication issues through staff development. To encourage teachers to talk to one another more about professional issues, Ellen sets as a schoolwide goal that each teacher informally observe one colleague three times over the course of the year. Ellen creatively uses the institutional structure and her position in it as principal to address the lack of community she feels in the school. Her response recognizes the interpersonal nature of the problem and demonstrates care, but it also underscores professional expectations.

In addition, during the two years before and the year of the study, Ellen begins, consciously or unconsciously, to relinquish some of her control by delegating work. Several teachers remark on this.

> And really last year and this year, I've seen a big difference in that she's learning to give some power up to other people, or just some responsibility. She says now, "I'm not going to do this, so-and-so can just take

care of this. I'm going to like let it go. It's not my baby anymore." And so I think she's maybe happier that she's been able to do that. (Teacher interview, 2/94)

Along with delegating some of her power, Ellen continues to run a staff council, composed of teacher representatives from each grade level. Council meetings provide a forum where teachers can raise concerns and issues, make some decisions, and receive information that they then communicate back to their colleagues. While some teachers feel that Ellen still needs to maintain control over this and other teacher groups in the school (e.g., the special education staffing meetings, the student assistance meetings), others see a better balance between her need to run the school and maintain control and her willingness to share decision making with the staff. These divergent perspectives seem to depend in part on how much the speakers feel involved in school processes, on whether or not decisions meet their needs, and on whether they view themselves and their colleagues in the school as requiring a firm hand or more autonomy. One teacher, for example, comments, "I think we have some people who are outspoken, and there's times where she just needs to say 'this the way it has to be.' I think if she lets too much go, people take advantage" (Teacher interview, 11/93). Like Jeanne's attempts to delegate and share power, Ellen's efforts are sometimes successful and sometimes undermined by the contradictions inherent in carrying out the role of the principal while meeting the goal of democratic management. Also like Jeanne, Ellen has to balance her own urge just to do what needs to be done with her understanding of teachers' desire for a share in decision making.

Gender is another factor in the way Ellen and her faculty interact. Teachers mention that because Ellen is a woman they sometimes feel comfortable approaching her with personal issues; her "sensitive side" allows her to empathize with their experiences (Teacher interview, 2/93). Like Ann's faculty, Fieldcrest teachers comment on the shift that occurs in their principal's style in the years just prior to the study away from a more direct managerial style and toward, in Ellen's case, a more democratic style. It may be that teachers generally prefer this style; it may also be that they see it as more appropriate for a woman principal. In fact, some of the literature suggests that teachers prefer working for women principals, perhaps because they tend to exhibit a more participatory and interpersonally oriented style of management (Gross and Trask, 1976).

Ellen tends to downplay the importance of gender in her life and career, although, as suggested in chapter 2, she frequently follows a statement saying gender has no influence with a story that illustrates the opposite. For instance, at our first meeting, when asked about the role of gender in her life and career, Ellen expresses doubts about gender influencing her actions and interactions at the school. Then, she recounts that when she first came to Fieldcrest, a parent said to her, "Well, I wonder it will be like to have two women in the office," meaning Ellen and the school secretary (Field notes, 5/6/93). She also mentions that she reads the folders for all children new to the school and assigns them to an appropriate teacher. Her male colleagues, by contrast, do not read each folder; they ask the school secretaries to assign the children as they come in. She attributes some of these differences to background, her training in reading for example, but recognizes that her approach to her work seems to differ from her male peers.

The possibility that gender influences her actions or others' responses to her sometimes worries Ellen, perhaps because gender complicates interactions or makes them less manageable.

> I do think sometimes. I do worry. I get, that whole gender thing. I mean, I guess sometimes if I have a conflict with somebody, then I do stick to myself and think, "Oh, gosh, I hope this isn't a female thing." Or that maybe I don't think it is with me, but what if the other person is interpreting it to be female or they don't see it. I wonder: is it more difficult for another woman to see a woman as an authority figure? (Interview, 8/93)

When, in the National Excellence study, people attributed typically female characteristics to Ellen, she responded with surprise, and perhaps, an attempt to downplay nurturing in favor of management.

> You know, it's interesting because when the parents were interviewed when that Excellence guy came, some of the qualities that he used to describe me in their observations of me were qualities of nurturance. Which kind of amused me because I guess I am, but I don't really think of that so much. That's like secondary. I wouldn't have thought of that as, but of course they don't have—they can't see my ability to schedule. And I guess that's something that gives them a comfort level, you know. You know the kids' names. (Interview, 8/93)

Ellen may want to avoid gendered explanations of actions and interactions for the same reasons she initially hesitated about teaching in general or teaching in an elementary school with many women colleagues. The connections between gender, lower status, and lack of power and control run deep in the field of education and create difficulties for someone who is trying to meet district demands and teacher and student needs, especially someone who has a fairly strong desire to control her own surroundings. Like Ann, Ellen may believe that distancing herself from gendered interpretations makes it easier to take on and use more traditional characteristics of leadership.

Serving the Community: Summary

As principal, Ellen tends to balance what the literature describes as "male" and "female" leadership styles in her interactions with parents and teachers (Hurty, 1995; Irwin, 1995; Regan and Brooks, 1995). Like Jeanne and Ann, her goal is to be an effective principal. She draws on interpersonal skills (what others describe as sensitivity, responsiveness, nurturing, and warmth), while also using a fairly authoritative and direct leadership style. This approach makes it possible for her to meet people's expectations of principals *and* women, and serve the children in her school well. Teachers and parents sometimes resist her assumption of a controlling form of management, and they sometimes speak with tongue in cheek of her use of her femaleness to establish relationships with people. For the most part, however, Ellen successfully negotiates issues of class, religion, gender, and role as she creates a leadership style that embraces a range of approaches to get the job done in the Fieldcrest community.

MEETING INSTITUTIONAL EXPECTATIONS: NEGOTIATING THE CULTURE OF SCHOOLING

Ellen, like Jeanne and Ann, is very conscious of her role as a middle manager, balancing district demands with her school's needs. She is a good building manager; she submits her budget when it is due, responds to central office memos with alacrity, gets orders in on time, follows the district's complicated rules regarding truancy and special education, and makes sure the building is well taken care of. She, too, works hard to play by the rules, to carry out district responsibilities and maintain good relationships with the central administrators, several of whom she likes and admires. One teacher explains,

> They're her bosses. . . . She'll say, "This is from here [central office], and that's why it's going to be." . . . And she would never give an outward sign if she disagreed with one. No she would never say, "Oh, I don't agree with this, but" and give you a—give it a negative content, you know. Criticize them, never. Never. Not even if she disagreed with it, you probably wouldn't know. (Teacher interview, 11/93)

On the other hand, she makes her teachers' and students' needs clear to the central office, and pushes the administration, when necessary, to help her meet them. She does not hesitate to raise her concerns about the new district-mandated math program in administrative meetings, in conferences with the math supervisor, and, eventually with her teachers. In each case, her goal is to improve teacher functioning and student learning. In these and other situations, Ellen holds to certain principles about what teachers and students need in order to develop and learn. In doing so, however, she has to take positions that do not always feel comfortable to her.

The story of Ellen's efforts to implement the district math program at Fieldcrest illustrates how she balances her interpersonal and authoritative approaches in negotiating the introduction of a new curriculum. She works to serve the needs of current and future students, of teachers who have to use the program, and of a central administration with a strongly gendered hierarchy, a culture of control, and a financial and philosophical commitment to demanding full compliance with the newly adopted curriculum. Ellen's work with these often competing groups demonstrates how she juggles the academic and affective needs of her constituents to achieve generally positive outcomes within the structure of the institution.

The District Mandate: Implementing the Math Program

In 1993–1994, the Edgemont School District implemented a new systemwide elementary math program. Key characteristics of the program include the introduction and drill of multiple skills and concepts within a single lesson and the existence of a "script." Teachers are given the exact words to say in each lesson and are instructed to use a signal, such as finger clicks, to elicit student group responses. In addition, program developers recommend that the program be taught to students grouped homogeneously by math ability. Creating homogeneous groups requires shifting students from classroom to classroom, an unusual practice at Fieldcrest and at most Edgemont elementary schools.[10] Finally, the program has its own language, formats, and formulas for learning math, most of which are quite unfamiliar to teachers and parents.

From the beginning, many Fieldcrest teachers express doubts about the program and reluctance to change their existing math approaches. They respond to the new curriculum with the attitude that it has been mandated by the central office and they will comply, perhaps proving the administration wrong when the program fails. Ellen, too, has concerns, but she feels it is her responsibility as principal both to execute the district's plan *and* to provide support for her teachers in the process. At the beginning of the year of the study, she lists successful implementation of the program at Fieldcrest as one of her annual goals:

> We just were adopting this new math program and . . . some of us are
> not too thrilled that we have to do it. I'm more not thrilled only
> because I have so many faculty members that are not so thrilled, but it

was a teacher committee and—it could be good. We got great test data
out of it, but it's a scripted thing. So, well you'll see. So that has to be
kind of a building effort." (Interview, 7/93)

In the first faculty meeting of the year, Ellen explains to teachers
that she does not want the program to limit their good teaching. Some
teachers argue that if they deliberately work around the new curriculum,
they will undermine the program. Ellen tries to serve as spokesperson for
the district decision but also as empathetic staff developer for her teachers. She explains that no one expects teachers to limit themselves to the
script. Acknowledging that the scripts depart from the natural voice of
the teacher, she assures the faculty that the goal is not to squelch all that
teachers have to offer. She admits that the scripting would drive her
crazy and points out that teachers can certainly do additional activities
that are not in the program after they finish a lesson. Ellen, saying she
can hear people getting ready to do primal screams and beat their chests,
assures the teachers that she does not intend to check up on how closely
people keep to the scripts—it is just not her style. One teacher reminds
Ellen that they were told not to deviate from the script because it would
jeopardize the program's quality. Ellen responds that the math supervisor told her that teachers could do more once a lesson was finished, such
as working on geometry or using manipulatives. The teacher persists,
arguing that such deviations could invalidate the final test results that
will be used to evaluate the program. Ellen reiterates that teachers can
do other things with and around the program. She describes this as a
learning year and ends the discussion by telling the assembled teachers,
"Do the best you can" (Field notes, 9/22/93).
    Ellen typically circulates through the school building once or twice
each day, looking in on classrooms; stopping to admire student work;
talking with teachers about students, parents, or other issues; and catch-
ing up with people. During the fall, as she moves in and out of classrooms, Ellen frequently asks teachers how the math program is going.
Some teachers complain, others express doubts. Some show Ellen the
ideas they have come up with to use as the clicker to elicit student
responses (e.g., a Snapple top, castanets). One teacher says that in her
advanced class, she "throws away the script half the time—the kids are
way past it" (Field notes, 10/6/94). Ellen purposely avoids doing her formal teacher observations during math lessons in the fall so that teachers
can become comfortable with the program. In October, Ellen teaches a
few lessons in the program at a couple of different grade levels to get a
feel for it herself.
    In January, Ellen puts the math program on her grade-level meeting
agendas to discuss teacher responses to it. She also begins observing in

teachers' math classes, choosing to observe high-level student groups taught by teachers who are comfortable with the program. She hopes, with this strategy, to minimize teachers' anxieties about how well they are doing. Her goal again seems to be to help teachers adapt to the program rather than to enforce one particular mode of implementation. In one third-grade class, she explains that the teacher has found that rather than doing the script for four days and then doing enrichment one day, she and the students enjoy it more if they go through the script more quickly then do some enrichment each day (Field notes, 1/25/94). In a fifth-grade classroom, Ellen observes that the veteran teacher seems less relaxed and less responsive to students when teaching the new curriculum. As Ellen and I observe in a first-grade class, Ellen points out that this math class is much more organized than many of the lessons this teacher often conducts.

During the course of the year, teachers give the program mixed reviews. Those most comfortable with it also seem to be the ones who feel confident about integrating their own materials and approaches into the given rubric. Others dislike the program for its rigidity, for what it leaves out, or because they feel that their students can not succeed within it. It is also unwieldy to administer as children move from one grade to the next at the end of the year. These impediments to curricular change, like the constraints on changes described in the other schools in earlier cases, are ignored by a central administration who decided to buy new texts and implement a new program.

Throughout the fall, Ellen supports the new program, emphasizing the obligation to work with it and give it a chance despite its problems. She tries to balance meeting the district's requirements and responding to her teachers' concerns, although she recognizes that teacher resistance makes her job more complicated.

> And I think that the math has created, you know, a lot of pressure for us. But I think we're managing. And we're getting a little bit looser about saying, "Well, this doesn't work so I'm going to complement the lessons with other things." Maybe people or—I don't know, not so much—well, some of them are a little resigned. But they're also kind of trying to make the best of it, which I kind of hoped would happen and I think in a way it has a little bit. (Interview, 1/94)

In January, Ellen begins to shift toward protecting and supporting her teachers and away from the district mandate. By the end of the year, Ellen is clearly more willing to articulate to teachers and to the central administration her own fairly negative feelings about the program, although she recognizes the areas in which it succeeds for some children and teachers.

I think it's very controlling. . . . It's the contrived part that bugs me. It's also the strategies, the way they teach these fractions and finding common denominators in division is really a trip. And multiplication—the way they're teaching multiplication it looks like division. I mean, I just don't think that's necessary to teaching kids how to think. I think they could have done the concept of lots of disparate skills and used the traditional strategies. . . . I mean, is a program going to fix kids or fix teachers? (Interview, 6/94)

Ellen's approach to the mandated math program illustrates her ability to balance the demands of competing constituencies within the context of the institution. She accepts the district's decision and works within institutional and district structures to make the new curriculum a success. She insists that her faculty use the program, but she cushions the process for them by not including math lessons in her observations and subsequent evaluations. She uses the existing process of teacher observation and feedback to examine how the new approach to math affects teachers' work and to solicit opinions and ideas about their classroom experiences with the program. She makes institutional changes, such as revising teachers' schedules so that they can group children effectively for math the following year. Ellen is comfortable in her role and in working within the institutional structure as she balances the district's demands to implement a new program with teacher concerns about its effectiveness. Her confidence in her own skills and her experience with both administrative and interpersonal responsibilities combine to make the implementation of the new math curriculum a reality, if not necessarily an educational success.

Negotiating with the Math Supervisor: Diplomacy and Care

In implementing the math program, Ellen serves as an intermediary between the district's math supervisor, George Bates, who is responsible for directing program adoption throughout the district, and her teachers. Again, she plays the referee between two conflicting groups. Although a committee of teachers and administrators had chosen the new curriculum from among several possibilities, Bates had favored the program selected; some teachers believe he had pushed strongly for its acceptance. Ellen works hard to maintain a positive relationship with the math supervisor while also supporting her teachers and raising her own questions and concerns about the program and the process of implementation. As she interacts with George Bates, she draws on her interpersonal skills, seeking to make him feel valued and needed. In this approach, Ellen echoes Jeanne's strategies for making her superintendent "feel like a hero." Women middle managers seem to make good use of their understanding of what their bosses need, working to maintain a relationship with them but continuing to focus on their own vision of what needs to be done. This may amount to adapting to the male-dominated culture and system, but it is also a strategy that allows a principal to use her skills to accomplish both district and school-based or personal goals.

Ellen stays in frequent touch with the math supervisor over the course of the year. In October, she contacts him to find out about math inservice programs for teachers. She also invites him to a Home and School meeting to talk with parents about the new math program. As the year progresses, and she and the teachers became more vocal about their concerns, Ellen has to work harder to keep the relationship positive. In one example of this process, Ellen negotiates with the math supervisor about his evaluation of a teacher in her school. Teachers at Fieldcrest can choose to have one of their three evaluation observations done by a central administrator.[12] In November, the math supervisor comes to Fieldcrest to observe one of Ellen's teachers, someone who is widely considered to be a very skillful teacher and a relative advocate of the new program. When Bates observes this teacher's math lesson, he discovers that she does not teach the program according to its design and script and is not using the materials appropriate to that lesson. He finds Ellen before meeting with the teacher to discuss the observation. At one point, he suggests that he rip up his notes and offer to come back another time. Ellen tells him that would indicate to the teacher that she had failed. Ellen listens to Bates's concerns and responds:

> I wonder if teachers are getting too many messages about the math program. I know that when you spoke at the principal's meeting yesterday I heard some new things; maybe they weren't new but I really heard it yesterday. . . . Teachers aren't going to the meetings that are available to them about [the math program]; I don't know why not. . . . You might want to talk to [this teacher] about how we need to do a better job of communicating to teachers what is expected. The message I get from this is that we need to do more explaining. . . . I may have contributed to the problem by overloading teachers and not providing enough explanations. . . . You should ask [the teacher] how clear she is on what's expected. (Field notes, 11/17/93)

Ellen also tells Bates that he, too, needs to take some responsibility for a situation in which a good teacher is not succeeding in the program. She ends the conversation by complimenting Bates on always being so positive and for providing teachers with such specific comments (Field notes, 11/17/93). During this conversation, Ellen manages to give the math supervisor direct suggestions about how to talk to the teacher about his observation, relays to him her concern that teachers feel overloaded and unclear about expectations, empathizes with both Bates and the teachers, and conveys to him that she values his actions and approach.

Later in the spring, two representatives from the publishing company responsible for the math program spend a day at Fieldcrest observing classes and talking to teachers. According to Ellen, the meetings are a disaster and the math supervisor is "a wreck."

> The teachers have some criticisms. The fifth-grade teachers are really good. They are professionals—not just griping. . . . The consultant could have said, "You seem to be having trouble here. Let me look at the lesson, see if I can find some other ways, work with a small group of kids." Instead she was just defensive. (Field notes, 4/5/94)

Bates comes to Fieldcrest later that same week and meets with the fifth-grade teachers, frustrated with them for their lack of cooperation. Ellen explains, "George feels he has to defend the program." She tells him that teachers have to talk and describes how one teacher, Paul, was literally down on the floor showing the consultants the specific problems he was having with lesson 57. A few days after Bates's meeting with teachers, Ellen calls him, starting the conversation by asking if he is still in one piece. She then recounts for him her conversation with the fifth-grade teachers, explaining that they had not meant to be offensive or problematic, although she could see how he could have taken it that way.

> I told Evelyn about the idea you gave to Ann about pulling out one skill from several lessons and teaching just the one skill at a time—it's nice you can offer the teachers this kind of suggestion. I was thinking that if you had time, maybe you could take one of the lessons Paul is having trouble with—you could take five kids out in the hall and do some diagnosis. Maybe you could tell what the problem is. . . . I know you're really busy. . . . For a classroom teacher it's even just moral support if you sit down with a few kids and see what's missing. (Field notes, 4/5/94)

She follows up this call with a letter to Bates, thanking him for the work he had done on a districtwide survey of math performance. She explains that once she had time to go through the survey carefully, she learned a lot from it; it allowed her to see her school in the district context. She tells Bates that she is considering holding a meeting for parents with one of the program consultants, and she thanks him for the suggestions he offered to two teachers who have been having difficulties. Commenting that the first year of any program is difficult, she says that she hopes he will continue to be available to work with them on the new curriculum again next year (Field notes, 4/12/94).

Ellen balances her role in the middle, protecting and defending her teachers, supporting the implementation of a new program, and using interpersonal skills to guide her own and her teachers' relationships with a central administrator in charge of overseeing the curriculum change. Her style of working with the math supervisor—listening to him, providing him with suggestions for working with people, and complimenting him on other aspects of his work whenever she can—helps to contain a potentially volatile conflict between teachers and the central administration. Her approach could be described as "caring," or leadership by empowering others, in that she considers the math supervisor's needs as a person and a professional as she works with him. It could also be considered a strategic use of the skills, often associated with female administrators and people in subordinate positions, of recognizing and providing what those in power need in order to be satisfied. This approach allows Ellen to maintain and continue to act upon the best interests of her school and teachers within an institutional structure that aims to control both process and product.

Negotiating with Administrative Colleagues and Central Administrators

Ellen must also negotiate with a predominantly male group of colleagues and central office staff at meetings held regularly to discuss district policy and procedures. These meetings are characterized by strongly gendered patterns of expectations and interactions that often complicate Ellen's middle management role. Ellen meets regularly with the other elementary school principals and the assistant superintendent, and with all of the principals in the district and the superintendent. The two women principals and two of the women central administrators often sit together. At a superintendent's meeting in December 1993, one of the women whispers to me as the meeting begins that if you sit where we are now (at one end of the square of tables) you have to cross your legs. In fact, this would have been true wherever we sat; her comment suggests a keen awareness of the constraints of gender in the meeting room. At another meeting the superintendent starts by noting that there is "a stranger here from the east." He then asks not Ellen, but the other woman elementary principal to introduce me. We remind him that I am working with Ellen, and Ellen introduces me and asks me to describe my project. I explain that I am developing case studies of principals. This produces laughter and comments around the table, including the jest, "Yes, she's a case." Later in the meeting, one of the female central administrators gives the curriculum and instruction report for the (male) assistant superintendent who is unable to attend the meeting. She prefaces her remarks by saying since she does not have his humor her report will be more straightforward. Some people clap; one of the male elementary principals jokes, "You're better looking." At another point, the superintendent talks about an environmental resource council meeting that included an exhibit of artwork from one of the district's middle school. He describes one sculpture, labeled a belly dancer, and explains that they had changed the name to exotic dancer to be more appropriate. The sculpture wore bells that jangled when turned on; he jokingly describes how someone turned it on during the keynote address and everyone laughed (Field notes, 12/9/93).

Both Marshall and Mitchell (1989) and Ortiz (1982) describe how women administrators must deal with a male-oriented culture that permits and supports language and patterns of interaction that denigrate women, often by focusing on their sexuality. In the "joking relationship" described by Ortiz (1982) and illustrated in the examples above, men reinforce values and positions of authority through teasing and jokes. All participants accept these comments as part of a friendly group conversation, but such interactions contribute to the maintenance of patterns of dominance and disrespect. It is acceptable to make jokes about a woman's looks, competence, talkativeness, and availability, and even, perhaps, to confuse one of two women principals with the other. In fact, such comments may raise the speaker's own stature in the eyes of his peers. Although the women may laugh along and "not mind," these interactions create and reinforce a culture of male dominance and a hierarchical pattern of interaction and status based on gender. The gender hierarchy interacts with the institutional hierarchy to make the middle management role of a female principal even more of a balancing act. Ellen therefore must meet, or challenge, gender expectations while trying to address both district demands and school needs.

At one administrative meeting, Ellen raises some of her concerns about the implementation of the new math program. She says that her learning specialists and teachers point out that "asking most kids to integrate six or seven things is a great idea, but for kids with language problems there is too much language and for many special education kids they are asked to make too many cognitive leaps in the program" (Field notes, 10/19/93). She explains that she has been suggesting to teachers that they do the script for thirty minutes and then do manipulatives. She also says that teachers remain unsure about how much they are allowed to deviate from the program. She considers, aloud, inviting the math supervisor and one of the curriculum administrators to observe and comment on lessons, to give teachers some feedback, and perhaps teach some sample lessons. No one responds to Ellen's misgivings or ideas. When another principal raises a concern about scheduling instrumental music lessons by pulling kids out of their classes, Ellen brings the discussion back to the math program, saying they could not take kids out of math classes, given the scripted programs. When the other principal complains that the program is a burden on the principals because of the scheduling difficulties involved in its implementation, Ellen adds, "and on the classroom teacher" (Field notes, 10/19/93).

In March, during an extended visit to the district by one of the senior writers and a sales representative for the program, the elementary principals devote one of their meetings to a discussion of the math program. The math supervisor and the senior writer talk about what seems to work best in the program. Both appear somewhat defensive as principals raise some of the logistical problems involved in implementing the program: scheduling to get homogeneous groups, covering material not in the program but on the Iowa tests and state competency tests, and determining proper placement of students within different levels of the program. In addition, Ellen again brings up a series of questions about how to use the program with her needier population of students. Noting that thirty-five new students have entered her school since January, Ellen points out, "It's really hard to enter a third- or fourth-grader into this program let alone give parents materials to help them catch up." The program representative explains that one tenet of the program is that any work that goes home should be work students feel completely confident about doing themselves; Ellen responds that it is overly idealistic to think that because students are doing this math program that they will be confident going home and remembering it all (Field notes, 3/30/94). Her strong statements and concerns discomfit those responsible for the program, her colleagues, and other senior administrators at the meeting. Like Jeanne, who is met with silence when she asks for support and training at an administrative council meeting, Ellen receives no verbal support or response to the issues she raises at this meeting.

Teachers and administrators in the district comment that Ellen is highly respected by her administrative colleagues and superiors. Some of their comments indicate that gender plays a key role, both positive and negative, in how other administrators view and respond to Ellen's style.

> I think she's well respected. This is a district where things are very political. And if you're a male, you'll probably get anything even if you have an IQ of 20. But to be a woman and have stayed here, you really have to be smart and assertive, and I think Ellen really wins out there. She's well respected. (Teacher interview, 10/93)

Some teachers suggest that Ellen draws on her femininity in her work with the central administration, saying that, "Given her personality I think she beguiles the guys up top" (Teacher interview, 11/93), or, "The way she interacts with other administrators—she acts like a goofy schoolgirl" (Teacher interview, 11/93). Just as Ann is criticized for not being female enough, and Jeanne for not being a true leader, Ellen experiences the mixed expectations of others. Female management strategies or the use of typical female traits are expected of women administrators, and they may be useful as survival strategies. They are also, however, seen as somewhat inappropriate by teachers and colleagues.

A number of teachers and administrators mention that Ellen talks a lot, and they frequently connect that characteristic to gender and to a lack of seriousness.

> It's almost a joke at the principals' meetings. Ellen will say something. Someone will say—and I must admit, it's usually the guys, "All right, Ellen, what are you going to say?" or "What do you think, Ellen?" It's like opening up the door. But that's done in good nature. It's not done behind her back, and she knows that. That's just Ellen. Maybe that's how she survived at Fieldcrest—she just outtalks them all (laughing). But she will get the last word out of anything. . . . I mean it's a joke: "Ask Ellen." You know you're going to get an answer. (Administrator interview, 10/93)

Despite the fact that men dominate (in terms of number and length of comments) most conversations and meetings, women continue to have the reputation of being the talkers (see, e.g., Hall, 1982). Overtalkativeness is also a stereotypical characteristic sometimes assigned to Jews. In administrative meetings, Ellen's willingness to speak her mind occasionally becomes the subject of discussion and teasing; one hears in the comments above that some of her ideas could even be dismissed given the perception that she "runs at the mouth" (Teacher interview, 4/94). After the principal's meeting on the math program, she comments, "And did I get any answers to my questions?" (Field notes, 4/5/94). She is certainly well respected, but a gender filter may prevent her ideas from being heard in the context of district meetings.

Meeting Institutional Expectations: Summary

Ellen is extremely successful at carrying out the demands of the institution within which she works. She meets district deadlines and guidelines and makes thoughtful contributions at administrative meetings. As she works with the new math program in her school, she operates within the limits of the program and the given process of implementation in ways that balance the needs of students, teachers, and the central administration. She is a strong advocate for her teachers with the district, and, in turn, she represents district policy to her teachers in clear terms.

In the process of negotiating the demands of her constituents, she operates within a hierarchical context in which gender and power are not normally seen as compatible. Ellen draws on characteristically male and female approaches to management; she is direct and authoritative, especially with teachers, even as she demonstrates her concern for them and for the administrators with whom she works. She considers others' emotional well-being as well as their professional needs, understanding the connections between the two. In a district culture that keeps women subordinate through patterns of interaction, formal procedures, and common values, Ellen maintains a strong, if sometimes undervalued, voice. As the next section suggests, the stands she takes demonstrate her strength and occasionally take their toll as she challenges institutional norms and hierarchies with the goal of ensuring a good education for all of her students.

BALANCING CONTINUITY AND CHANGE: NEGOTIATING WITHIN THE SYSTEM

Implementing the district's new math program involves a change in practice. In many ways, however, it also reflects business as usual in this school district. The process draws on existing norms, structures, and roles; teachers' and administrators' responses suggest that they are used to carrying out mandates from above that do not always reflect the best educational practice or the realities of their particular school situations. Even when Ellen and some of her colleagues raise concerns about the program and its implementation, the central administration continues to look for ways to make the program fit into existing school structures, routines, and goals. Ellen works hard to help her teachers balance their need for continuity with the change they have to make, but the district as a whole emphasizes maintaining a stable structure and process.

During the year of the study, however, Ellen initiates another change that is anything but "business as usual." Motivated by her own moral and educational vision of what constitutes best practice for children, Ellen gathers information toward the ultimate dismissal of a veteran teacher. She carries out this project virtually unassisted, despite her requests for support from the central administration. In the process, she discovers the difficulties in challenging the system and its cultural norms; although she believes that her decision and actions are right, she sometimes questions her own style and role in the institutional structure. For any principal, challenging the system by initiating and carrying through a significant change is a daunting task. A woman principal faces an additional set of questions and barriers raised by the male-dominated norms and structures that define schools as institutions (Adler et al., 1993; Ballou, 1989; Shakeshaft, 1989).

Philip Washington: Dismissing a Teacher

Philip Washington, a third-grade teacher at Fieldcrest Elementary, has taught in the Edgemont School District for twenty years. In 1990–1991, Ellen gave him an unsatisfactory evaluation for his inability to maintain discipline and teach effectively. Because of health problems and, perhaps, a need to recuperate from his personal and professional difficulties, he left school eight weeks early that year. When he returned in the fall of 1991, things seemed better. Still, teachers, administrators and parents in the district refer to him as a "legend," a teacher who is clearly problematic but difficult to do anything about. Teachers and administrators explain that Ellen has worked continuously with this teacher "to remediate and to bring him along" but that he has made little progress (Administrator interview, 9/93). Ellen describes conversations she had with Washington two years earlier about looking into other career possibilities, such as real estate or travel, since he had done some work in those areas. Washington insisted that he wanted to continue to teach.

In September 1993, during my first visit to the school, Ellen's secretary enters her office saying that a parent had come in concerned about negative comments she had heard about her child's teacher, Philip Washington. Although Ellen agrees that this teacher is indeed a problem, she emphasizes that she "won't accept untruths and slander from parents" (Field notes, 9/7/93). In October, after her first observation in Philip's class, she asks the part-time reading teacher to provide support for him by reading with some of his students. She explains that his management problems make it difficult for him to work with the range of students in his class. She also points out that her memo to the reading teacher has gone into Philip's file, which is about three times thicker than most teachers' cumulative files.

In November, Ellen does a second formal observation in Philip's class. Her written evaluation of this observation, like the reports that she writes for all of the teachers, includes a detailed discussion of the classroom process. In Philip's case, however, rather than praising specific teacher actions and student outcomes and behaviors as she does in most other teacher evaluations, Ellen points out a number of things Philip could do to be more effective. She concludes by writing that the class is "satisfactory in a marginal sense" (Field notes, 11/17/93). When she conferences with him about her written report (something she does with each teacher following an observation) she finds that his only response is to disagree with her use of the word "reprimand" in regard to an action he had taken. Ellen tells Philip that she thinks the reprimand was one of the best spots of the lesson, because Philip set some limits. Nevertheless, she agrees to change the wording to "spoke sternly" (Field notes, 12/5/93). Also in November, Ellen writes three memos to Philip. The first asks him for his feedback on a situation in which a child had complained to Ellen that Philip had "chucked him under the chin pretty hard in math class, although he knew Philip wasn't mad at him but was mad at some other boys who were acting up." The second memo requests that he gather some information for a Tuesday staffing meeting about a child—information initially requested from him in September that he has yet to provide. The third memo comments on two children in his room who need to be separated and provides suggestions about what Philip should do for and with these students (Field notes, 12/5/93). All of these memos became a part of Philip's file.

During informal visits throughout the fall and early winter Ellen (and I, on occasion) observe Philip's inability to maintain a classroom atmosphere conducive to learning. For example, during one observation, it takes him twenty-five minutes to shift the class from reading to a science lesson. Students take advantage of his ineffectual management techniques (e.g., repeatedly saying "shh" or calling out an individual child's name) to bother one another, wander around the class, and ignore his frequently repeated instructions. When students do work, they seem disengaged; they do not volunteer answers to Philip's questions and their work (in one case filling in a worksheet on the parts of the human body) is rote and frequently incorrect.

At this point in the year, Philip's actions are not unlike his work in past years. By March, however, the problems and Ellen's responses to them escalate, partly as a result of parents' concerns about both behavior and academic work in Philip's class. In one incident, for example, a child Philip sends to the office tells Ellen and his parents that he had called Philip a bad name. The boy says that Philip told him that if he was his child he would beat him when he got home. In a March 7th memo to Philip, Ellen documents conversations she has had with this student, his mother, and two other children. They all talk about Philip hitting and pushing students. In a memo responding to Ellen, Philip states that he has not hit this child. In the same week, Ellen receives a call from another child's parents, who request a meeting with Ellen and Philip. Philip, they claim, hit their son. At that meeting, on March 9th, Ellen informs the parents that she will arrange for their child to be moved to another class. When Philip joins the meeting and describes this child's behavior in his class, the parents are appalled. The child has been verbally and physically abusive to his peers and to Philip, who, in turn, has been unable to stop or change his behavior. The parents are angry with both Philip and their son, and they want to know why Philip did not contact them or take action sooner. Philip shifts between self-righteousness (having had to tolerate this child), confusion (over what he did and did not say or do in response), and defensiveness in this meeting. He frequently appears close to tears; at one point, Philip is so shaken and upset that he leaves the room, returning a few minutes later when he has calmed down. He, Ellen, and the parents agree that the child will change classrooms, since his relationship with Philip has deteriorated beyond repair (Field notes, 3/9/94).

During the rest of March, Ellen writes Philip a series of memos. Some address student behavior problems and subsequent meetings with parents; others focus on the academic problems she discovers as she begins to talk to students and spend more time in Philip's classroom. Several of the memos arrange support for him and the students, continuing the pattern Ellen began in the fall of simultaneously documenting problems and trying to improve the situation. For example, she learns that Philip does not know that his students have done no work in their workbooks, because he never checks them. In a March 14th memo, Ellen describes his routine of waiting until the workbooks are completed before checking them as "unsound instructional practice" because it "provides no feedback to children or parents." To ensure that he follow a more regular schedule, Ellen instructs him to develop a plan to help the students complete their work. Beginning this Friday he is "to issue a weekly workbook grade based on those week's pages. . . . In addition, work out a plan for children to make up incomplete pages and inform parents of this endeavor. . . . Finally turn in weekly plans every Monday to Ellen" (Field notes, 3/30/94). She summarizes his instructional problems, which include the need to move lessons along with greater purpose, provide more opportunity for sustained reading and writing, and help students work toward finished products. She notes that he spends too much time on things like having students correct each other's papers, and that he provides a poor quality of related language arts activities. Ellen also offers Philip a number of sources of help. She contacts the district's Language Arts director and arranges for her to talk with Philip about a program that might be helpful; she gives him examples of activities she has seen in other teachers' classes that could work for him; she provides feedback to him on the lesson plans he has begun to hand in to her; and she asks that he observe his own class in art and music and his grade-level partners' classes for ideas about how to work more effectively with his students.

Early in March, Ellen thinks she has enough documentation to give Philip an unsatisfactory evaluation at the end of the year. By late March, she has contacted senior administrators in the district and arranges to meet with the district lawyer to see if she can give Philip an unsatisfactory evaluation immediately for "creating an unsafe environment," and then give him a second at the end of the year on instructional issues.

Two unsatisfactories constitute grounds for dismissal. She comments at this point that doing all of the documentation has been a lot of work and many nights staying up until midnight. She has "covered herself," but, she acknowledges, this kind of situation "emotionally drains you" (Field notes, 3/30/94).

Throughout the year, parents seemed to feel that Ellen is her doing her best with a difficult situation. They do not appear to be aware of the severity of the problem nor of Ellen's plans to dismiss Philip. Teachers are generally attentive to what is happening, and, while it is an uncomfortable situation for them, they quietly support Ellen. The one teacher who openly questions Ellen's actions is the same person with whom she had conflicted during her first year. This teacher feels that there are some teachers Ellen "is after—she hounds them" (Teacher interview, 4/94). For the most part, though, teachers find it a relief to have action taken at last.

> She has been in there a lot. I know some people think he's picked on or barraged. But when you see the nonsense that goes on in his room. The only reason to feel sorry for him is that this has gone on so long—he should have been out twenty years ago. . . . I once requested a room change when I was next to him—it made me sick to watch what was going on. He does nothing in our grade, nothing for kids, there is nothing pleasing in his room. He has done nothing to change; I don't think he has the desire to change. (Teacher interview, 4/94)

Ellen's decision to dismiss Philip Washington is a major challenge to the norms of a system that generally protects all teachers, even poor ones. Few principals would undertake such a change; it could jeopardize their relationship with the other teachers in the school, with the teachers' union, with parents, and with a central administration that usually prefers to have principals handle personnel problems without involving the district or its legal structure.

Involving the System in Change

In April and May, Ellen continues the process of finding external support for Philip and his students, documenting problems, and meeting with concerned parents when they contact her. She also forces the central administration to get involved. She repeatedly telephones the assistant superintendent and director of personnel to discuss the case with them. She realizes that only with their support, even their reluctant support, will she be able to carry out this change; she also knows that despite the respect others have for her, she sometimes runs up against the bureaucracy in ways that limit her efficacy. She points out that while teachers in her building may perceive her as strong both in the school and in relation to the central office, they do not necessarily know what she is up against: "I mean I have egg on my face sometimes here, and they don't know why" (Interview, 6/94). The bureaucracy of schools can frequently overpower the voice of a single woman principal (Marshall and Mitchell, 1989; Schaef, 1985; Ferguson, 1984).

Ellen requests that several administrators observe in Philip's class, and she sends them his schedule. She worries a bit that she is "setting Philip up" by asking them to come in during transition times, such as when students return to his class from music. She reasons, though, that since Philip often takes up to forty-five minutes to settle the class down to work at those points, the observations would not be unfair. In mid-May she sends a follow-up memo to two senior administrators that includes the anecdotal notes she has kept on Philip for the last month and an addendum to an earlier memo saying that no one from the administration has come to observe Philip yet. She notes that she is worried that the "degree of supervision will be insufficient in showing our efforts to help him improve." The memo describes three issues in Philip's classroom: the kids are in physical danger, they are having a poor educational experience, and they are suffering emotionally. She tells me that it is "shameful" she has to write this memo, that the central administration has not yet come to observe (Field notes, 5/11/94).

Eventually, a senior administrator does visit Philips classroom, and he agrees that the situation is "just terrible" (Field notes, 5/17/94). In June another administrator observes Philip and is concerned because "it wasn't terrible." Ellen tells her not to worry; the lawyer has said that it is fine to have acceptable observations in his file as well. Ellen also talks to the union president and to a member of the union's executive committee who teaches in her building. The president assures her that "they don't want to win one they shouldn't" (Field notes, 3/30/94).

By the time Ellen gathers up the final file in early June to give to the lawyer, she has accumulated seventy documents from the year. By then, senior administrators have agreed with Ellen's request to dismiss Philip. Philip himself will not be told until June 20th, the last day of school, when he will be given his final evaluation by Ellen with a senior administrator and the union head present (Field notes, 6/94). When this meeting finally occurs, Ellen describes feeling fairly unemotional; she has used up all of her energy in the months before.

> Well, we went through the dismissal thing, and that went well. He was very restrained and kept his head down. And they sent this Bob Pierce with him, who's a sweet man, but he's the [union] grievance person, [and] he's new. And I just thought that was so symbolic because if you were really going to rescue someone, you'd send more than just

Bob. . . . I think that they, like us, have been trying to raise his consciousness. . . . It's really interesting. [The senior administrator]
turned to him and said something like, "You know, this is not a personal thing. I know it's hard for you not to take it personally, your
job," and that seemed to be it. No emotion. I wasn't nervous about it.
(Interview, 6/96)

At the meeting, Ellen shows Philip the documentation file,

. . . and there were times that I read from it. I said I felt it was important. And I would say, "You know, you're going to need to read some
of these things more closely when you get home," like my personal
notes. We would have been there until four [if I had read the whole
thing]. They [the senior administrator and union representative] were
very complimentary when they left, so that was nice, you know. I got
a hug from each of them, and they left. (Interview, 6/94).

In retrospect, Ellen describes Philip's dismissal as both a goal that
she achieved and a low point for the year.

I'm surprised at how emotionless I am. But I mean, that was achieved,
that was a goal. I never, I always feel like I never spend enough time
with the teachers. . . . He took some time in the fall, but nothing like
the spring. And that's always his pattern, it's always his worst. . . . The
Washington thing was a low and what happened to those kids. It was
really a tragedy, I think. Their peer relationships, almost more than
how they treated him. They treated each other so badly. And they
weren't bad kids. They were nice kids. (Interview, 6/94)

She also feels that she did the work involved by herself, with little
support from the district. A few weeks later she feels betrayed by the
same administration when she tries to hire a former Fieldcrest teacher to
replace Philip Washington, and is turned down by the central administration because her candidate would cost too much. Ellen loses her temper with the personnel director, who calls to give her the news. She
describes the conversation with him:

I really went berserk! And in the middle of it I said, "I'm probably
telling the wrong person. I think you would probably do anything for
me. It's probably the superintendent that I should be telling." And he
actually says to me, "Well, maybe you should tell him." You see,
because they only have so much influence on him. . . . I said, "I cannot
believe that yesterday I get rid of a teacher that nobody got rid of for
twenty five years, and today I ask for one thing, and they're going to
renege." "So, can't you get somebody's who's just as good?" I said,
"No, not like him." And I actually said to him, I said, "You know
what? Not that I have an offer, but if I had one right now, I would
wheel around and turn my back. I would not look behind me." I said,

"I have had it. I'm down here all by myself, doing a great job. . . . If I get one more compliment, I don't want to hear it. It's really not worth anything." (Interview, 6/94)

Ellen does take her concern to the superintendent, only the third time in her many years in Edgemont that she has done so. She goes to the meeting carrying an index card listing the issues she wants to be sure to raise. She recalls that at one point she says to the superintendent, "'And I'm going to tell you something.' I said, 'I would have been disappointed anyway, but on the heels of the Washington situation,' I said, 'I don't mean to sound puffed up or over—like—egotistical. And I don't want to diminish some of the support I got from people. But essentially, I did this alone'" (Interview, 6/94).

Despite her belief that she is right to insist that Philip Washington be dismissed, and despite others' perceptions of her as a strong leader, Ellen describes feeling "pushy," "emotional," and "guilty" when she insists on being heard by the administration in situations like those surrounding Philip Washington's dismissal (Field notes, 6/8/94). She says she felt that "she reacted fifty percent emotionally and fifty percent intentionally" in reaction to the decision not to let her hire her chosen replacement for Philip Washington. Following another run-in with a central administrator she remarks to me that she feels "she was acting more like a mom" (Field notes, 6/8/94) nagging and reminding and following up on every detail.

In reflecting on why she feels uncomfortable when she responds strongly with her own opinions, she says,

> I always thought of myself as this, I don't know, that I just sort of get along with everybody, and I don't make a big deal about things. And I really came up against people in the central administration and I had to take a stand on things. And it was a really new experience for me. So, maybe it was good, maybe it was bad. It's like, you know, it's like when you get your way, you're still not really comfortable with that role. (Interview, 6/94)

When she challenges administrative decisions, perhaps acting in ways that she herself and others consider either unfeminine or stereotypically feminine but unprofessional (like a nagging mother), she seems to worry about whether or not those in control will still like and respect her. It seems important to her, for example, that the administrators who came to Philip Washington's final dismissal meeting compliment her afterwards; that she can have a good conversation with the assistant superintendent after having pushed for a change in the hiring process for the head teachers; and that she can maintain a positive relationship with the math supervisor despite her (and her teachers') criticisms of the math program. But equally important is the fact that Ellen, like Jeanne and Ann, depends on maintaining these relationships in order to carry out her work. Ellen recognizes, perhaps intuitively, the tensions involved in taking a strong, definitive stance in effecting change and how that approach might make others, particularly senior male administrators, feel. Thus, she works to interact in ways that both support her needs and allow others to accept her actions. The process, however, sometimes undermines her own sense of who she is and how she wants to present herself in the role of principal.

Balancing Continuity and Change: Summary

The bureaucracies of schools, like all bureaucracies, resist change. Women administrators may be less likely than their male counterparts to initiate change, given that others may already see their very presence as a challenge to the norm. Expectations about acceptable behavior for women principals may also deter actions that appear authoritative or that challenge the status quo. In order to be accepted in the system, be effective in their daily work, and maintain relationships that aid them in the process, women may, consciously or unconsciously, choose to adapt rather than resist.

Ellen, however, like Jeanne, appears to feel secure enough in her roles and firm enough in her convictions about what constitutes good education that she can challenge the institutional structures and work toward a change in practice. Interestingly, the changes Ellen and Jeanne make that truly affect the process of education in their schools are not the major mandated changes of their districts: school-based management and a new math program. They are, instead, the goals these principals initiate themselves and believe in very strongly. It may be necessary to have this kind of commitment in order to resist the bureaucracy and hierarchy that tend to constrain change, especially change initiated by a woman in a culture that values the male voice, male patterns of interaction, and male administrative styles.

Jeanne experiences the system as more of an outsider, despite her many years in it, which, perhaps, allows her to take the risks of initiating change. Ellen is more of an insider, both in the district and in the style she uses. But even with her comfortable assumption of the role of the principal, her insider status, and her conviction about the need to dismiss Philip Washington, Ellen sometimes finds it difficult to take the actions necessary to implement change. Because the change results from personal commitment rather than administrative mandate, it feels to Ellen like she must draw on personal actions, like being pushy, that do not mesh with how she usually sees herself as a person or an administrator. Nor do these descriptions match those of a leader in the traditional sense. Ellen experiences the tension of negotiating change in a stable system; she also balances who she wants to be and how she feels she must act in order to make change happen. Many of these tensions arise out of the dilemma of being a woman in a highly male-dominated system. But Ellen, like most women in her position, tends to attribute the discomfort she feels to her own shortcomings or particular experiences, rather than to any limitations imposed by the system within which she operates.

SUMMARY

The literature on gender and school management often emphasizes either the male-dominated culture of schools to which women must adapt or the new definitions of leadership that emerge when we examine women administrators at work. Ellen's experience provides an example of what it might look like if we merge these two conceptual frameworks. Ellen works within a hierarchical and patriarchal system that privileges men, their language, their patterns of interaction, and their styles of leadership. She accepts these norms, and, given her own interests, background, training and style, she often operates comfortably within them. To have status, to be in control, to be heard in the hierarchy require adapting to the structure of power.

Ellen recognizes, however, that she is not exactly "one of the boys." Her attention to individual students' classroom placements, her involvement with curriculum development and implementation, her understanding and use of democratic leadership, and her strong use of interpersonal skills to care for and maintain relationships with every constituent reflect a style of leadership different from that of many of her colleagues in the district. Although Ellen may be less collaborative, sharing less responsibility with others than do those who describe themselves as feminist leaders, she does work to empower others. The balance she strikes recognizes the importance of maintaining enough control to satisfy her own needs and to be effective in the system within which she works.

Ellen both adapts to and challenges the system. She gives the district, and the players in it, what they want, and is respected as a result. She also acts and speaks out for what she believes is right, even when doing so runs counter to cultural norms and expectations. She negotiates the balance of working within and resisting the structure and culture of the school district through the maintenance of interpersonal relationships. In the process, gender plays contradictory roles. It constrains her, as others undermine her actions and beliefs, and it allows her to succeed in establishing and nurturing the connections and behaviors that make her effective in the multiple contexts within which she works.

CHAPTER 6

Conclusions:
Redefining the Principalship

Were Jeanne, Ann, and Ellen effective principals? We could examine data on student achievement in each school to find out. We could survey parents, teachers, and central office staff for another perspective. We could analyze the tasks they perform, the skills they demonstrate, and the roles they take in their schools to see if they match those identified in other research on effective leadership. But the case studies presented here suggest that we would miss much of the depth and breadth of the principals' work if we examined it using only these relatively static frameworks. Instead, their cases provide us with an understanding of the principalship as a dynamic process that evolves over time within multiple contexts. Principals must balance their own personal backgrounds and identities with the demands of the people and communities with whom they work. They must also develop ways to adapt to and resist institutional constraints and find places for themselves both within and outside of the boundaries of historically and socially defined norms.

A process view of the principalship does not ignore the fact that a principal may have certain traits, exercise important skills, and play prescribed roles in her position. Jeanne, for example, develops listening skills, organizational skills, and skills for facilitating group discussions that help her respond to parents when they demand more discipline in the cafeteria and to the school district mandate for school-based management. Ann uses strong communication and interpersonal skills with parents, and she begins to use more of these same skills with teachers, making them feel more included and cared for. Ellen draws on excellent organizational skills to document and bring about Philip Washington's dismissal. She also demonstrates thoughtful interpersonal skills in her work with teachers and supervisors to implement the unpopular math program.

Focusing only on discrete skills and traits, however, limits our understanding of the constant process of negotiation that occurs within the multiple contexts of the principalship. How a principal practices any given skill might change when she uses it in a different context, with dif-

ferent people, at a different point in a time. For example, Jeanne's negotiations with the superintendent are both similar to and yet different
from her negotiations with demanding parents. Working within multiple contexts may call for distinct—and even opposing—skills. The
authoritative stance Ellen takes with Philip Washington, for instance,
would not have been successful if she had used it with the math supervisor concerned about the implementation of the new math program.
And Ann consciously uses one set of interpersonal skills with parents, to
whom she must market the school, and teachers, who, she believes, have
a specific job to do.

A static view of the principalship also fails to illustrate how the contexts within which a school leader works change over time. A school's
processes, demands, rituals and roles may shift and vary in importance
over the years, requiring different kinds of negotiations. Jeanne, for
example, reaches a stage in her principalship in which she is ready to
take a more direct approach to leadership, at least in some areas. But at
that moment, the district mandates school-based management, which
requires a participatory, democratic leadership style in the school. In
response to changes in the personal and institutional context, Jeanne
modifies her approaches, negotiating this tension in ways that allow her
to maintain her own voice and respond to district demands.[1]

During Ellen's eight years as principal, the school experiences
increasingly overcrowded conditions and a growing population of troubled children. As the school community changes, so do teachers'
responses to Ellen's direct style of leadership. While they happily join
her in the work necessary to accomplish the building renovation and the
National Excellence self-study, they complain in later years that her
demands feel controlling. Ellen's approach may have changed over time,
but so has the community context within which she works. For Ann,
too, the changing context requires new negotiations. Mark Rubin's
arrival creates a new set of institutional demands. Ann's increased
warmth and openness with her faculty during the year of the study
serves as one strategy for coping with these changes. She struggles,
though, to find ways to adapt a previously effective management style
to the changing institutional context. The constantly shifting personal,
community, and institutional contexts within which these three principals work play an important role in shaping their actions and opportunities.

Studies that focus on an examination of school culture, especially
those that see that culture as a part of larger social systems of power and
interaction, offer a conceptual framework for understanding the contexts within which a principal works (see, e.g., Marshall, 1993, 1988;
Ballou, 1989; Shakeshaft, 1989; Weiler, 1988; Connell, 1985). Specify-

ing the patterns of discourse and interaction and the hierarchies that dominate schools helps clarify that the individual principal, regardless of particular skills and personal attributes, is constrained by larger systemic structures. But these studies, too, have limitations. The cultural perspective sometimes makes it difficult to see the person as an active agent, someone who redefines and restructures meanings and procedures in the course of her negotiations. A dynamic understanding of school leadership must also include the person—her background, her training, her beliefs and values, and her ways of interacting with people and systems—in order to have a complete picture of the principalship.

Imagine, for example, that Jeanne was hired as principal of Edgemont, or that Ellen went to Pepperdine. The contexts would remain the same, but the dynamic would be completely different. Jeanne's facilitative rather than directive style might clash with the expectations and needs of Edgemont's parents and teachers. It is doubtful, for example, that she could get a parent committee to take on discipline issues in that community or that she would agree with the results if such a committee were to form. Ellen's combination of authority and interpersonal skills might not mesh well with the demands of Pepperdine's community; she would, no doubt, take a more proactive stance with the head, Mark Rubin, than Ann did. Speculations like these force us to acknowledge the importance of the individual in any examination of the principalship. While the contexts and their demands frame the negotiations that occur, the person must respond, bringing her own perspectives and beliefs to the process.

Examinations of the role of gender in school administration begin to provide some insight into the interaction between the individual and the institutional and social structures within which she works (see, e.g., Grogan, 1996; Chase, 1995; Dunlop, 1995; Schmuck and Schubert, 1995). Gender influences the principal's life and work within every context. It affects her personal experience and entry into the profession, her interactions with the school community, the institutional framework within which she works, and her negotiation of historically and socially constructed norms and expectations. Jeanne, given her use of more traditionally female patterns of interaction, strikes some as less than a "real leader." Ann looks for ways to present a professional self, often trying to minimize her femininity in the process. Male-dominated patterns of interaction and expectations constrain Ellen's work with her colleagues and superiors and influence her sense of what a principal is allowed to do.

As an analytical lens, gender provides important insights into the process of the principalship, enriching our understanding of the balancing act each principal undertakes. Gender also represents one challenge to the system, a factor that allows women principals to be change agents in schools. (This aspect of gender is explored more below.) As an explanation of a principal's experience, however, gender cannot stand alone. It is a variable variable (Schmuck, 1981), one of the factors that principals balance as they work with various constituencies and develop a sense of who they are within different contexts.

Each of the women principals described in this book experiences her gender differently, as mediated by her own personal background and individual characteristics such as race, age, religion, and class. All three principals encounter socially constructed and sometimes conflicting expectations of women and of women administrators, but they respond differently, given different personal styles and the particular contexts within which they work. Ellen uses the fact that she is a woman to tell mothers—her "girlfriends"—to wash their children's clothes even as she can surprise parents with her strength and firmness. Ann responds to her community, whose members differ from her in both personal style and class background, with professionalism and reserve. She could never be a "girlfriend," nor would parents expect it of her. Jeanne's race and gender together make her an anomaly in her community and among her fellow administrators in the district. These differences influence her goals for the school, her interactions with the central administration, and her negotiations with teachers and parents.

In the rest of this chapter I return to the four themes described in chapter 1 and used to frame the case studies. Reviewing the findings theme by theme clarifies some of the issues that have emerged and highlights the insights provided by a process approach to the principalship. Each theme draws attention to one of the key contexts within which the principal functions: *Becoming a principal* focuses on the principal's negotiation of her personal background, experience, and training. *Serving the community* looks at her work within the context of her school community. *Meeting institutional expectations* examines how each principal balances the demands of the institutional context with her personal approach and her community relationships and expectations. And *Balancing continuity and change* explores how principals can contribute to school change within institutional and social frameworks that emphasize the status quo. Within these themes, I describe the similar patterns experienced by the three principals, but I also consider the differences in their lives and work. These differences illustrate that the principalship is a dynamic process, one in which the principal is limited by the expectations, structures, and social systems within which she operates, but also one in which she is an actor, an agent who defines her own role and actions and contributes to a modification of those same systems.

BALANCING ACTS: THE PRINCIPAL IN CONTEXT

Becoming a Principal: Negotiating the Personal Context

None of these three principals planned to become administrators when they entered the field of education; two of the three had not even expected to be teachers. All three taught for longer than most men do before becoming principals. Ellen, the only one to have significant experience outside of the classroom, worked as a reading specialist for a number of years before entering administration. Jeanne, Ann, and Ellen each describe the importance of people "pushing" them into administration when they did not necessarily feel ready, personally or professionally, to take on the role. In many ways, then, their experiences reflect the literature's description of women's access and entry into the principalship (Bell and Chase 1993; Edson, 1988, 1981; Marshall, 1984; Stockard and Johnson, 1981; Wheatley, 1981; Clement 1980).

These broad similarities are only part of the picture. Significant differences exist among these principals' career paths and experiences, differences stemming from variations in the women's personal needs, styles, and work contexts. Of the three, Jeanne may have been the least prepared temperamentally and experientially to take on a leadership role. Teaching had been central to her adult life; she was, and still is, the consummate teacher. But once hired, she is determined to succeed as principal. At first, succeeding means running the school in ways that meet with the approval of the central office, teachers, and parents. Over time, succeeding comes to mean balancing the demands of others with her own voice and vision. Race and gender are key factors in Jeanne's case. Central administrators may have hired her because they believed she would be easy to manipulate, but among some parents, her race and gender give her an extra cachet. Jeanne is aware of both sides of this equation. She uses her insights gained as a woman of color to negotiate the conflicting expectations people have of her as she develops her leadership stance.

Ann, once pushed into the principalship, needs little additional encouragement to leave most of her earlier life behind. Administration fulfills needs for her that had not been met by marriage, parenting, or teaching, and she is willing to sacrifice personal relationships for the controlled isolation she believes the position demands. Her dedication to her work and her clear enjoyment of management and organization make her successful in responding to the crisis situations she faces in her principalships. When the context demands an approach that matches her style, she seems to thrive. When the context changes, as it does with the arrival of Mark Rubin as headmaster of Pepperdine, Ann's approach makes it difficult for her to adapt. She meets her goal of getting the school up and running efficiently, only to discover that this accomplishment is not enough to win Mark's approval. She struggles to adjust her skills and interests to meet the demands of the changing context in which she finds herself.

Ellen's career path is more traditionally male than either Jeanne's or Ann's. Following many years in typically female work as a teacher and reading specialist, Ellen becomes an assistant principal and a summer school principal. She also has more consistent mentoring in administration along the way. These experiences provide her with resources, networks, and a self-confidence in working within the system that Jeanne and Ann do not have when they enter the principalship. Ellen's personal style, her middle-class status in a working-class community, and her prior work experience allow her to take on major projects during her first five years as principal, establishing herself as a directive and caring leader.

While all three women experience some of the career trajectory described by Parkay et al. (1992) and Kremer-Hayon and Fessler (1992), their different experiences and contexts require a more complex understanding of career path, one that considers interactions among gender, age, experience, and context. The first five years do appear to be a time of survival and growth, but they are also a time for a principal to discover a style that fits both the context and herself. Jeanne's facilitative style during her first five years allows her to develop skills and goals she needs in order to become more directive when necessary and more focused in the years to come. Ellen's cooperative (though somewhat directive) style during her first five years shifts to a more controlling stance, according to her teachers, and eventually to a balance between authority and delegation. It may be that for some women, the early years of the principalship provide an opportunity to develop a voice and a vision that can be carried into the next phase of their work. These years may also give them a sense of the level of control necessary to meet demands, respond to others' needs, and carry out their own goals. This balancing act may be more salient for women than for men, because women experience greater conflicts in the expectations they have of themselves and others have of them in the role of principal. Finding a solid stance is more complicated when the system, the expectations, and the self do not neatly align.[2]

Age, too, seems to influence these principals' experience. Age has different meanings for women and men in society in general and in the principalship in particular. Young men may be seen as confident, energetic, almost precocious when they take on the principalship; Ellen once commented that she could never have taken the assertive stance assumed by some of the young male principals in her district during their first few years. Women, constrained by family responsibilities, hiring expectations and practices, and internalized perceptions of their role, generally become principals later than do men (see, e.g., Pavan, 1991; Yeakey et al., 1986; Edson, 1981; Wheatley, 1981). Younger women may thus be seen (and see themselves) as inexperienced, lacking in confidence, and underqualified. Ellen, for example, felt she needed more years of experience before moving into each new position although others repeatedly assured her she was well prepared. Both Ellen and Ann seem to remain conscious of age-related issues even when they are firmly situated in their jobs. Ellen sees her changing relationship to her faculty in terms of her age, and Ann worries that if people knew her age they would no longer feel she had anything to offer. What are the cultural expectations of women in their forties, fifties, and sixties? Do these women garner the wisdom attributed to older men in our society, or are they seen as idiosyncratic and querulous when they develop a voice and style of their own? Becoming a principal later may give a woman the advantage of a broader or deeper experience and the wisdom of more years of living and working, but it may also affect how others perceive her and how she feels about herself as a leader. Differences in age among women principals also affect how they respond to and experience the role. Ann, age sixty-seven, and Jeanne, age fifty, each in her fifth year as principal at the time of this study, respond differently to administrative and teacher demands for change. The differences stem mainly from their own backgrounds, races, and work contexts, but they may also be affected by these women's ages and their expectations regarding their futures as principals.

Negotiating the personal context involves making choices and decisions about career path, family and work conflicts, and initial approaches to leadership. Historically and socially constructed expectations about women, about teachers and teaching, and about school administration sometimes constrain those choices and create common experiences and pathways for women entering the principalship. Race and class also affect the dynamic, influencing both the decisions made and the ways in which those decisions are experienced.

What the cases illustrate most dramatically, though, is that each individual's negotiation of these expectations, roles, and paths is unique, in part of because of her own life history and in part because of the different contexts within which she lives and works. Even within shared social and institutional frameworks, the interaction between individual and context results in a dynamic process of principaling, one in which the individual has some power to create a balance that works for her.

Serving Others: Defining Leadership in the Community Context

Each of the three principals in this study demonstrates the characteristics of female leadership described by researchers who have moved away from the more hierarchical, management-oriented definitions developed during the nineteenth and twentieth centuries (see, e.g., Hurty, 1995; Astin and Leland, 1991). Jeanne and Ellen, especially, focus on developing a school community that welcomes all constituents and considers how to best involve them in the learning and teaching process. People describe these women as caring, interested in students and people, and responsive to the needs of others. Ann, too, wants to develop an effective educational community, although she has a different perspective on what each constituent needs to do in order to make that happen. Her conception of caring involves creating an organized environment within which people can do their jobs, rather than one in which she, personally, takes care of individuals. In different ways and to different extents, Jeanne, Ann, and Ellen each seek to empower those with whom they work to be the best teachers, parents, and students they can be.

In addition, all three experience the mixed expectations parents and teachers have of women in the role of principal. The school community wants a woman to be a "girlfriend," to care about them and their children as a mother would, to share her life with them and allow them to share hers, to consult with them about decisions. Teachers and parents also want a principal who uses her position of authority to act decisively and often unilaterally, providing direction, expertise, and firm decisions. When a principal tends toward one approach or the other, parents and teachers question her validity as either woman or principal. Jeanne, therefore, is sometimes seen as less than a leader, given her warmth and her willingness to delegate decision-making power to parents and teachers. Ann is seen as unfeminine, given her impersonal approach and focus on management issues. Even Ellen, who demonstrates both authority and care in ways that appeal to teachers and parents, is seen as using her femininity to "beguile" administrators or as controlling when she exerts authority. These contradictory perspectives, arising from socially and historically constructed expectations of women and administrators, make people uncomfortable, in part because these opposing views of "women" and "leaders" are irreconcilable. Each principal responds to the contradictions in ways that work for her as an individual within a particular community.

Gendered descriptions of leadership, those that contrast male and female styles and those that call for redefinitions based on women's experience as leaders, clearly provide new insight into how principals negotiate their roles within schools. The case studies demonstrate, however, that no one definition of leadership, nor any single construct like gender, fully explains the style and relationships demonstrated by these three principals. Both their own personal contexts and the community contexts within which these women work shape the ways in which they present themselves, affect their relationships, and influence others' responses to them as women administrators. Jeanne, for example, has learned in her own personal life and her work as a teacher how to "give them what they want" *and* hold on to her own sense of self. It is a process she brings with her to the principalship and uses as she balances authority and care. In addition, Jeanne is both an insider and an outsider in her community. She has lived and worked in Greenfield-Weston for twenty-five years and is well respected as a teacher. As an African American woman, however, she is an outsider within (Collins, 1991). This position may allow others to question (and at times stereotype) her actions, but it also allows her to resist traditional notions of what it means to run a school. Perhaps Jeanne takes advantage of her position in the white, relatively liberal community in which she works as she begins to challenge the school to better meet the needs of African American students, drawing on her understanding that she will not be overtly challenged in this work.

Ann is also an outsider, in terms of class and educational background, in the community of parents she serves. She responds by adapting, presenting herself as a professional who can look and act like those around her, in order to be effective in her interactions with them. She, more than Jeanne or Ellen, chooses to manage her femininity, controlling her emotions, her relationships, and her dress in ways that minimize the effects of being female on her work (Marshall, 1988). Ann's actions do not usually reflect the more female management styles described in the literature, but she is clearly influenced by gender and context in the adaptations she makes in order to feel comfortable and successful in the role of principal. When Ann does begin to exhibit more care and warmth toward teachers, they respond very positively, perhaps because this approach better fits their expectations of how a woman principal should respond to them. For Ann, as for Jeanne and Ellen, defining oneself as a principal is an interactive process that occurs as the individual negotiates the contexts within which she works.

Ellen, like Ann, resists any expectations that she will demonstrate typically female patterns of nurturance or need. Despite her initial responses that gender makes no difference in her work, she contrasts her own approaches and those of her male colleagues. She is aware, for example, that she pays more attention than they do to curriculum and to the needs of parents, teachers, and children. Teachers and parents expect and respond to her demonstrations of care and occasionally raise concerns when she appears to be making unilateral decisions, wanting her to play the role of sensitive woman, and sometimes mother. Ellen uses an authoritative stance that works well with parents in this working-class community. Like Jeanne, she takes advantage of her outsider status as a middle-class woman to surprise parents with her strength and firmness. Because she combines this approach with empathy and understanding, she meets people's expectations of women and of principals in many of her interactions.

The individualized ways in which these women leaders balance the multiple and sometimes conflicting demands of the contexts within which they work are reflected in the different metaphors used to describe them. Ann handles people and events *graciously*, a term applied predominantly to women to connote style, elegance, and skill in managing others. She both uses and denies her femininity, adapting to the community context and using patterns of interaction that have worked for her in the past. Jeanne *dances on water*, trying to create a self that meets her own demands while responding to a constantly shifting set of expectations from other contexts. Ellen *plays the referee*, working to find a balance among members of the community, using a range of approaches that allow her to feel comfortable and in control and that meet the needs of others. As the dance or the game develops, each principal negotiates a balance among her personal style or background, social constructions of gender and administration, and the community context within which she works.

Meeting Institutional Expectations:
Negotiating the Culture of Schooling

Principals function within formal and informal institutional structures that influence patterns of interaction, behavioral norms, and definitions of success. They must also work with people in positions of equal or greater power who want to maintain the existing hierarchical structures from which they benefit (Marshall and Mitchell, 1989; Ortiz, 1982). The process of negotiation becomes more complex as a principal balances the demands of these structural regularities with her own personal needs and approaches and with the demands, expectations, and interactions she experiences within the school community. Jeanne, Ann, and Ellen each struggle to maintain an independent voice within an institutional structure that privileges traditionally male-oriented discourse, bureaucracy, and relationships. In doing so, each develops unique coping strategies that result from her individual style and the specific contexts within which she works.

Jeanne, for example, receives a mandate from her district to implement a school-based management plan. Her general tendency is to do what her superiors tell her to do; this approach has allowed her to survive and succeed in her own family, in school, and in her teaching career. She also respects the central administrators in her school district, appreciates the chance they have given her to be a principal, and is usually willing to play by their rules. Under Jeanne's leadership, Greenfield-Weston is the first school in the district to implement many aspects of school-based management, even though Jeanne and her teachers often find the process awkward and uncomfortable. Still, an undercurrent of resistance flows beneath Jeanne's apparent compliance with institutional demands and acquiescence to the role of supplicant and "rookie" that the central administrators tend to assign to her. She explains that she listens, provides acceptable responses, and then carries out the ideas that matter to her. She uses the school-based management plan and structure to argue with the superintendent about the number of teachers she can have in her building, turning an institutional mandate to her own advantage. She acknowledges that the system's requirements weigh upon her, but she insists that she will not allow the bureaucracy to force her out. She will not leave until she feels she has done what she wants to do in the school and district. The process of leadership takes an emotional toll, but Jeanne is determined to maintain a balance between the institutional demands, her personal goals, and the needs of her community.

Ann is less successful at balancing personal and institutional demands. Pepperdine, because of its size, its private school culture, and its more direct lines of control between the headmaster and the head of the lower school, seems to provide less room for negotiation than do the institutional structures Jeanne and Ellen face.[3] Mark Rubin, the school head, has a great deal of power and control over Ann's tenure and the parameters of her job. He uses his maleness and his youth to support his position, and Ann has difficulty finding and maintaining her own voice or vision in the face of his authority. Like both Jeanne and Ellen, she has learned to play by the rules and to respond to power (usually wielded by males) with obedience. It is a strategy that fits her personal style and one that helped her achieve her goals in the other schools in which she has worked. Although when she talks to me she is articulate and self-assured, Ann is unable to find a way to negotiate with Mark, the embodiment of the institution, or to work through their conflicting expectations and needs. It may be, as I discuss below, that Ann's goal of creating and maintaining a well-organized school does not provide her with a personal or professional vision that would allow her to challenge the institutional norms. It may also be that her own personal needs and approaches prevent her from taking on the hierarchy. She knows how to adapt and perform within it but not how to challenge it.

Of the three principals, Ellen operates most comfortably within the institutional context, the result, perhaps, of having worked in the same district for many years in a range of capacities. Her path to the principalship has given her experience in balancing personal, community, and institutional demands; she seems to enjoy the challenge of meeting multiple expectations. Ellen, more than either Jeanne or Ann, derives pleasure from successes within the system. These achievements include projects, events, and student achievement scores; parent and teacher satisfaction; and her own sense that children are benefiting from whatever change she has engineered. In order to be successful, Ellen, too, plays by the rules, goes along with the jokes, and works long hard hours to do the job in the way she feels it should be done. Her implementation of the district's new math program demonstrates her ability to juggle the needs and demands of the central administrative staff, the teachers, and the children in the school. She is at her best as she uses authority and warmth, directness and responsiveness to make the program work.

Ellen works successfully within the institutional structure most of the time, adapting when possible and pushing at its boundaries when necessary in order to balance her own values, the community's needs, and the district's demands. At the same time, the institutional context constrains her ability to be the principal she would like to be, and even to be as successful as she might like within the system. Gendered patterns of interaction and male-dominated power structures are more overt in Edgemont than they are in the other two cases. Ellen is subtly silenced and unsupported as she raises questions about the math program or solicits help in the case of Philip Washington. She feels undermined and unacknowledged at the end of the process of dismissing Washington, when her request for a particular teacher replacement is denied. In order to achieve her goals, she acts in ways that feel "pushy" or like a "nagging mother," gendered terms that describe a woman making people do something they would rather not. While she, like Jeanne, is willing and able to challenge or subvert the system in order to reach a goal, Ellen feels uncomfortable and unprincipal-like in the process.

Although the gendered nature of the community and institutional contexts seems very apparent to me in these cases, none of the three principals chooses to interpret her experience through this analytical lens. The institutional norm is a male norm, a set of values, beliefs, communication patterns, and behaviors that these principals accept as the given way of life in schools (Bem, 1993; Schaef, 1985; Ferguson, 1984). Women do not always consciously choose to adapt to or resist this structure; they may assume that any trials and tribulations they experience are either commonplace or idiosyncratic rather than the result of institutional discrimination or patterns of behavior that reflect larger historical and social constructs (Chase, 1995; Dunlop, 1995; Schmuck and Schubert, 1995). Assuming a gendered framework of analysis also appears to undermine one's own individual success within the system, since it takes control away from the individual and her own interpretation of events. When these principals challenge the hierarchy or bureaucracy, they see their actions as individual and locally important rather than as challenges to a larger social or institutional structure. Despite their more personal analyses, however, their actions can sometimes be seen as acts of resistance that call into question the validity, the effectiveness, and the benefits of the existing institutional framework within which they work. Just as they both adapt to and push the boundaries of expectations within the community context, they conform to and challenge the institution norms that frame their positions. The result is, again, a balancing act influenced by personal needs and styles, community expectations, and the institutional culture.

Balancing Continuity and Change:
Negotiating within the System

I have frequently been struck by parallels between the characteristics of leadership described by researchers and practitioners who want to restructure schools and those who study women administrators. School restructuring projects look for principals who can facilitate interaction among teachers and between parents, teachers and children. They call for leaders who can share decision making and power and develop learning environments that empower students and teachers (see, e.g., Lieberman, 1995, 1992, 1990; Griffin, 1990; Lieberman and Miller, 1990). Those studying woman administrators explain that women leaders demonstrate the ability to empower teachers, create school communities that focus on people and learning, and develop relationships with constituencies that lead to greater interaction (see, e.g., Hurty, 1995; Regan and Brooks, 1995; Astin and Leland, 1991). Given the similar lists of principals' skills and roles in the work on school change and the research on women in educational administration, why do we not see more demand for women principals as a way of improving schools, or hear of women principals who have been unusually successful in implementing such changes?

One problem with this parallel set of characteristics is that it, like other lists of key traits and skills, tends to minimize both the personal history of the individual and the variable contexts within which she acts. The cases illustrate that essentialized descriptions of women principals, while they have some validity, limit our ability to see women administrators negotiating their leadership approaches in ways that meet their own needs and the demands of the communities and institutions within which they work. Calls for school-based reform recognize some of these contextual variables but may leave out the role of the individual in school change. Research on women in administration must continue to explore the relationship between the individual and the contexts within which she works and examine the resulting variations that occur in women's styles, approaches, and definitions of leadership. Only then will we be able to judge the validity of parallel descriptions of leadership for change and women's multiple management approaches.

Another response to the question of the relationship between school change and women administrators is that women principals, like all principals, are limited by the given institutional regularities that inhibit change in schools (see, e.g., Sarason, 1971). In addition, women function within a system that privileges traditionally male patterns of interaction, styles of leadership, and values. This structural frame further hinders women's ability to act as agents of change (Adler et al., 1993; Ballou, 1989; Marshall, 1985; Schaef, 1985; Ferguson, 1984). Whether women enter administration as feminists with clear goals and changes in mind or whether they become principals without a specific political agenda, they face systemic constraints that limit their power.[4] As these three cases demonstrate, even women who do not use gender as a framework to explain their own experiences are aware of needing to manage, use, or compensate for their gender as they negotiate the principalship. In a system that sees a dichotomy between women and power, women principals may have difficulty bringing about systemic change.

The more incremental changes they do implement, however, have meaning to them as people, as educators, and in some cases, as conscious or unconscious agents of change. In making these relatively small school-level changes, they may actually be contributing to a gradual shift in the discourse about schools and administration that will allow us to realize some of the connections between school leadership and school change described above. It may be that some women principals can and do demonstrate alternative visions, paths, and approaches that lead to better schools for students and teachers.

For Jeanne and Ellen, the willingness to pursue change comes from a personal commitment to a vision of what education should be. Jeanne is willing to use a more directive approach to decision making in addressing Alan's needs and encouraging the school to be more responsive to issues of diversity. She challenges a caring teacher, breaks school district rules to keep Alan in her school, and works around faculty and parent grumbling about her investment in children of color and a multicultural curriculum. She sees her actions as serving all members of the community; her goal is to provide everyone with the best education in an environment that recognizes and supports every child and adult. Her own personal and professional experiences give her the insight and the strength needed to pursue these changes. She operates within existing structures, challenges them when they get in her way, and creates new ones (such as the monthly all school meetings) in order to meet her goals. Race and gender influence her aims and vision, her responses to the system, and her willingness to pursue the incremental changes that she hopes will lead the school and community to embrace her sense of what education should be. As someone who is "dancing on water," she aims to create a new vision of education within the confines of the school system.

Ellen, too, works to translate her vision of good education into action. In her work implementing the new math program, she truly "plays the referee," moving the game along by clarifying the rules, keeping all constituents informed and engaged, and managing crises as they arise. There is little sense that this math program is a significant educational change in this school or district, however. Although teachers must adopt different approaches and a specific language, they generally do so in a resistant and often rote manner that minimizes the impact of the changes. Neither the teachers nor Ellen view the program as having much effect on student learning after the first year of the program.[5]

When Ellen decides to take the steps necessary to dismiss Philip Washington, however, she acts on a conviction that this teacher harms children socially and educationally. Her view of good education includes a positive classroom and school environment, appropriate relationships between children and between a child and her teacher, learning centered curricular design and implementation, and teacher-parent relationships that provide both parties with the information needed to best support each child. When she determines that Philip Washington's classroom lacks these key elements, Ellen moves simultaneously to provide them and to remove Washington from his position. All of her actions take place within acceptable system guidelines: she documents and collects necessary materials following the district's legal framework and uses district resources to try to bolster Washington's teaching for the rest of the year. Again, she serves as a referee between this teacher and parents, children, and district supervisors. But she moves beyond the role of referee when she chooses to dismiss Washington, an action that if not unprecedented is certainly unusual. She plays within the rules of the system, but she also forces a change in the status quo by insisting that an incompetent veteran teacher be dismissed. This change, while focused on a particular teacher and school, has systemic repercussions. The central administration cannot ignore Ellen's values, her actions, and her calls for support as she handles Washington's case.

Ann has created changes in the schools in which she has been a head, providing new organizational structures and hiring and firing teachers to develop a staff that she feels works successfully. She, too, has a vision of what schools should look like and has, in the past, acted on that view. Her vision, however, is a somewhat less responsive one than Jeanne's or Ellen's. She aims to build an administrative organization within which people can function effectively. Because this goal leads her to focus on structures rather than people and processes, the kinds of changes she initiates seem more concrete and finite than either Jeanne's or Ellen's.

Ann is comfortable with her vision of schools; it is one that has allowed her to function effectively and to remain in control of the changes needed. When asked, therefore, to consider curricular change, or changes in the student population and school ethos around issues of diversity, Ann responds with discomfort and some resistance. These changes are not included in her own vision, nor are they within her realm of expertise or under her control. When both Jeanne and Ellen are asked by the central administration to implement changes not of their own choosing (school-based management and the math program, respectively), they adapt to those mandates by drawing on prior skills and working with and around the mandates in ways that require a sense of the school as a responsive organism. In addition, each implements some changes in which she is invested and which represent what she believes schools should look like. The changes Ann faces, however, seem to undermine her efficacy as a principal. She has little investment in the new approaches and programs Mark asks her to implement, in part because she does not initiate them. Just as important, though, Ann does not see what value these changes would have in maintaining the stable environment in which she is invested, a setting that allows her to feel confident and competent. Her inclination is to focus on stability and organization, rather than educational change. While she "handles things graciously" she avoids taking action that would lead to significant curricular or philosophical change.

Thus, the case studies suggest that while women principals are constrained by school structures and limited by male-dominated norms, they can balance continuity and change by responding to systemic demands *and* acting upon convictions about best practice. Jeanne and Ellen seem to make both conscious and unconscious use of their gender, race, and class positions to take actions that set them apart from their colleagues. Some of their ability to act stems from personal style and experience, some from the power of being the outsider within, and some from the community and institutional contexts within which they operate. Ann, conversely, has always experienced her gender as something to be controlled, managed, and compensated for, not a difference that gives her an edge. Her age, another difference (one seen by some of her teachers as giving her greater wisdom), is also something she feels the need to hide rather than use. Gender alone certainly does not determine leadership style and approach. But the cases illustrate that it does play a role in how a school leader negotiates the process of providing continuity and creating changes that affect individual children, teachers, and schools. The leadership styles Jeanne and Ellen demonstrate could, perhaps, lead to school restructuring in a context that supported and encouraged them to develop their visions and continue their work.

IMPLICATIONS

A process orientation to the principalship forces us to see the position as extremely complex; many variables influence the way a principal does her job. Defining effectiveness becomes more difficult, which makes it harder to develop direct implications for policy and training. The three principals themselves worried, when they read their cases, that others who read this book might not want to become principals. They explained that the cases make it sound like too hard a job, perhaps because they reveal the complexities of a principal's relationships, interactions, and negotiations. This process approach makes us focus on understanding the individual, the multiple contexts within which she works, and the interactions between the two. It also gives us insight into some of the limitations, or forced adaptations, a principal experiences in order to survive and have some success within the system.

On the other hand, understanding the principalship as a dynamic process of interaction provides a very positive sense of what principals can do to maintain their own voices, act upon their own values and make changes in seemingly immutable systems. Jeanne's commitment to African American children and to the education of students and faculty around issues of diversity quietly challenges a community and an institution that has other concerns and issues in mind. Ellen's efforts to dismiss Philip Washington illustrate an approach that pushes the edges of the system, but still allows her to work within it. These shifts in discourse, in purpose, and in style bring into focus and open to debate the structures within which school administrators must work. The resulting insights contribute to further discussion of the role and purpose of schools, how to best carry out the negotiations between individual and context, and how to challenge historical and social frameworks that do not clearly serve the needs of students, parents, teachers, or administrators.

As I have suggested, this approach to the principalship is consonant with a school or district-based approach to reform. An understanding of the multiple contexts within which the principal functions expands the notion of school culture and the need to consider the behavioral and institutional regularities that often constrain school or systemic change. Reflecting on the personal, community, institutional, and social-historical contexts within which teachers and principals work provides a better sense of the barriers to and the opportunities for change in a given school or district. We need to consider how any proposed changes will be played out in these different contexts, and how an educational leader can adapt, support, resist, or work toward school or systemic change. Leadership training might be aimed at providing aspiring principals with an in-depth understanding of these contexts. It might, in addition, help principals and those considering the principalship develop the skills needed to explore how each context affects a school leader and shapes school change. Perhaps we can teach leaders how to handle the work graciously within the system and still have the resources to create—to play and dance—in ways that provide children, parents, teachers, and fellow administrators with new ideas and options for growth.

Women principals may be especially well positioned to see and respond to the need for school change, although race, class, age, religion, and context influence the impact of gender as a support or catalyst for an educational vision that encompasses change. The person and the contexts within which she lives and works interact to produce a unique set of administrative practices. At some points this interaction is adaptive and at others it challenges the status quo. An understanding of the dynamic process of the principalship gives us insight into the possibilities inherent in the multiple approaches to leadership demonstrated by these three women principals.

NOTES

INTRODUCTION

1. Names of the principals, their colleagues, and their school districts have been changed. In addition, certain identifying characteristics of places and people have been altered, as necessary, to ensure anonymity.

2. Others who have studied this issue have examined how women entering nontraditional occupations face dilemmas and contradictions as a result of conflicting expectations (see, e.g., Reskin and Roos, 1990; Charlton, 1978; Hughs, 1945).

3. Margaret Grogan (1996) suggests that we focus on the positive implications of the voices of women in educational leadership rather than the difficulties they experience. In doing so, we emphasize the possibility for resistance and change in a traditionally male-dominated structure and field.

4. I have chosen to use *she* to refer to all principals in this text. I find that doing so jars my own ear as I read, since principals have, in practice and in the literature, traditionally been he's. Learning to hear the principal spoken of as a women seems like a valuable experience, a way of unsettling the normative discourse about school leaders.

CHAPTER 1

1. These studies parallel work on women managers in the field of management and organizational behavior (e.g., Kanter, 1977).

2. Of course, this may reflect researchers' penchant for finding differences (always more interesting to report than no difference).

3. Regan (1990) draws on McIntosh's (1983) work in which she uses the metaphor of a broken pyramid to describe human experience. The pyramid, in Regan's interpretation, represents the basis of role differentiation in our society. Above the faultline in the pyramid, people, predominantly white males, operate within competitive, hierarchical norms of interaction. Below the faultline, women, people of color, and low-status white males, interact more collaboratively and focus on maintaining relationships and building community.

4. Neither Schaef (1985) nor Ferguson (1984) explores questions about variations *within* women's experiences. Although they do not explicitly describe the Female System they present as white and middle class, their work does not recognize or describe the multiplicity of women's experiences. Neither addresses the impact of race, ethnicity, class, or sexual orientation on women's lives and work.

5. As I explain in the introduction, I include both parents and teachers under the heading of community. I focus here on the notions of relationship and interaction, examining how these concepts both constrain and empower a principal. While the perspectives of teachers and parents sometimes differ, a principal must consider both as she negotiates with and serves these constituencies. In the process, she defines herself as a principal, even as she responds to the expectations others have of her in that role.

6. The emphasis here on relationships is not entirely a gender difference; some of it stems from the research methods used. Case studies based on ethnographic data will yield a different and probably more interpersonally focused picture of the principalship than broader survey studies of large numbers of school leaders.

7. Several authors have examined the differences between school cultures in public and private schools (see, e.g., Bryk et al., 1993; Coleman and Hoffer, 1987; Cookson and Persell, 1985). A key difference focuses on the private school as an intentional community that can choose its values, its clientele, and its approaches to teaching and learning. Despite these differences, I believe many similarities exist in the hierarchical roles and structures that shape teachers' and administrators' experiences in public and private schools.

8. These newer studies suggest that the process of change, is, itself, part of the content of change. For example, involving teachers in decision making is both a change in process that will lead to different outcomes and an important change in and of itself that affects teachers' lives and work. The paradigm shifts from an input-output model of change to a systems approach that involves people, context, and interaction. The latter approach makes it possible to reexamine the role of the principal in ways suggested by this study, leading to redefinitions of the principal's role and effectiveness in context.

CHAPTER 2

1. There are also a few collections of first person accounts of women in educational administration. See, for example, Ozga, 1993.

2. It seems clear that no single method or set of methods constitute feminist research; both quantitative and qualitative studies can, for example, serve feminist and nonfeminist goals. But common themes emerge in feminist work in the social sciences. Feminist researchers generally aim to carry out research that contributes to social change, in particular the improvement of women's experience and position in society (Kelly et al., 1994; Acker et al., 1991; Fonow and Cook, 1991; Lather, 1991; Weiler, 1989). In some cases, they call for work that is action-oriented, focused on explicit change in people's understanding and actions and in the social institutions within which they operate. Feminist social scientists ground their work in an understanding of the historical and contemporary oppressive social structures that influence what we know, how we act and interact, and what we value: "To do feminist research is to put the social construction of gender at the center of one's inquiry" (Lather, 1991). In doing so, they reject the notion of value-free research, and depend on a process of con-

tinuous reflexivity about their own perspectives, actions and choices as researchers (Oleson, 1994; Stewart, 1994; Fonow and Cook, 1991; Lather, 1991; Weiler, 1989).

3. I found it interesting that the central administrators agreed so readily to this project. Some of their acquiescence indicated a certain level of principal autonomy; if the principal chose to participate, the central administrator agreed. On the other hand, as the cases demonstrate, when central administrators chose they could wield a great deal of direct and indirect power and control over the principals and their decisions. Perhaps central administrators were assured by my promises of anonymity or wanted to make a contribution to educational research. But I tend to believe that despite my letters and phone calls explaining my research goals and design, few central office administrators had a clear sense of the depth of information a researcher could gather over the course of the year. They may have been correct if they assumed that my presence would have little long-term impact on the daily working of the schools, but I do not think they understood the detailed level of data collection and analysis that would occur. The principals themselves, while also relatively inexperienced in the process of qualitative research, were more aware of the immediate implications of having me there; they had to consider how it would feel to have me present and watching as they carried out their daily routines.

4. Regardless of the level of collaboration and participation across the various stages of the research project, control of the project and the final report most often remains with the researcher. Josselson (1996) points out that writing about the people whom she has interviewed is sometimes a painful process, because she knows she might hurt someone with whom she has shared an "intimate relationship." Some researchers have coped with this dilemma by acknowledging that a distance exists between the researcher and the researched, even in relatively collaborative research processes based on mutual trust and care. Chase (1996), in her examination of women superintendents, found that her analysis and interpretation focused on the cultural meanings that framed her subjects' experiences, not just on the meanings that the superintendents themselves gave to their daily actions and interactions. She argues that this analytic role, while not always comfortable, is the responsibility of the researcher. "The question then becomes how to produce an analysis which goes beyond the experience of the researched while still granting them full subjectivity. How do we explain the lives of others without violating their reality?" (Acker et al., p. 142).

CHAPTER 3

1. Jeanne never referred to these courses or talked about using what she had learned in them as she took on the role of principal. Unlike Grogan's (1996) women aspirants to the superintendency, none of the three women in this study seemed to think that their training had provided them with more than the certification necessary for the position.

2. Parents shared these views of the superintendent at the time of the study, five years after Jeanne had been appointed as principal. Their statements

seemed to reflect their discomfort with the superintendent's intentions toward the Greenfield and Weston communities both at the time of Jeanne's selection in 1986 and five years later, in 1991.

3. I interviewed parents from both Greenfield and Weston in doing this case study. In general, responses about Jeanne and the school were consistent across the two communities. Middle-/upper-middle-class Greenfield parents tended to have a slightly more positive reaction to Jeanne's management style than did working-class Weston parents, who more often praised Jeanne as a person but questioned her ability to lead. This parallels other research suggesting that class influences parental expectations of schooling (Metz, 1990; Lareau, 1989). However, the small number of parents interviewed here precludes a clear generalization about the effects of class and community on parents' views of Jeanne.

4. The proposal for school-based management was approved by the Board of Managers in 1991. This formal written plan was not published until 1993, however, two years after the district's schools had been asked to begin implementation.

5. None of the other schools in the district convened an active advisory council during the spring of 1992, despite the fact that it was part of the district plan.

6. Jeanne made this comment when I met with her in October 1993 to discuss her reactions to an earlier draft of the case study.

CHAPTER 4

1. Ann's trip to this school was unusual for her in her role as head of Pepperdine's lower school. She went to observe a child with multiple disabilities who had applied to Pepperdine for the following year. Pepperdine ultimately rejected the child's application.

2. As explained in chapter 2, most of the data for this case was collected between June 1993 and June 1994. My final interview with Ann occurred in July 1994 as a result of Ann's need to help her daughter through an illness in June 1994. In addition, we had several informal conversations during the 1994–1995 school year as she negotiated her departure from Pepperdine.

3. For more discussion of women's adaptation to existing administrative structures, see, for example, Adler et al. (1993), Ballou (1989), and Marshall (1985).

4. During her fourteen years of teaching, Ann taught fourth and fifth grade in two different schools, both within the same district.

5. The school is governed by a board of directors, who appoints a head of the school. During the year of the study, I rarely heard teachers or administrators speak of the board as involved in any of the daily decisions or administration of the school. Although they did vote on major policies (e.g., tuition, faculty benefits, etc.), they seemed relatively uninvolved in issues of curriculum, staffing (below the position of headmaster), and program. The headmaster is responsible for appointing heads for the upper, middle, and lower school divi-

sions, supervising curriculum and program, and maintaining relationships with parents and community members. Division heads are given a very small discretionary budget and primary responsibility for hiring, evaluating, and dismissing teachers and staff. The school also has administrators responsible for admissions, public relations, and finances, all of whom report to the headmaster. Power over all major decisions in this school seems to reside in the headmaster's office.

6. For example, each year the fifth-grade class takes a trip costing $225 per child. The school offers no assistance, although aid may be supplied if parents request it. "In the past they have sometimes asked parents to donate extra money to help those who might not be able to afford it, but that gets in the way of the development office" (Field notes, 9/93). Parents are also expected to spend time and money on school fundraising activities that range from selling $35 stadium blankets ($5 additional for monogramming) to running an annual three day sale where local merchants set up stands on campus to sell their products and then donate some of the profits to the school. (In the year before the study, the merchants' contribution amounted to $35,000.)

7. It is interesting to contrast Mark's imposition of a policy with the school board's imposition of school-based management in Jeanne's case or the district's imposition of a math curriculum in Ellen's case. In the public school situations, there is, at least, the semblance of community or teacher involvement in decision making; school-based management was discussed and approved by the Boyerton-Greenfield school board, and the math program was chosen by a committee of teachers and administrators in Edgemont. At Pepperdine, as at most private schools, the school head seems to have the prerogative to make and impose policies unilaterally if he chooses to do so.

8. As I mention in chapter 2, Ann asks me to read this letter and to help her think about how to respond to it.

9. For additional description and analysis of ways in which the bureaucratic structures of schools can limit the change women leaders can facilitate, see Marshall and Mitchell (1989), Schaef (1985), and Ferguson (1984).

10. Ann does sit on several of the K–12 curriculum committees formed by Mark to develop and articulate the curriculum. During these meetings, she tends to defer to those who she feels have more expertise in the particular field under discussion.

11. This interview was carried out by undergraduate students in a course I taught in 1991. They interviewed Ann as part of an ethnography of Pepperdine.

CHAPTER 5

1. Reading Buddies is a school district program in which senior citizens come to the school weekly to read with children. Chapter 1 is a federally funded, state-administered program to support low-income special needs students.

2. See Ortiz and Marshall (1988), Spring (1986), and Hoffman (1981) for further discussion of teaching as a woman's profession and of teaching and administration as separate (and gendered) professions.

3. Ellen discovers, for example, that two of the male elementary principals nominate a candidate and lobby for him with the other male principals and the central administration. Ultimately, the district hires one male assistant principal (the one for whom the male principals had lobbied) and one female to be shared by four of the elementary schools (including Fieldcrest). The female candidate Ellen supports does not get either of the two available positions. In the spring, when the district decides to hire four vice principals for the coming year, Ellen again discovers that several of the male principals and central administrators have discussed privately which schools will have vice principals, who the appropriate candidates might be, and how the hiring process will proceed. She protests the private proceedings, and manages to force the administration to change both the schools served and the hiring process.

4. The National Elementary School Recognition Program was initiated by the Department of Education during the Reagan administration. It aimed to promote excellence by recognizing those schools that fulfill certain standards of achievement. Schools could apply for a National Excellence Award, or "Blue Ribbon," if they met one of three criteria: (1) during the last three years, 75% of the students in the school achieved standardized test scores at or above grade level during the last three years; (2) during the last three years the number of children achieving standardized test scores at or above grade level in math and reading increased an average of 5% annually, and during the last year, 50% or more of the students achieved scores at or above grade level in both areas; or (3) the school could demonstrate exemplary progress and growth of students as individuals or a group through a documented system of evaluation. In both 1 and 2, the school had to state which tests they used to measure student achievement. Fieldcrest applied under the second set of criteria. Application involved completing a self study in response to a given set of questions. Schools that passed the first round of the assessment were visited by an outside evaluator who used the self-study as a guide for judging the school.

5. Despite Ellen's avowal that she has moved away from a process approach to leadership, she continues to use several organizational structures that give staff opportunities to engage in decision making. For example, she has a staff council, consisting of one representative from each grade level, that meets once a month to share issues and concerns and contribute to school policy. She also meets regularly with each grade-level group of teachers to discuss curriculum, students, and programs.

6. At Fieldcrest, 15.7% of the children receive Aid to Families with Dependent Children, compared to 5.9% districtwide.

7. In 1989–1990, the school served 638 students, compared to 737 in 1993–1994. Between 1989 and 1994 the school opened up only two new classes; generally the increased population meant larger class sizes.

8. At Fieldcrest, 4 to 6 individuals teach at the same grade level. In some cases, those working at a grade level form strong personal and professional attachments, friendships facilitated by common preparation and lunch periods during the day. Some teachers affected by Ellen's decision felt that they would never be able to build new relationships to replace those she had disrupted; they sometimes formed relatively tight cliques based on these prior friendships.

9. This committee plans all faculty social events, including holiday and end of the year parties. It also recognizes birthdays, marriages, and other special events that occur for faculty during the year. In the two or three years before the study, teacher attendance at all school gatherings had declined significantly.

10. In order to create homogeneous math groups at Fieldcrest, teachers at a particular grade level would often regroup their students across classrooms. That is, one teacher would teach the high-ability third-grade students, another the middle-ability third-graders, and a third the lower-ability third-grade students. Students were rarely moved up or down grade levels to accommodate math abilities.

11. The chosen math program was one of several evaluated by a committee of district administrators and teachers. The program was piloted in classrooms in several schools (not Fieldcrest) the year before the study, and recommended to the superintendent by the committee on the basis of student performance in those classrooms.

12. The district's contract requires that principals observe and write an evaluation of each tenured teacher three times per year (nontenured teachers receive five formal observations per year).

CHAPTER 6

1. The question of how the changing contexts affect the process of principaling would be an interesting one to pursue using longitudinal case studies. In Jeanne's case, for example, seven years after the study, there is a new (male) superintendent in the district and new principals in every school but Greenfield-Weston. Jeanne is now one of the most experienced administrators in the district. All but one of the district's principals are women, whereas at the time of the study Jeanne was the only woman. A longitudinal or follow-up study would provide valuable information, including the relative importance of the particular people in the roles versus the consistent historical and social structures of the system in determining the influence of the institutional context.

2. It is interesting to consider that perhaps because Ann worked in each of her principalships for only 5–6 years, she did not experience this shift in style or stance that would have allowed her to adapt to the changing context as she moved into her fifth and sixth years at Pepperdine. Perhaps because she frequently changed jobs just as she established a solid status quo, her sense of the principalship remains at the stage of developing one's position and, in the situations in which she has worked, reorganizing the school context.

3. The heads of the middle and upper schools at Pepperdine, while under the same institutional constraints, did negotiate more with Mark, however, working with him on a more equal basis to make decisions and plans for their part of the school. The institutional structure itself, therefore, does not unilaterally determine how an individual functions within it. Ann's personal style and values certainly influence the process.

4. An interesting contrast to the three principals in this study can be found in Jane Strachan's work on three feminist principals in New Zealand (Strachan,

1998). She describes how these principals' commitment to feminist ideals lead them to challenge the systems within which they work and the constraints they, too, face.

5. In 1996, two years after implementing the new math program, the district decided to abandon it (citing many of the problems Ellen had raised two years earlier). The district based its decision to end the program on teacher concerns, rather than test data on student achievement. Although the program seemed to work for average students, strong math students found it boring and weaker students struggled with the multiple concepts presented in each lesson. The curriculum coordinator explained that because it was not an expensive program to run (because it was workbook- rather than textbook-based) and because teachers generally did not like it, the transition back to a basal math series was relatively smooth.

BIBLIOGRAPHY

Acker, J., Barry, K., and Esseveld, J. (1991). "Objectivity and truth: Problems in doing feminist research." In M. Fonow and J. Cook (eds.), *Beyond Methodology*. Bloomington: Indiana University Press. 133–153.

Acker, S. (1990). "Managing the drama: The headteacher's work in an urban primary school." *Sociological Review*, 38. 247–271.

Adler, S., Laney, J., and Packer, M. (1993). *Managing Women*. Buckingham, England: Open University Press.

Aisenberg, N., and Harrington, M. (1988). *Women of Academe: Outsiders in the Sacred Grove*. Amherst: University of Massachusetts Press.

Astin, H., and Leland, C. (1991). *Women of Influence, Women of Power*. San Francisco: Jossey-Bass.

Ball, S., and Goodson, I. (1985a). *Teachers' Lives and Careers*. London: Falmer Press.

———. (1985b). "Understanding teachers: Concepts and contexts." In S. Ball and I. Goodson (eds.), *Teachers' Lives and Careers*. Lewes, England: Falmer Press. 1–26.

Ballou, M. (1989). "Male administrative orientation: Patriarchy in school administration." *Contemporary Education*, 60(4), pp. 216–217.

Barth, R. (1990). *Improving Schools from Within*. San Francisco: Jossey-Bass.

Bastian, A., Fruchter, N., Gittell, M., Greer, C., and Haskins, K. (1985). *Choosing Equality*. Philadelphia: Temple University Press.

Beck, L., and Murphy, J. (1993). *Understanding the Principalship: Metaphorical Themes 1920–1990s*. New York: Teachers College Press.

Becker, H. S. (1951). "Problems of inference and proof in participant observation." *American Sociological Review*, 23, pp. 652–660.

Bell, C., and Chase, S. (1993). "The underrepresentation of women in school leadership." In C. Marshall (ed.), *The New Politics of Race and Gender*. London: Falmer Press. 141–154.

Bem, S. (1993). *The Lenses of Gender*. New Haven: Yale University Press.

Beynon, J. (1985). "Institutional change and career histories in a comprehensive school." In S. Ball and I. Goodson (eds.), *Teachers' Lives and Careers*. London: Falmer Press. 58–179.

Biklen, S. (1980). "Introduction: Barriers to equity—Women, educational leadership, and social change." In S. Biklen and M. Brannigan (eds.), *Women and Educational Leadership*. Lexington, MA: D.C. Heath and Co. 1–23.

———. (1995). *School Work: Gender and the Cultural Construction of Teaching*. New York: Teachers College Press.

Blackmore, J. (1993). "In the shadow of men: The historical construction of educational administration as a 'masculinist' enterprise." In J. Blackmore and J. Kenway (eds.), *Gender Matters in Educational Adminstration and Policy*. London: Falmer Press. 27–48.

Blase, J., and Kirby, P. (1992). *Bringing Out the Best in Teachers: What Effective Principals Do*. Newbury Park, CA: Corwin Press.

Bloom, L. R., and Munro, P. (1995). "Conflicts of selves: Nonunitary subjectivity in women administrator's life history narratives." In J. A. Hatch and R. Wisniewski (eds.), *Life History and Narrative*. London: Falmer Press. 99–112.

Blumberg, A. (1987). "The work of principals: A touch of craft." In W. Greenfield (ed.), *Instructional Leadership*. Boston: Allyn and Bacon. 38–55.

———. (1989). *School Administration as a Craft*. Boston: Allyn and Bacon.

Blumberg, A., and Greenfield, W. (1986). *The Effective Principal: Perspectives on School Leadership*. Boston: Allyn and Bacon.

Boyan, N. (1988). "Describing and explaining administrative behavior." In N. Boyan (ed.), *Handbook of Research on Educational Administration*. New York: Longman. 77–98.

Boyer, E. (1983). *High School: A Report on Secondary Education in America*. New York: Harper & Row.

Bryk, A., Lee, V., and Holland, P. (1993). *Catholic Schools and the Common Good*. Cambridge: Harvard University Press.

Buell, N. (1992). "Building a shared vision: The principal's leadership challenge." *NASSP Bulletin*, 76, pp. 88–92.

Burawoy, M. (1991). "The extended case method." In M. Burawoy (ed.), *Ethnography Unbound*. Berkeley: University of California Press. 271–290.

Burlingame, M. (1987). "Images of leadership in effective schools literature." In W. Greenfield (ed.), *Instructional Leadership*. Boston: Allyn and Bacon. 3–16.

Charlton, J. (1978). "Women entering the ordained ministry: Contradictions and dilemmas of status." Paper presented at the Annual Meeting of the Society for the Scientific Study of Religion, Hartford, CT.

Charters, W.W., and Jovick, T. D. (1981). "The gender of principals and principal-teacher relations in elementary schools." In P. Schmuck, W. W. Charters, and R. Carlson (eds.), *Educational Policy and Management*. New York: Academic Press. 307–332.

Chase, S. (1995). *Ambiguous Empowerment: The Work Narratives of Women School Superintendents*. Amherst: University of Massachusetts Press.

———. (1996). "Personal vulnerability and interpretive authority in narrative research." In R. Josselson (ed.), *Ethics and Process in the Narrative Study of Lives*. Thousand Oaks, CA: Sage. 45–59.

Chusmir, L. H. (1989). "Male-female differences in the association of managerial style and personal values." *The Journal of Social Psychology*, 129(1), pp. 65–78.

Clement, J. (1980). "Sex bias in school administration." In S. Biklen and M. Brannigan (eds.), *Women and Educational Leadership*. Lexington, MA: D.C. Heath and Co. 131–138.

Cohen, R.M. (1991). *A Lifetime of Teaching: Portraits of Five Veteran High School Teachers*. New York: Teachers College Press.

Coleman, J., and Hoffer, T. (1987). *Public and Private High Schools*. New York: Basic Books.

Collins, P. H. (1991). "Learning from the outsider within: The sociological significance of black feminist thought." In M. Fonow and J. Cook (eds.), *Beyond Methodology: Feminist Scholarship as Lived Research*. Bloomington: Indiana University Press. 35–59.

Connell, R. (1985). *Teachers Work*. London: Allen and Unwin.

Cookson, P., and Persell, C. (1985). *Preparing for Power*. New York: Basic Books.

Coursen, D., Mazzarella, J., Jeffress, L., and Haddreman, M. (1989). "Two special cases: Women and blacks." In *School Leadership: Handbook for Excellence*. Washington, D.C.: Office of Educational Research and Improvement. 85–106.

Datnow, A., and Karen, R. (1994). "Responsibility and sensitivity in case study research." Paper presented at the Annual Meeting of the American Educational Research Association, New Orleans, LA.

Deal, T. (1987). "Effective school principals: Counselors, engineers, pawnbrokers, poets . . . or instructional leaders?" In W. Greenfield (ed.), *Instructional Leadership*. Boston: Allyn and Bacon. 230–248.

Donaldson, G. (1991). *Learning to Lead: The Dynamics of the High School Principalship*. New York: Greenwood Press.

Donmoyer, R. (1990). "Generalizability and the single-case study." In E. Eisner and A. Peshkin (eds.), *Qualitative Inquiry in Education: The Continuing Debate*. New York: Teachers College Press. 175–200.

Doughty, R. (1980). "The black female administrator: Women in a double bind." In S. Biklen and M. Brannigan (eds.), *Women and Educational Leadership*. Boston: D.C. Heath and Co. 165–174.

Dunlop, D. (1995). "Women leading: An agenda for a new century." In D. M. Dunlap and P. A. Schmuck (eds.), *Women Leading in Education*. Albany: State University of New York Press. 423–435.

Dunlop, D. M., and Schmuck, P. A. (1995). *Women Leading in Education*. Albany: State University of New York Press.

Eagly, A. H., Karua, S. J., and Johnson, B. T. (1992). "Gender and leadership style among school principals: A meta-analysis." *Educational Administration Quarterly*, 28(1), pp. 76–102.

Edson, S. (1981). "If they can, I can: Women aspirants to administrative positions in public schools." In P. Schmuck, W. Charters, and R. Carlson (eds.), *Educational Policyand Management*. New York: Academic Press. 169–185.

———. (1988). *Pushing the Limits: The Female Administrative Aspirant*. Albany: State University of New York Press.

———. (1995). "Ten years later: Too little, too late?" In D. M. Dunlap and P. A. Schmuck (eds.), *Women Leading in Education*. Albany: State University of New York Press. 36–48.

Fauth, G. (1984). "Women in educational administration: A research profile." *The Educational Forum*, 49(1), pp. 65–79.

Ferguson, K. (1984). *The Feminist Case against Bureaucracy*. Philadelphia: Temple University Press.

Fine, M. (1994). "Working the hyphens: Reinventing self and other in qualitative research." In N. Denzin and Y. Lincoln (eds.), *Handbook of Qualitative Research*. Thousand Oaks, CA: Sage. 70–82.

Fonow, M., and Cook, J. (1991). "Back to the future: A look at the second wave of feminist epistemology and methodology." In M. Fonow and J. Cook (eds.), *Beyond Methodology*. Bloomington: Indiana University Press. 1–15.

Franz, C., Cole, E., Crosby, F., and Stewart, A. (1994). "Lessons from lives." In C. Franz and A. Stewart (eds.), *Women Creating Lives: Identities, Resilience, and Resistance*. Boulder, CO: Westview Press. 325–334.

Gilligan, C. (1982). *In a Different Voice*. Cambridge: Harvard University Press.

Glaser, B. G., and Strauss, A. L. (1967). *The Discovery of Grounded Theory: Strategies for Qualitative Research*. New York: Aldine.

Goodlad, J. (1984). *A Place Called School*. New York: McGraw-Hill.

Goodson, I. (1991). "Teachers' lives and educational research." In I. Goodson and R. Walker (eds.), *Biography, Identity and Schooling*. London: Falmer Press. 137–149.

———. (1992). *Studying Teachers' Lives*. New York: Teachers College Press.

Gosetti, P., and Rusch, E. (1995). "Reexamining educational leadership: Challenging assumptions." In D. M. Dunlap and P. A. Schmuck (eds.), *Women Leading in Education*. Albany: State University of New York Press. 11–35.

Grant, L. (1984). "Black females' place in desegregated classroom." *Sociology of Education*, 57, pp. 98–111.

Grant, R. (1989). "Alternative model of 'career.'" In S. Acker (ed.), *Teachers, Gender and Careers*. Lewes, England: Falmer Press. 35–50.

Greenfield, W. (1987). "Moral imagination and interpersonal competence: Antecedents to instructional leadership." In W. Greenfield (ed.), *Instructional Leadership*. Boston: Allyn and Bacon. 56–73.

Griffin, G. (1990). "Leadership for curriculum improvement: The school administrator's role." In A. Lieberman (ed.), *Schools as Collaborative Cultures: Creating the Future Now*. London: Falmer Press. 195–212.

Grogan, M. (1996). *Voices of Women Aspiring to the Superintendancy*. Albany: State University of New York Press.

Gross, N., and Trask, A. E. (1976). *The Sex Factor and the Management of Schools*. New York: John Wiley and Sons.

Grundy, S. (1993). "Educational leadership as emancipatory praxis." In J. Blackmore and J. Kenway (eds.), *Gender Matters in Educational Administration and Policy*. London: Falmer Press. 165–180.

Hall, R. (1982). "The classroom climate: A chilly one for women." Washington, D.C.: Project on the Status and Education of Women, Association of American Colleges.

Hare-Mustin, R., and Marecek, J. (1990). *Making a Difference: Psychology and the Construction of Gender*. New Haven: Yale University Press.

Hatch, J. A., and Wisniewski, R. (1995). "Life history and narrative: Questions, issues and exemplary works." In J. A. Hatch and R. Wisniewski (eds.), *Life History and Narrative*. London: Falmer Press. 113–133.

Hoffman, N. (1981). *Women's True Profession*. Old Westbury, NY: The Feminist Press.

hooks, b. (1989). *Talking Back*. Boston: South End Press.

Hughs, E. (1945). "Dilemmas and contradictions of status." *The American Journal of Sociology*, March, pp. 353–359.

Hurty, K. S. (1995). "Women principals—leading with power." In D. M. Dunlap and P. A. Schmuck (eds.), *Women Leading in Education*. Albany: State University of New York Press. 380–406.

Irwin, R. (1995). *A Circle of Empowerment: Women, Education, and Leadership*. Albany: State University of New York Press.

Josselson, R. (1996). "On writing other people's lives." In R. Josselson (ed.), *Ethics and Process in the Narrative Study of Lives*. Thousand Oaks, CA: Sage Publications. 60–71.

Kanter, R. (1977). *Men and Women of the Corporation*. New York: Basic Books.

Katz, M. (1987). *Reconstructing American Education*. Cambridge: Harvard University Press.

Kaufman, S. (1993). *The Healer's Tale*. Madison: University of Wisconsin Press.

Kelly, L., Burton, S., and Regan, L. (1994). "Researching women's lives or studying women's oppression? Reflections on what constitutes feminist research." In M. Maynard and J. Purvis (eds.), *Researching Women's Lives from a Feminist Perspective*. London: Taylor and Francis. 27–48.

Kincheloe, J., and McLaren, P. (1994). "Rethinking critical theory and qualitative research." In N. Denzin and Y. Lincoln (eds.), *Handbook of Qualitative Research*. Thousand Oaks, CA: Sage. 138–157.

Kremer-Hayon, L., and Fessler, R. (1992). "The inner world of school principals: Reflections on career life stages." *International Review of Education*, 38, pp. 35–45.

Lareau, A. (1989). *Home Advantage*. Lewes, England: Falmer Press.

Lather, P. (1991). *Getting Smart*. New York: Routledge.

Lieberman, A. (ed.) (1990). *Schools as Collaborative Cultures*. Lewes, England: Falmer Press.

———. (1992). "The meaning of scholarly activity and the building of community." *Educational Researcher*, 21(6), pp. 5–10.

———. (ed.) (1995). *The Work of Restructuring Schools: Building from the Ground Up*. New York: Teachers College Press.

Lieberman, A., and Miller, L. (1990). "Restructuring schools: What matters and what works." *Phi Delta Kappan*, 71(10), pp. 759–764.

Lieblich, A. (1996). "Some unforeseen outcomes of conducting narrative research with people of one's own culture." In R. Josselson (ed.), *Ethics and Process in the Narrative Study of Lives*. Thousand Oaks, CA: Sage. 172–184.

Lightfoot, S. (1980). "Socialization and education of young black girls in school." In S. Biklen and M. Brannigan (eds.), *Women and Educational Leadership*. Lexington, MA: D.C. Heath and Co. 139–164.

Lobel, A. (1993). *Ming Lo Moves the Mountain*. New York: William Morrow and Co.

Lomotey, K. (1989). *African-American Principals: School Leadership and Success*. New York: Greenwood Press.

Lortie, D. (1975). *School Teacher: A Sociological Study*. Chicago: University of Chicago Press.

Lyons, N. (1983). "Two perspectives on self, relationships, and morality." *Harvard Educational Review*, 53(2), pp. 125–145.

Marshall, C. (1984). "The crisis in excellence and equity." *Educational Horizons*, 63(1), pp. 24–30.

———. (1985). "The stigmatized woman: The professional woman in a male sex-typed career." *Journal of Educational Administration*, 23(2), pp. 131–152.

———. (1988). "Analyzing the culture of school leadership." *Education and Urban Society*, 20(3), pp. 262–275.

———. (1993). "Politics of denial: Gender and race issues in administration." In C. Marshall (ed.), *The New Politics of Race and Gender*. London: Falmer Press.

Marshall, C., and Mitchell, B. (1989). "Women's careers as a critique of the adminstrative culture." Paper presented at the Annual Meeting of the American Educational Research Association, San Francisco.

Matthews, E. N. (1995). "Women in educational administration: Views of equity." In D. M. Dunlap and P. A. Schmuck (eds.), *Women Leading in Education*. Albany: State University of New York Press. 247–273.

Maynard, M. (1994). "Methods, practice and epistemology: The debate about feminism and research." In M. Maynard and J. Purvis (eds.), *Researching Women's Lives from a Feminist Perspective*. London: Taylor and Francis.

McIntosh, P. (1983). *Interactive Phases of Curriculuar Re-vision: A Feminist Perspective*. Wellesley, MA: Wellesley Center for Research on Women.

Mehan, H. (1996). *Constructing School Success: The Consequences of Untracking Low Achieving Students*. New York: Cambridge University Press.

Meier, D. (1995). *The Power of Their Ideas*. Boston: Beacon Press.

Merriam, S. (1988). *Case Study Research in Education: A Qualitative Approach*. San Francisco: Jossey-Bass.

Metz, M. H. (1990). "How social class differences shape teachers' work." In M. McLaughlin (ed.), *The Contexts of Teaching in Secondary School*. New York: Teachers College Press. 40–110.

Middleton, S. (1989). "Educating feminists: A life-history study." In S. Acker (ed.), *Teachers, Gender and Careers*. Lewes, England: Falmer Press. 53–68.

Miklos, E. (1988). "Administrator selection, career patterns, succession, and socialization." In N. Boyan (ed.), *Handbook of Research on Educational Administration*. New York: Longman. 53–76.

Mitchell, J. P., and Winn, D. D. (1989). "Women and school administration." *Journal of Instructional Psychology*, 16, pp. 54–71.

Mortimore, P., and Sammons, P. (1987). New evidence on effective elementary schools. *Educational Leadership*, 45(1), pp. 4–8.

National Association of Elementary School Principals (1990). *Principals for 21st Century Schools*. Arlington, VA: National Association of Elementary School Principals.

National Center for Education Statistics (1994). "Public and Private School Principals: Are There Too Few Women?" Statistics Issue Brief 1-94. Washington, D.C.: U.S. Department of Education.

National Commission on Excellence in Education. (1983). *A Nation at Risk.* Washington, D.C.: The National Commission on Excellence in Education, U.S. Government Printing Office.

Noddings, N. (1988). "An ethic of caring and its implications for instructional arrangements," *American Journal of Education,* 96(2), pp. 215–229.

Oja, S. N., and Smulyan, L. (1989). *Collaborative Action Research: A Developmental Process.* London: Falmer Press.

Oleson, V. (1994). "Feminisms and models of qualitative research." In N. Denzin and Y. Lincoln (eds.), *Handbook of Qualitative Research.* Thousand Oaks, CA: Sage. 158–174.

O'Rourke, C., and Papelewis, R. (1989). "Women and their stories: Nine case studies in educational administration." Paper presented at the Annual Meeting of the California Educational Research Association, Burlingame, California.

Ortiz, F. (1982). *Career Patterns in Education.* South Hadley, MA: J. F. Bergin, Publishers.

Ortiz, F., and Marshall, C. (1988). "Women in educational administration." In N. Boyan, (ed.), *Handbook of Research on Educational Administration.* New York: Longman. 123–141.

Orum, A. M., Feagin, J. R., and Sjoberg, G. (1991). "Introduction: The nature of the case study." In J. Feagin, A. Orum, and G. Sjoberg (eds.), *A Case for the Case Study.* Chapel Hill, NC: University of North Carolina Press.

Ozga, J. (1993). *Women in Educational Management.* Buckingham, England: Open University Press.

Paddock, S. (1981). "Male and female career paths in school administration." In P. Schmuck, W. Charters, and R. Carlson (eds.), *Educational Policy and Management.* New York: Academic Press. 187–198.

Parkay, F. W., Currie, G. D., and Rhodes, J. W. (1992). "Professional socialization: A longitudinal study of first-time high school principals." *Educational Administration Quarterly,* 28(1), pp. 43–75.

Pavan, B. (1991). "Reflections of female school administrators regarding their careers." Paper presented at the Annual Meeting of the American Educational Research Association, Chicago. ED334–676.

Plummer, K. (1983). *Documents of Life.* London: George Allen & Unwin.

Polczynski, M. (1990). "Getting There," *Momentum,* 21, pp. 28–30.

Porter, A. W., Lemon, D. K., and Landry, R. G. (1989). "School climate and administrative power strategies of elementary school principals." *Psychological Reports,* 65, pp. 1267–1271.

Powell, A., Farrar, E., and Cohen, D. (1985). *Shopping Mall High School.* Boston: Houghton Mifflin.

Powell, G. N. (1988). *Women and Men in Management.* Newbury Park, CA: Sage.

Prolman, S. (1983). "Gender, career paths, and administrative behavior." Paper presented at the Annual Meeting of the American Educational Research Association, Montreal.

Regan, H. (1990). "Not for women only: School administration as a feminist activity." *Teachers College Record,* 91(4), pp. 565–577.

Regan, H., and Brooks, G. (1995). *Out of Women's Experience: Creating Relational Leadership*. Newbury Park, CA: Corwin Press.

Reinharz, S. (1992). *Feminist Methods in Social Research*. New York: Oxford University Press.

Reissman, C. K. (1993). *Narrative Analysis*. Newbury Park, CA: Sage.

Reskin, B., and Roos, P. (1990). *Job Queues, Gender Queues: Explaining Women's Inroads into Male Occupations*. Philadelphia: Temple University Press.

Richardson, M., Short, P., and Prickett, R. (1993). *School Principals and Change*. New York: Garland Publishing.

Rossman, G. (1993). "Building explanations across case studies: A framework for synthesis." ERIC Document ED373115. Colorado University School of Education.

Sarason, S. (1971). *The Culture of the School and the Problem of Change*. Boston: Allyn and Bacon.

Sassen, G. (1980). "Success anxiety in women: A constructivist interpretation of its source and significance," *Harvard Educational Review*, 50(1), pp. 13–24.

Schaef, A. W. (1985). *Women's Reality: An Emerging Female System in a White Male Society*. San Francisco: Harper & Row.

Schatzman, L., and Strauss, A. (1973). *Field Research: Strategies for a Natural Sociology*. Englewood Cliffs, NJ: Prentice Hall.

Schmuck, P. (1981). "The sex dimension of school organization: Overview and synthesis." In P. Schmuck, W. W. Charters, and R. Carlson (eds.), *Educational Policy and Management*. New York: Academic Press. 221–234.

Schmuck, P., Charters, W. W., and Carlson, R. (eds.) (1981). *Educational Policy and Management*. New York: Academic Press.

Schmuck, P., and Schubert, J. (1995). "Women principals' views on sex equity: Exploring issues of integration and information." In D. M. Dunlap and P. A. Schmuck (eds.), *Women Leading in Education*. Albany: State University of New York Press. 274–287.

Schofield, J. W. (1990). "Increasing the generalizability of qualitative research." In E. Eisner and A. Peshkin (eds.), *Qualitative Inquiry in Education: The Continuing Debate*. New York: Teachers College Press. 201–232.

Schultz, K. (1998). "Silence, voice and methodological issues and dilemmas in conducting research 'with' students." Paper presented at the Annual Meeting of the American Educational Research Association, San Diego, CA.

Sergiovanni, T. (1990). "Advances in leadership theory and practice." In P. Thurston and L. Lotto (eds.), *Advances in Educational Administration, Volume 1, 1990. Part A: Perspectives on Educational Reform*. Greenwich, CT: JAI Pres. 1–26.

Shakeshaft, C. (1987). "Theory in a changing reality." *Journal of Educational Equity and Leadership*, 7(1), pp. 4–20.

———. (1989). *Women in Educational Administration*. Newbury Park, CA: Sage.

Sikes, P. (1985). "The life cycle of the teacher." In S. Ball and I. Goodson (eds.), *Teachers'Lives and Careers*. Lewes, England: Falmer Press. 27–60.

Sizer, T. (1984). *Horace's Compromise*. Boston: Houghton Mifflin.

Smith, D. (1977). "Some implications of a sociology for women." In N. Glazer and H. Waehrer (eds.), *Women in a Man-Made World: A Socioeconomic Handbook*. Chicago: Rand-McNally.

Smith, R. (1991). "Principals need to be good followers." *The High School Journal*, October–November, pp. 24–27.

Smulyan, L. (1990). "Moving the mountain: The individual and school change." Paper presented at the Implementing Educational Change Conference. Centre for Educational Development, Appraisal and Research, University of Warwick, England.

——. (1992). "The artist as INSET coordinator: A problem in design." *Journal of Teacher Development*, 1(2), pp. 95–110.

Spring, J. (1986). *The American School, 1643–1985*. New York: Longman.

——. (1989). *American Education*. New York: Longman.

Stacey, J. (1988). "Can there be a feminist ethnography?" *Women's Studies International Forum*, 11(1), pp. 21–27.

Stake, R. (1994). "Case studies." In N. Denzin and Y. Lincoln (eds.), *Handbook of Qualitative Research*. Thousand Oaks, CA: Sage. 236–247.

Stewart, A. (1994). "Toward a feminist strategy for studying women's lives." In C. Franz and A. Stewart (eds.), *Women Creating Lives: Identities, Resilience, and Resistance*. Boulder, CO: Westview Press. 11–36.

Stockard, J., and Johnson, M. (1981). "The sources and dynamics of sexual inequality in the profession of education." In P. Schmuck, W. Charters, and R. Carlson (eds.), *Educational Policy and Management*. New York: Academic Press. 235–254.

Strachan, J. (1998). "Witches, whacko or wonderful? Women educational leaders in 'new right' New Zealand." Paper presented at the Annual Meeting of the American Educational Research Association, San Diego, CA.

Sweeney, J. (1982). "Research synthesis on effective school leadership." *Educational Leadership*, 39(5), pp. 346–352.

Swiderski, W. (1988). "Problems faced by women in gaining access to administrative positions in education." *Education Canada*, 28, pp. 24–31.

Tibbetts, S. (1980). "The woman principal: Superior to the male." *Journal of the NAWDAC*, 43(4), pp. 15–18.

Traquair, N. (1993). "The primary head." In J. Ozga (ed.), *Women in Educational Management*. Buckingham, England: Open University Press. 68–72.

Tyack, D. (1974). *The One Best System*. Cambridge: Harvard University Press.

Valverde, L., and Brown, F. (1988). "Influences on leadership development among racial and ethnic minorities." In N. Boyan (ed.), *Handbook of Research on Educational Administration*. New York: Longman. 143–157.

Walker, C. (1993). "Black women in educational management." In J. Ozga (ed.), *Women in Educational Management*. Buckingham, England: Open University Press. 16–24.

Walker, R. (1986). "The conduct of educational case studies: Ethics, theory and procedures." In M. Hammersley (ed.), *Controversies in Classroom Research*. England: Open University Press. 187–219.

Weber, M., Feldman, J., and Pling, E. (1981). "Why women are underrepresented in educational administration." *Educational Leadership*, 38(4), pp. 320–322.

Weiler, K. (1988). *Women Teaching for Change: Gender, Class and Power.* South Hadley, MA: Bergin and Garvey.

Wheatley, M. (1981). "The impact of organizational structures on issues of sex equity." In P. Schmuck, W. Charters, and R. Carlson (eds.), *Educational Policy and Management.* New York: Academic Press. 255–272.

Wolcott, H. (1973). *The Man in the Principal's Office.* IL: Waveland Press.

Wolf, D. (1996). "Situating feminist dilemmas in fieldwork." In D. Wolf (ed.), *Feminist Dilemmas in Fieldwork.* Boulder, CO: Westview Press. 1–55.

Wooster, M. (1991). "First principals: The leadership vacuum in American schools." *Policy Review,* 57, pp. 55–61.

Yeakey, C., Johnston, G., and Adkison, J. (1986). "In pursuit of equity: A review of research on minorities and women in educational adminstration." *Educational Administration Quarterly,* 22(3), pp. 110–149.

Yin, R. (1984). *Case Study Research: Design and Methods.* Beverly Hills, CA: Sage.

Young, B. (1990). "Chance, choice and opportunity in the careers of four women educators." Paper presented at the Annual Meeting of the Canadian Society of Studies in Education, Victoria, British Columbia.

INDEX